DESCENDING STORIES

SHOWA GENROKU RAKUGO SHINJU

Haruko Kumota

THE STORY SO FAR

YOTARO'S ODYSSEY

Yotaro falls in love with Yakumo Yurakutei VIII's *rakugo* when he hears it in prison. Once free, he becomes Yakumo's apprentice, and is soon made a *zenza*. As his appreciation for *rakugo* grows, the incredible *rakugo* of the late Sukeroku takes hold of him, and he commits an unthinkable faux pas at a solo recital by his teacher. Facing expulsion, Yotaro begs for forgiveness. Yakumo relents, but extracts three promises from his student. Then he begins to tell the tale of his own promise with Sukeroku...

YAKUMO AND SUKEROKU

On the day Yakumo Yurakutei VII accepts young Kikuhiko as an apprentice, the scruffy Hatsutaro wheedles his way into the household, too. Hatsutaro's *rakugo* is so rude and boisterous that even uptight Kikuhiko laughs. Having thus joined Yakumo VII as apprentices on the same day, the two of them begin to walk the path to *rakugo* artistry together.

CAST OF CHARACTERS

Yakumo and Sukeroku

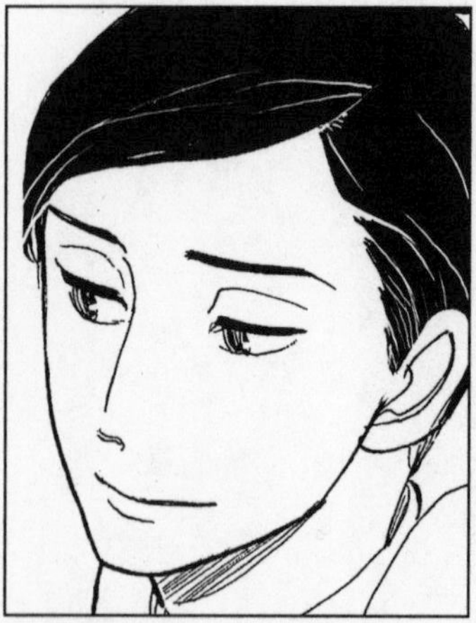

Kikuhiko
Yakumo Yurakutei VIII's stage name during his *futatsume* days. Frustrated by the artistic plateau he feels himself to be on.

Yotaro's Odyssey

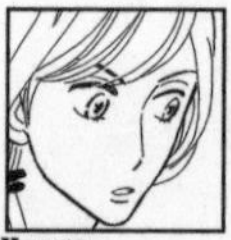

Konatsu
Sukeroku's only daughter, taken in by Yakumo.

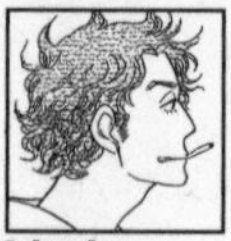

Sukeroku Yurakutei
Legendary *rakugo* artist hailed as a genius before his untimely death.

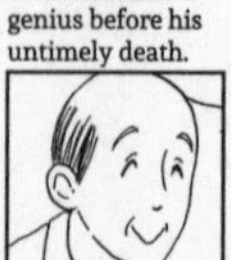

Matsuda
Faithful servant and driver of Yakumo VIII, and Yakumo VII before him.

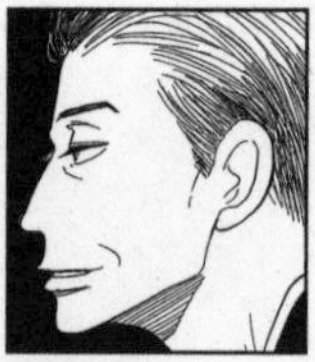

Yakumo Yurakutei VIII
Renowned as the Showa period's last great master of *rakugo*.

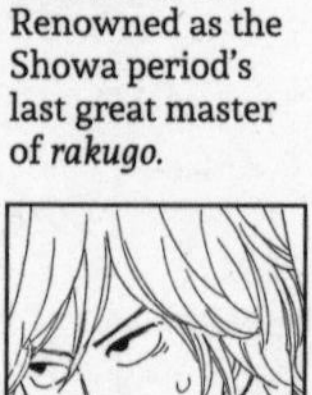

Yotaro (Kyoji)
Reformed street tough who became Yakumo's apprentice.

"We want to become futatsume."

But as Kikuhiko and Hatsutaro are struggling to become *futatsume*, the shadow of war falls on the *rakugo* world. As senior apprentices are drafted and disappear one by one, Yakumo VII takes Hatsutaro to Manchuria with him to entertain the troops. Kikuhiko remains behind with Yakumo VII's wife, and Matsuda-san, his faithful servant, and as they wait for Yakumo VII and Hatsutaro to return, the war comes to an end.

The dark times are over, and Hatsutaro declares cheerfully: the age of *rakugo* is here. Even more skilled after his Manchurian tour, he becomes a rising star among the *futatsume*. Kikuhiko, however, has yet to discover a *rakugo* of his own. Then, one day, a geisha named Miyokichi that Yakumo VII knew in Manchuria turns up on their teacher's doorstep...

Cast of Characters

Miyokichi
Future mother of
Konatsu. Works as a
geisha.

Yakumo Yurakutei VII
Kikuhiko and
Sukeroku's shisho
(master).

Sukeroku
Changed his stage name from
Hatsutaro. Still a *futatsume*, but
already a popular draw at the *yose*
(*rakugo* hall).

DESCENDING STORIES

SHOWA GENROKU RAKUGO SHINJU

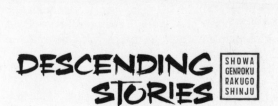

Contents

Yakumo and Sukeroku

SHOWA GENROKU RAKUGO SHINJU

DESCENDING STORIES

YAKUMO & SUKEROKU: 3

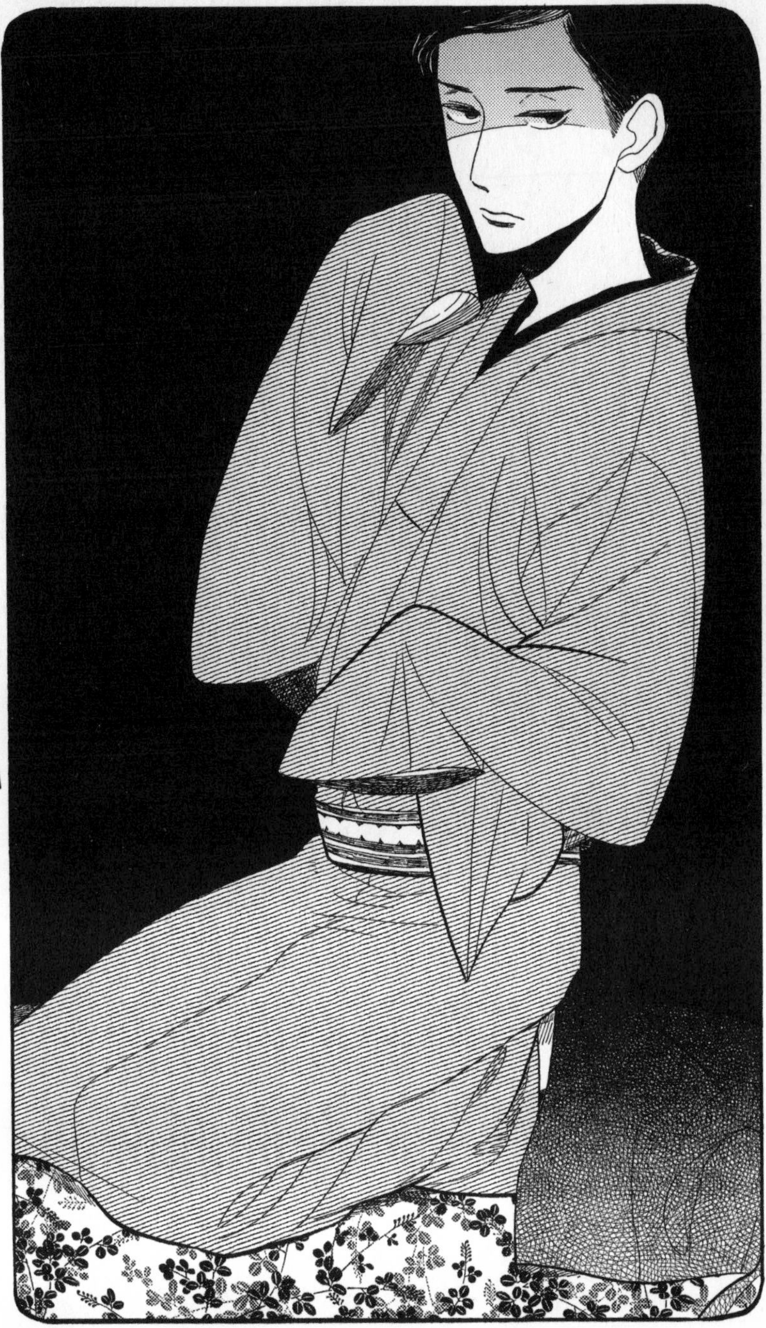

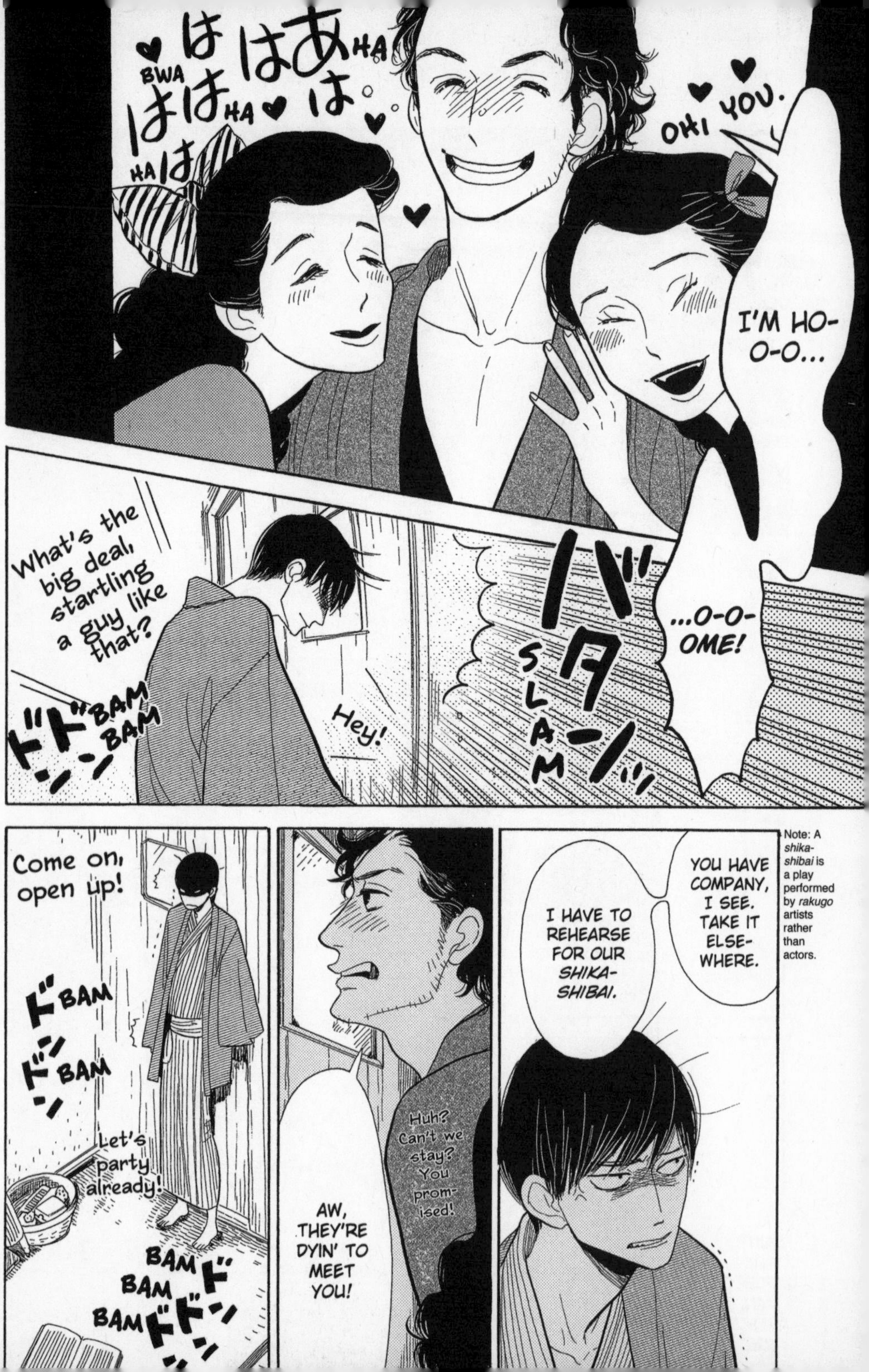
BWA HA HA HA
OH! YOU.
I'M HO-O-O...
...O-O-OME!
SLAM
Hey!
What's the big deal, startling a guy like that?
BAM BAM
YOU HAVE COMPANY, I SEE. TAKE IT ELSEWHERE.
I HAVE TO REHEARSE FOR OUR SHIKA-SHIBAI.
Huh? Can't we stay? You promised!
AW, THEY'RE DYIN' TO MEET YOU!
Come on, open up!
BAM
BAM
Let's party already!
BAM
BAM
BAM

Note: A *shika-shibai* is a play performed by *rakugo* artists rather than actors.

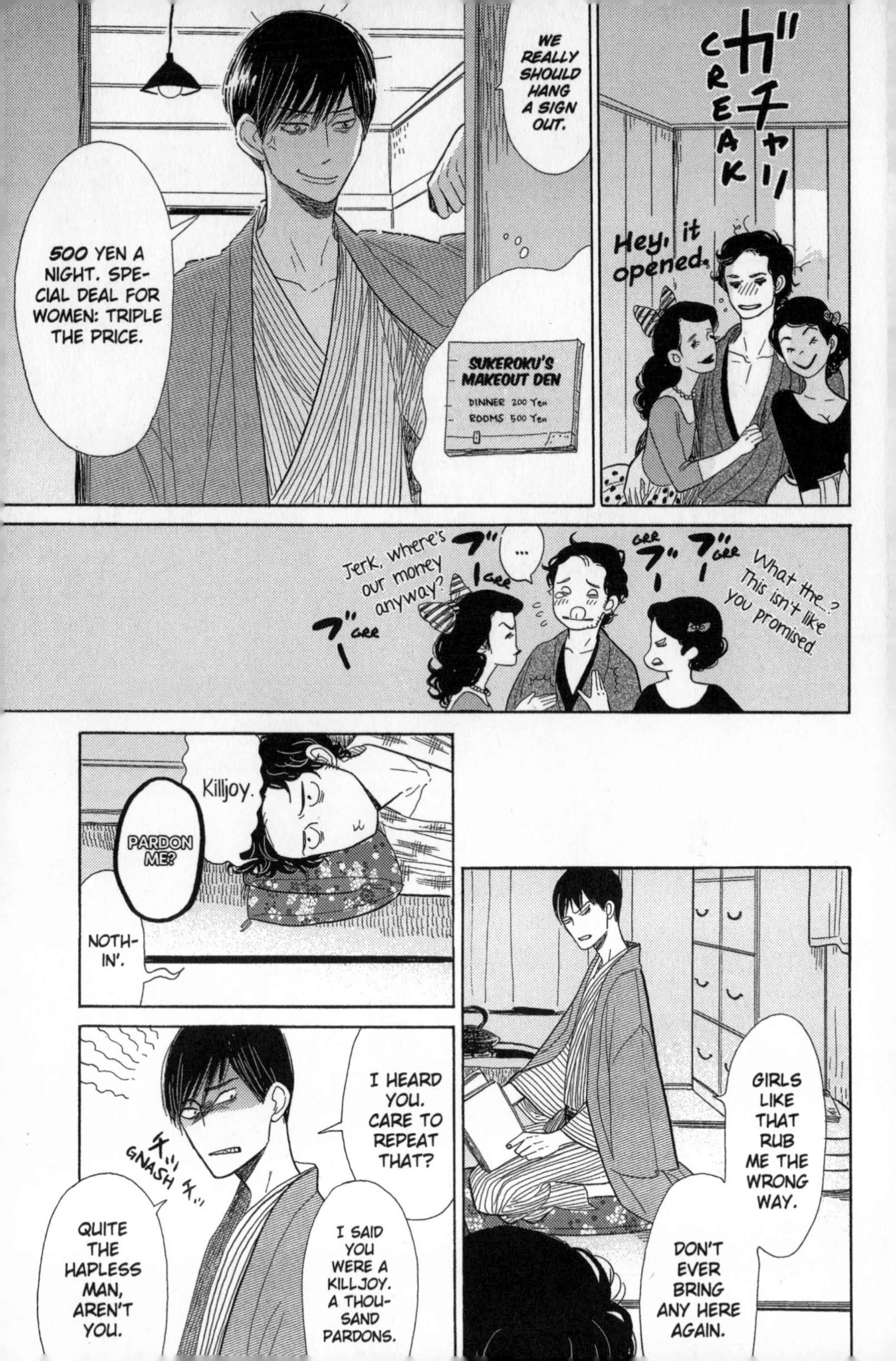

CREAK
Hey, it opened.
WE REALLY SHOULD HANG A SIGN OUT.
SUKEROKU'S MAKEOUT DEN
DINNER 200 Yen
ROOMS 500 Yen
500 YEN A NIGHT. SPECIAL DEAL FOR WOMEN: TRIPLE THE PRICE.
What the...? This isn't like you promised.
GRR
GRR
...
GRR
Jerk, where's our money anyway?
GRR
GIRLS LIKE THAT RUB ME THE WRONG WAY.
DON'T EVER BRING ANY HERE AGAIN.
Killjoy.
PARDON ME?
NOTHIN'.
I HEARD YOU. CARE TO REPEAT THAT?
GNASH
I SAID YOU WERE A KILLJOY. A THOUSAND PARDONS.
QUITE THE HAPLESS MAN, AREN'T YOU.

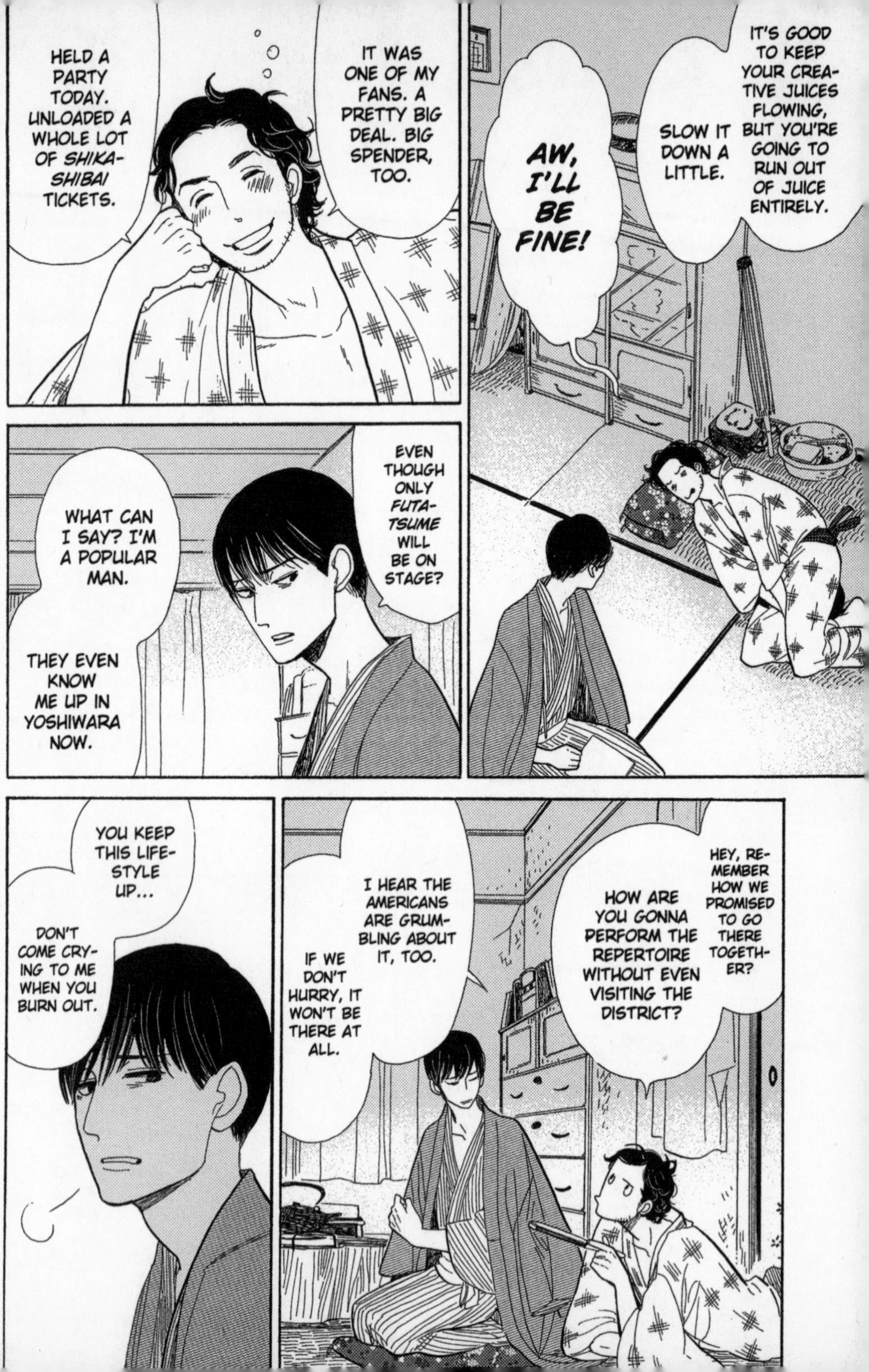

IT'S GOOD TO KEEP YOUR CREATIVE JUICES FLOWING, BUT YOU'RE GOING TO RUN OUT OF JUICE ENTIRELY.
SLOW IT DOWN A LITTLE.
AW, I'LL BE FINE!
IT WAS ONE OF MY FANS. A PRETTY BIG DEAL. BIG SPENDER, TOO.
HELD A PARTY TODAY. UNLOADED A WHOLE LOT OF *SHIKA-SHIBAI* TICKETS.
EVEN THOUGH ONLY *FUTATSUME* WILL BE ON STAGE?
WHAT CAN I SAY? I'M A POPULAR MAN.
THEY EVEN KNOW ME UP IN YOSHIWARA NOW.
HEY, REMEMBER HOW WE PROMISED TO GO THERE TOGETHER?
HOW ARE YOU GONNA PERFORM THE REPERTOIRE WITHOUT EVEN VISITING THE DISTRICT?
I HEAR THE AMERICANS ARE GRUMBLING ABOUT IT, TOO.
IF WE DON'T HURRY, IT WON'T BE THERE AT ALL.
YOU KEEP THIS LIFESTYLE UP...
DON'T COME CRYING TO ME WHEN YOU BURN OUT.

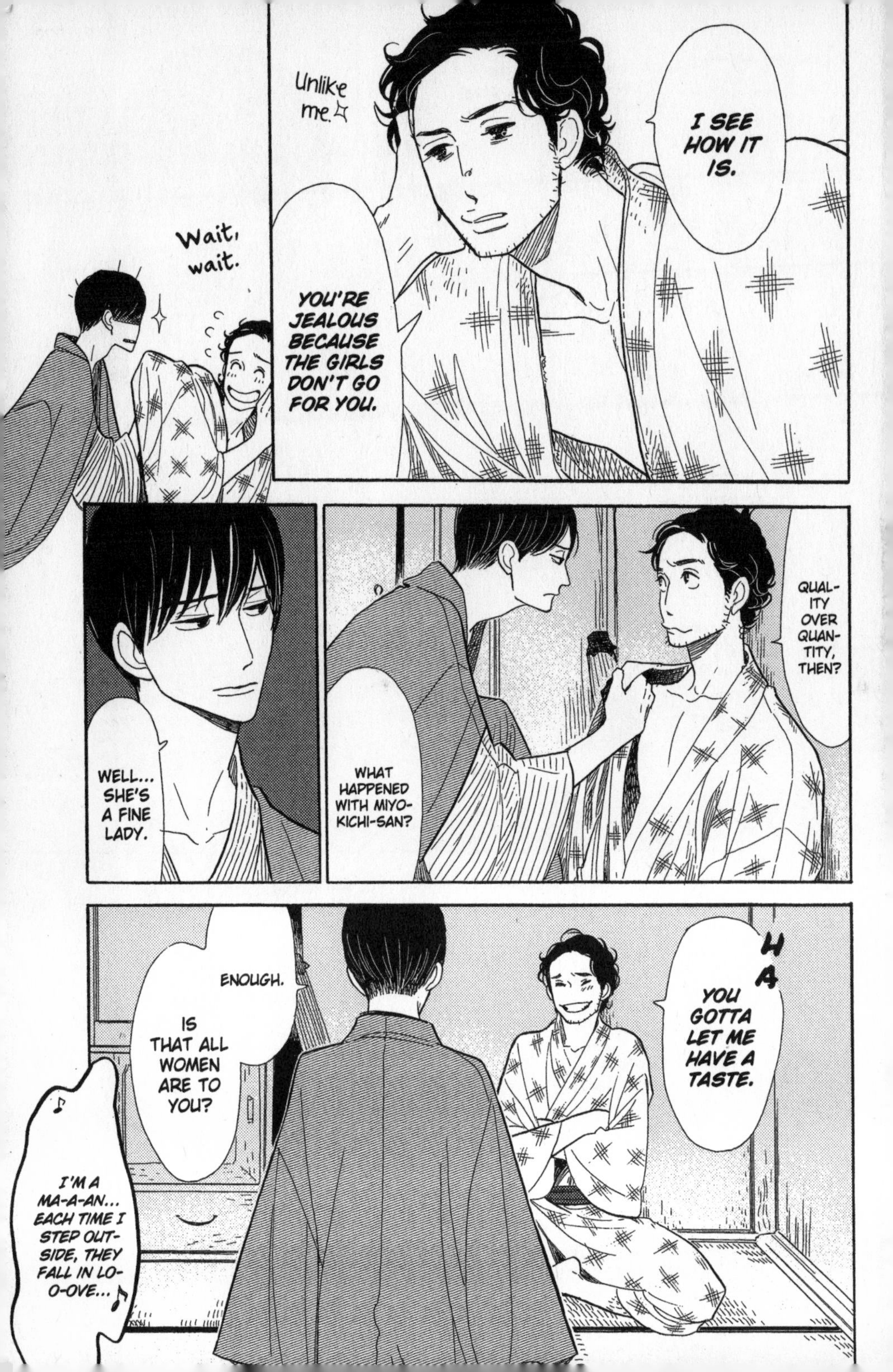
I SEE HOW IT IS.
Unlike me.
YOU'RE JEALOUS BECAUSE THE GIRLS DON'T GO FOR YOU.
Wait, wait.
QUALITY OVER QUANTITY, THEN?
WHAT HAPPENED WITH MIYOKICHI-SAN?
WELL... SHE'S A FINE LADY.
HA
YOU GOTTA LET ME HAVE A TASTE.
ENOUGH.
IS THAT ALL WOMEN ARE TO YOU?
I'M A MA-A-AN... EACH TIME I STEP OUTSIDE, THEY FALL IN LO-O-OVE...

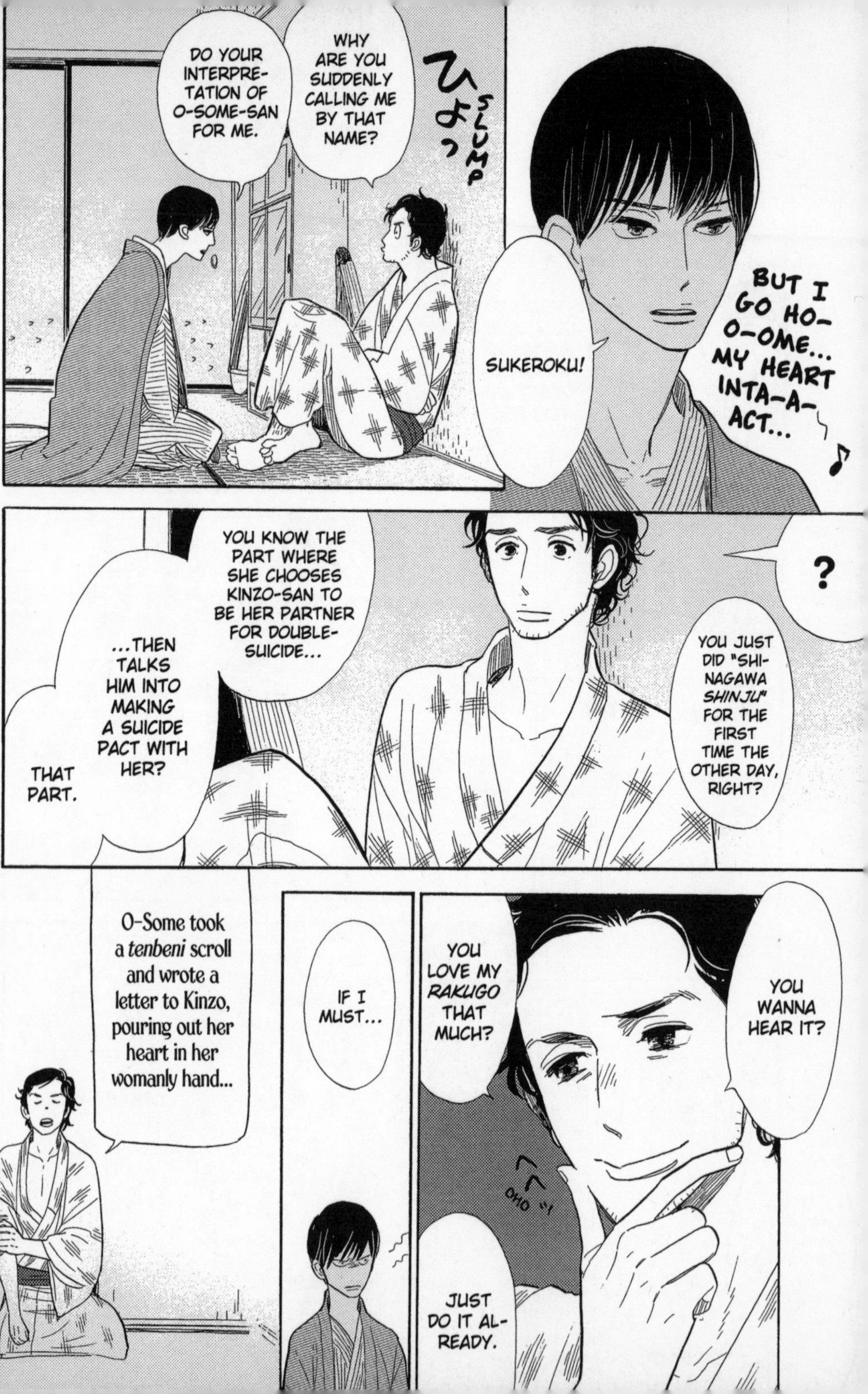
BUT I GO HO-O-OME... MY HEART INTA-A-ACT... ♪
SUKEROKU!
ひょっ SLUMP
WHY ARE YOU SUDDENLY CALLING ME BY THAT NAME?
DO YOUR INTERPRETATION OF O-SOME-SAN FOR ME.
?
YOU JUST DID "SHI-NAGAWA *SHINJU*" FOR THE FIRST TIME THE OTHER DAY, RIGHT?
YOU KNOW THE PART WHERE SHE CHOOSES KINZO-SAN TO BE HER PARTNER FOR DOUBLE-SUICIDE...
...THEN TALKS HIM INTO MAKING A SUICIDE PACT WITH HER?
THAT PART.
YOU WANNA HEAR IT?
OHO
YOU LOVE MY *RAKUGO* THAT MUCH?
JUST DO IT AL-READY.
IF I MUST...
O-Some took a *tenbeni* scroll and wrote a letter to Kinzo, pouring out her heart in her womanly hand...

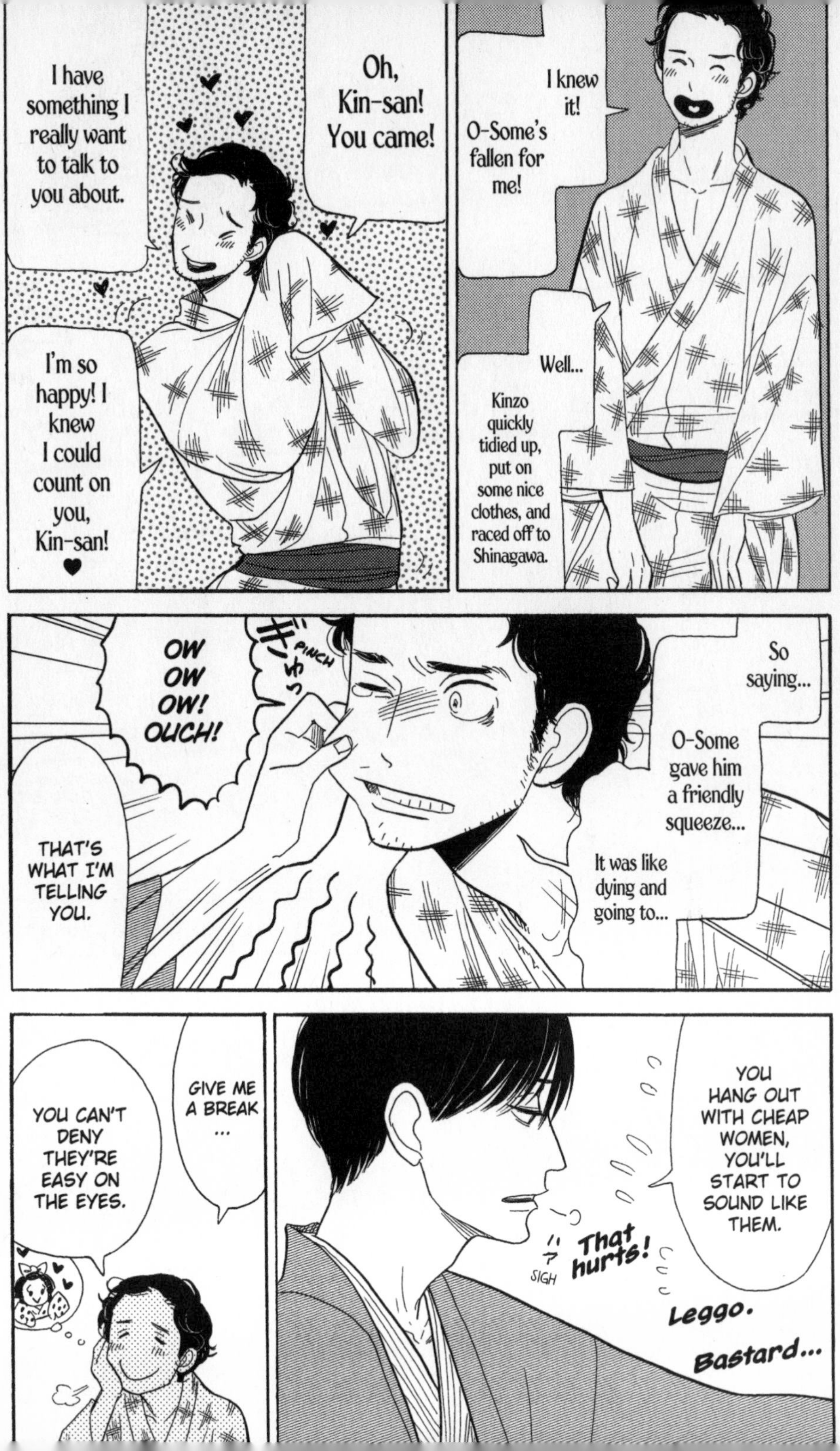
I knew it!
O-Some's fallen for me!
Well...
Kinzo quickly tidied up, put on some nice clothes, and raced off to Shinagawa.
Oh, Kin-san! You came!
I have something I really want to talk to you about.
I'm so happy! I knew I could count on you, Kin-san! ♥
So saying...
O-Some gave him a friendly squeeze...
It was like dying and going to...
PINCH
OW OW OW! OUCH!
THAT'S WHAT I'M TELLING YOU.
YOU HANG OUT WITH CHEAP WOMEN, YOU'LL START TO SOUND LIKE THEM.
SIGH
That hurts!
Leggo.
Bastard...
GIVE ME A BREAK ...
YOU CAN'T DENY THEY'RE EASY ON THE EYES.

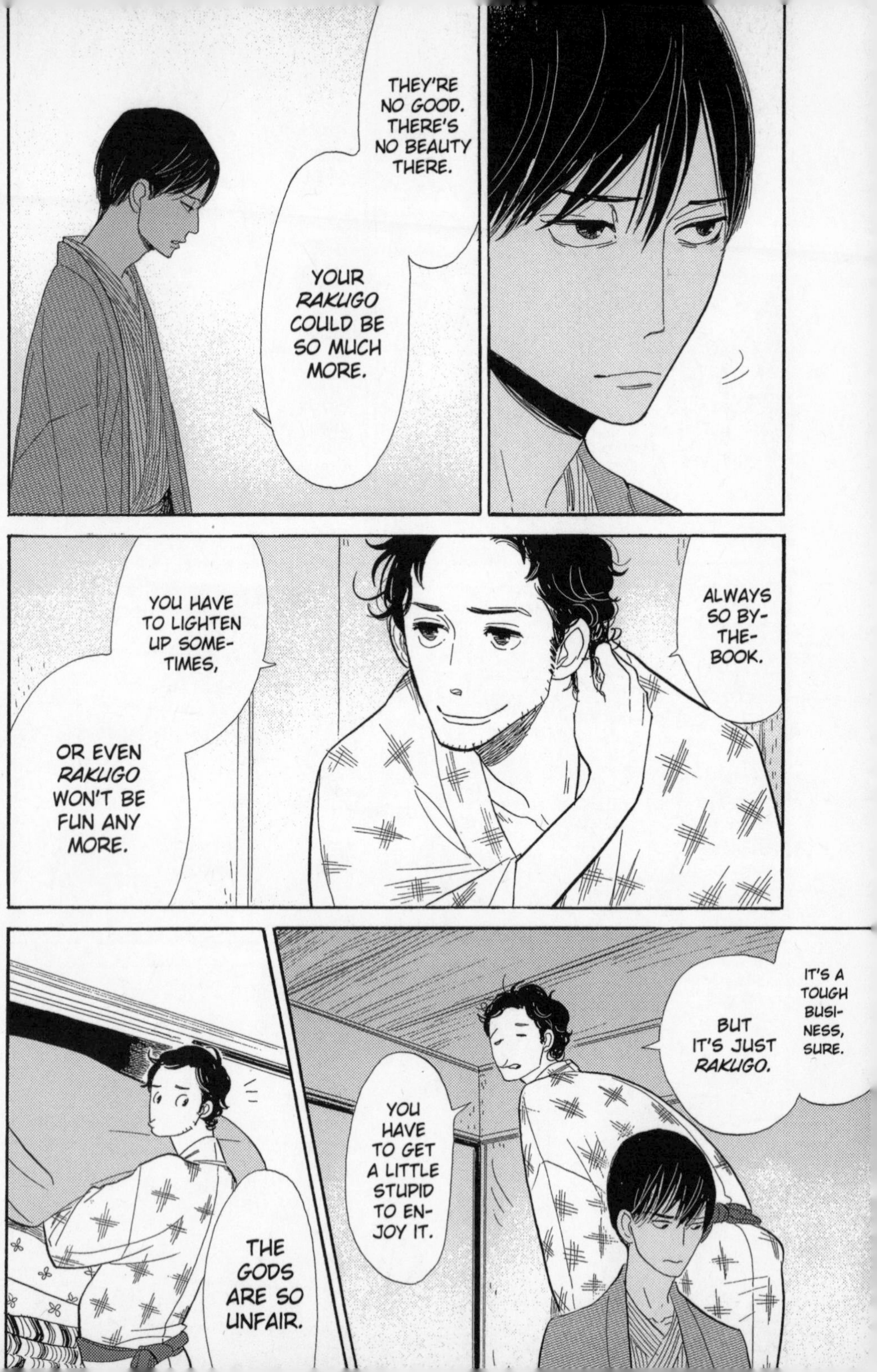
THEY'RE NO GOOD. THERE'S NO BEAUTY THERE.
YOUR *RAKUGO* COULD BE SO MUCH MORE.
ALWAYS SO BY-THE-BOOK.
YOU HAVE TO LIGHTEN UP SOMETIMES,
OR EVEN *RAKUGO* WON'T BE FUN ANY MORE.
IT'S A TOUGH BUSINESS, SURE.
BUT IT'S JUST *RAKUGO*.
YOU HAVE TO GET A LITTLE STUPID TO ENJOY IT.
THE GODS ARE SO UNFAIR.

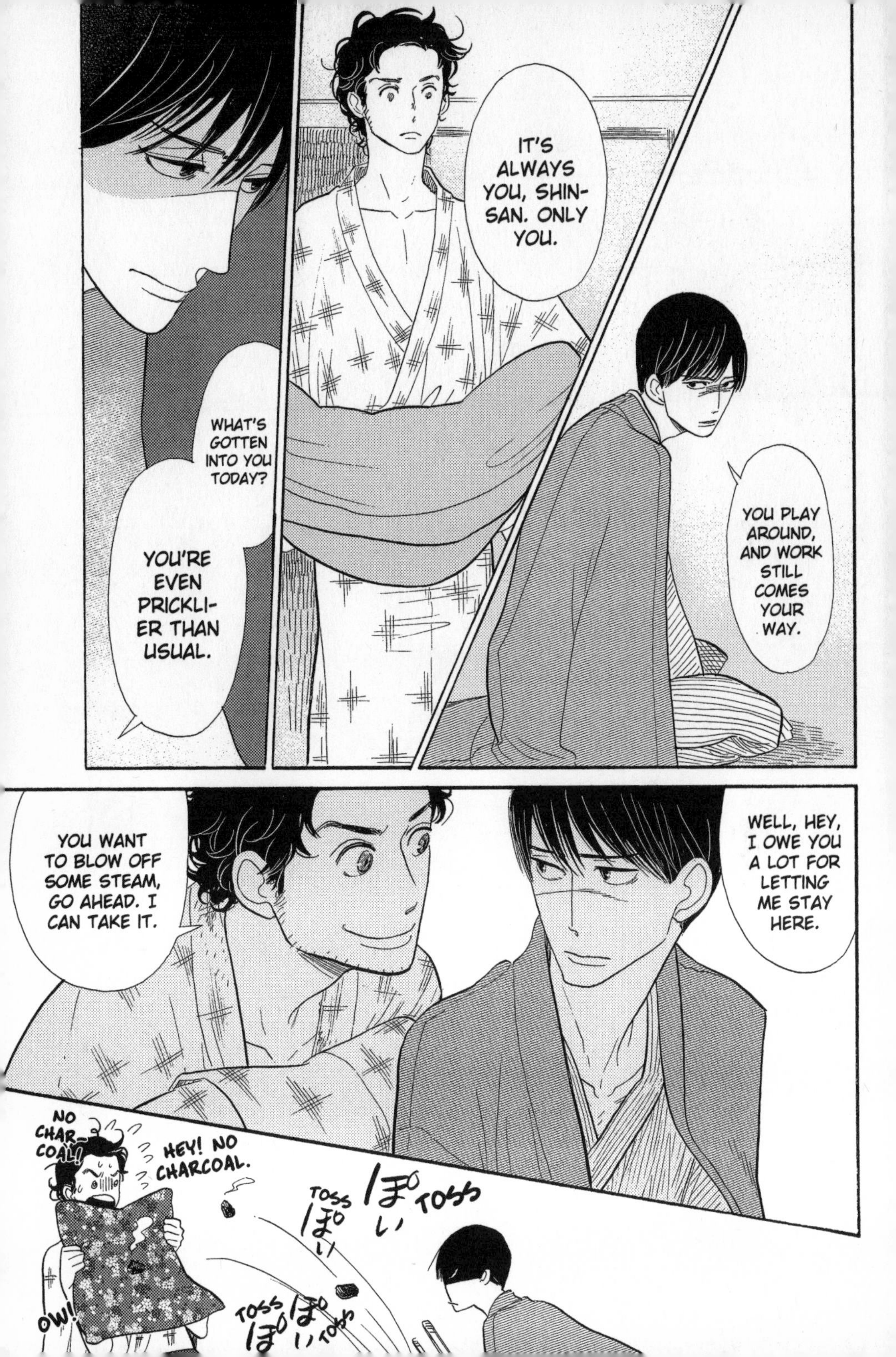
YOU PLAY AROUND, AND WORK STILL COMES YOUR WAY.
IT'S ALWAYS YOU, SHIN-SAN. ONLY YOU.
WHAT'S GOTTEN INTO YOU TODAY?
YOU'RE EVEN PRICKLI-ER THAN USUAL.
WELL, HEY, I OWE YOU A LOT FOR LETTING ME STAY HERE.
YOU WANT TO BLOW OFF SOME STEAM, GO AHEAD. I CAN TAKE IT.
ぽい TOSS
TOSS ぽい
HEY! NO CHARCOAL.
NO CHAR-COAL!
ぽ ぽい TOSS TOSS
OW!

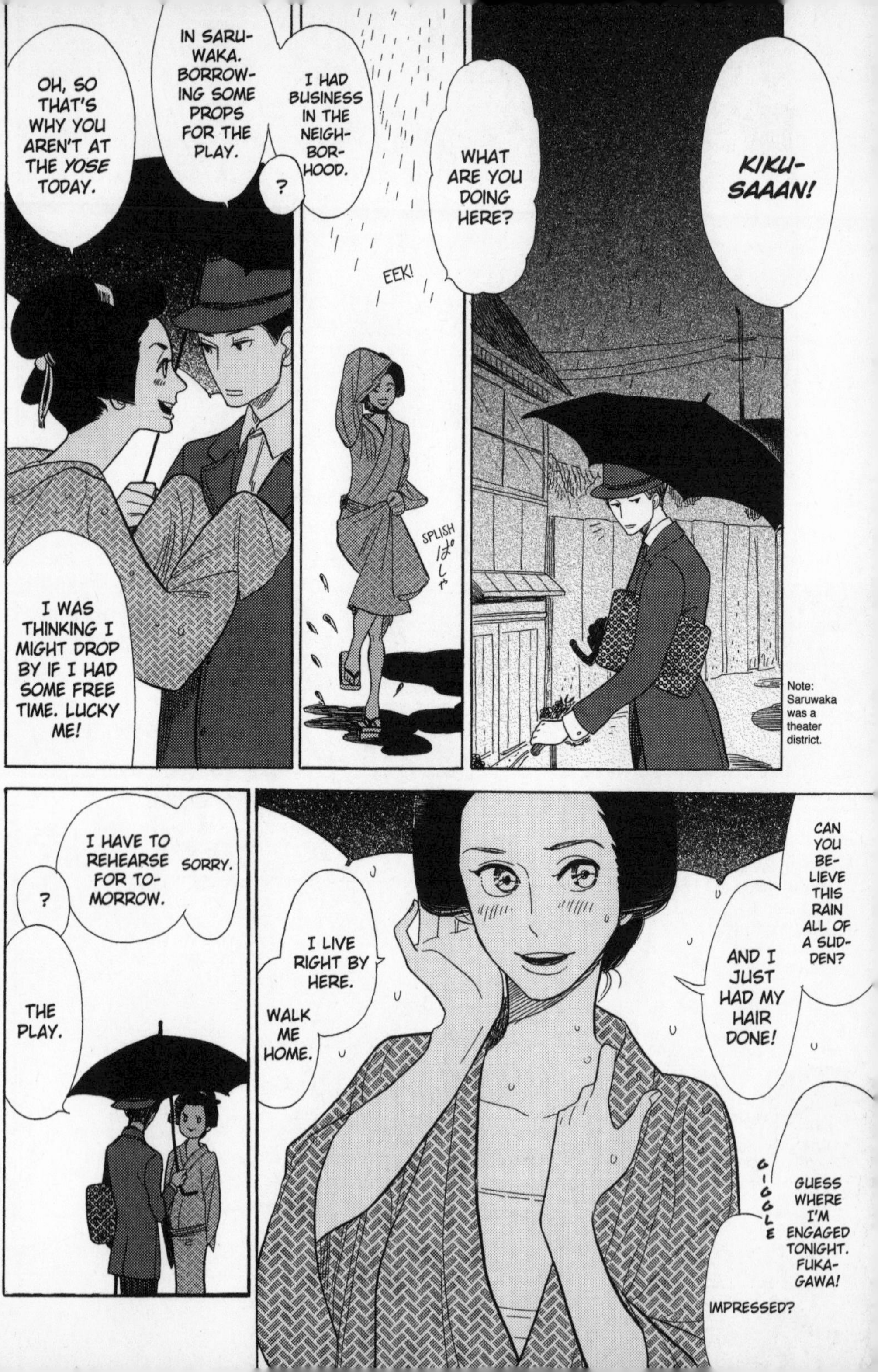
KIKU-SAAAN!
WHAT ARE YOU DOING HERE?
I HAD BUSINESS IN THE NEIGHBORHOOD.
EEK!
SPLISH
ぱしゃ
?
IN SARUWAKA. BORROWING SOME PROPS FOR THE PLAY.
OH, SO THAT'S WHY YOU AREN'T AT THE *YOSE* TODAY.
I WAS THINKING I MIGHT DROP BY IF I HAD SOME FREE TIME. LUCKY ME!
CAN YOU BELIEVE THIS RAIN ALL OF A SUDDEN?
AND I JUST HAD MY HAIR DONE!
I LIVE RIGHT BY HERE.
WALK ME HOME.
GUESS WHERE I'M ENGAGED TONIGHT. FUKAGAWA!
GIGGLE
IMPRESSED?
SORRY.
I HAVE TO REHEARSE FOR TOMORROW.
?
THE PLAY.

Note: Saruwaka was a theater district.

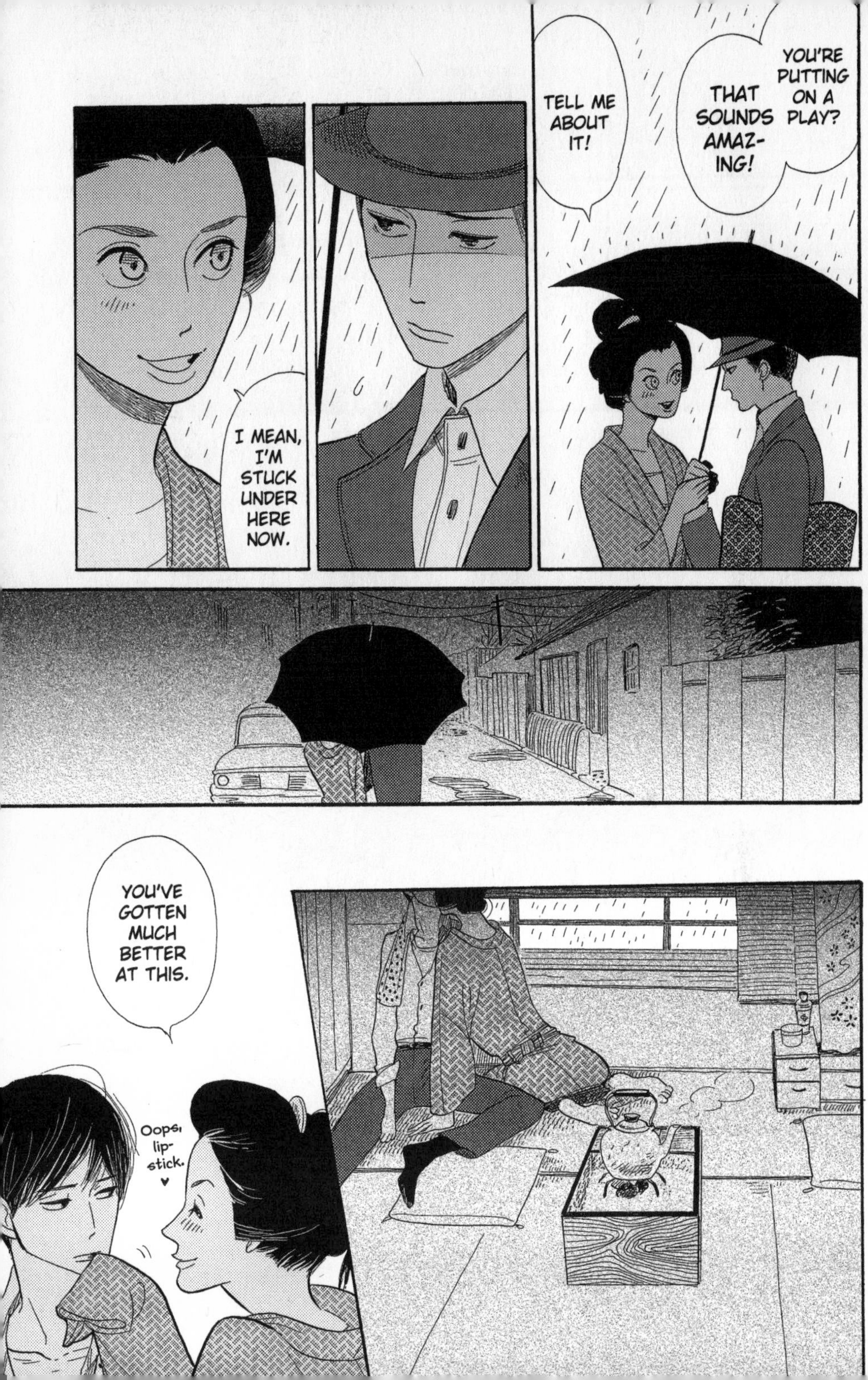
YOU'RE PUTTING ON A PLAY?
THAT SOUNDS AMAZ-ING!
TELL ME ABOUT IT!
I MEAN, I'M STUCK UNDER HERE NOW.
YOU'VE GOTTEN MUCH BETTER AT THIS.
Oops, lip-stick.

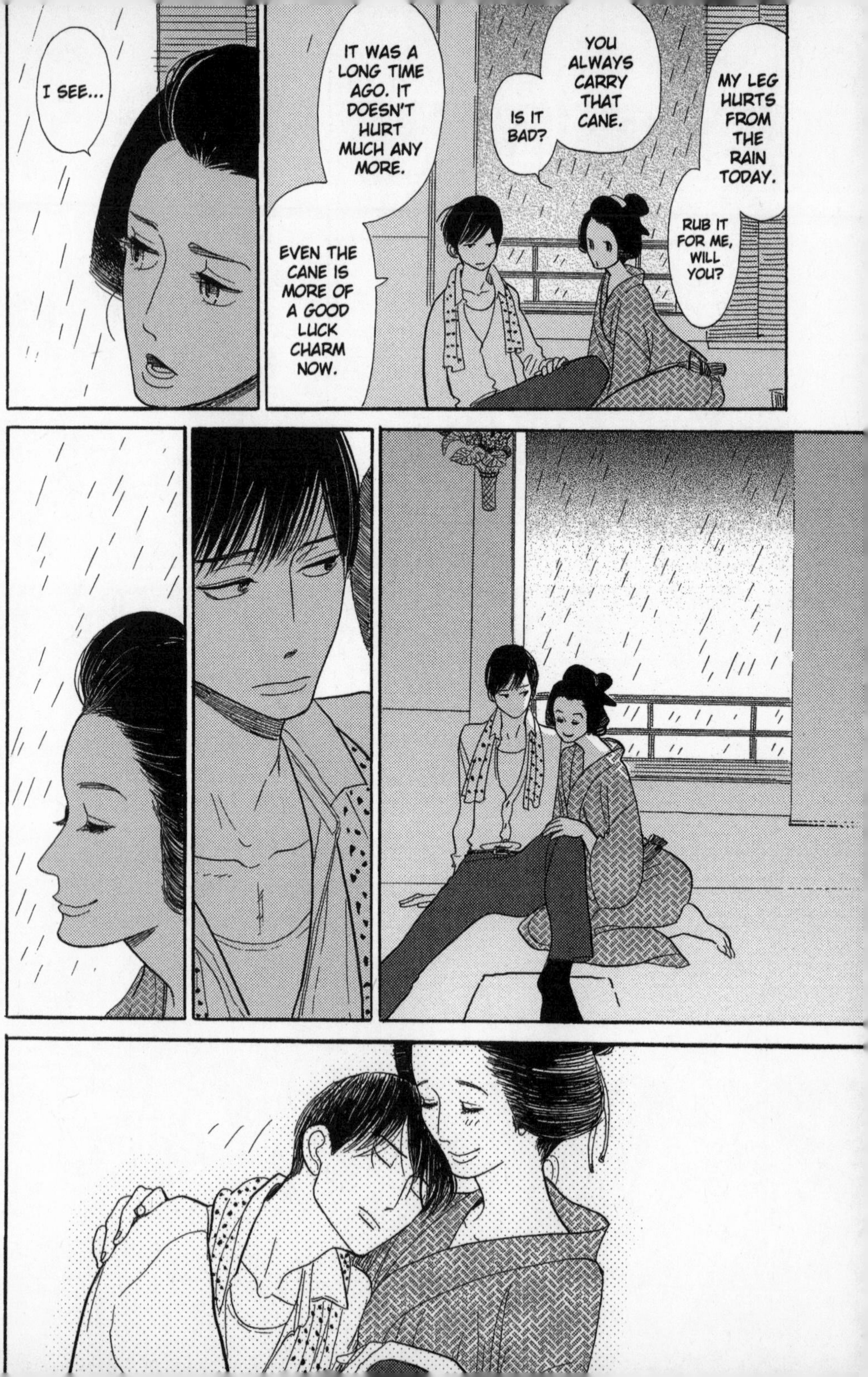
MY LEG HURTS FROM THE RAIN TODAY.
RUB IT FOR ME, WILL YOU?
YOU ALWAYS CARRY THAT CANE.
IS IT BAD?
IT WAS A LONG TIME AGO. IT DOESN'T HURT MUCH ANY MORE.
EVEN THE CANE IS MORE OF A GOOD LUCK CHARM NOW.
I SEE...

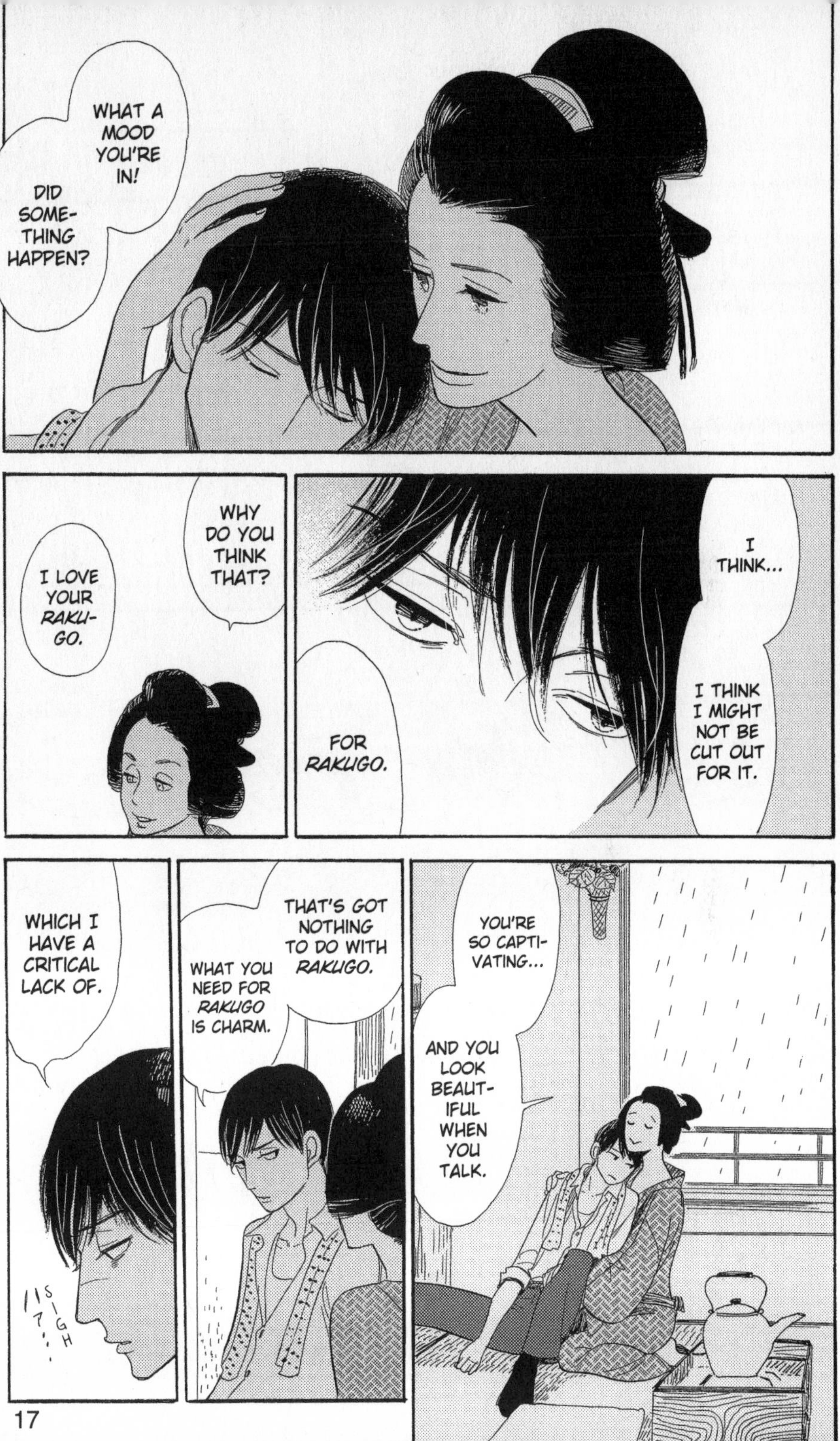
WHAT A MOOD YOU'RE IN!
DID SOMETHING HAPPEN?
I THINK...
I THINK I MIGHT NOT BE CUT OUT FOR IT.
FOR *RAKUGO*.
WHY DO YOU THINK THAT?
I LOVE YOUR *RAKUGO*.
YOU'RE SO CAPTIVATING...
AND YOU LOOK BEAUTIFUL WHEN YOU TALK.
THAT'S GOT NOTHING TO DO WITH *RAKUGO*.
WHAT YOU NEED FOR *RAKUGO* IS CHARM.
WHICH I HAVE A CRITICAL LACK OF.
SIGH...

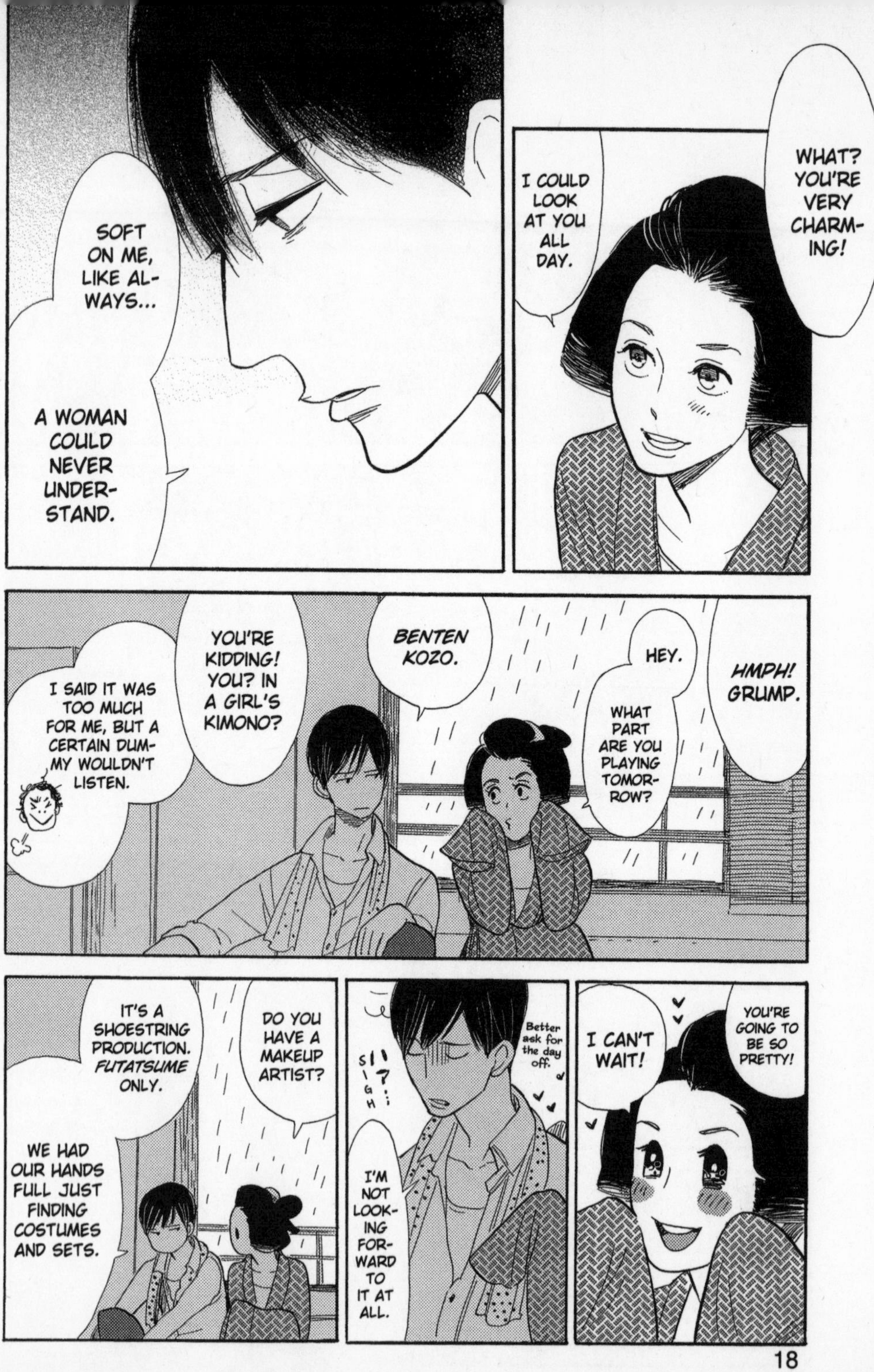
WHAT? YOU'RE VERY CHARMING!
I COULD LOOK AT YOU ALL DAY.
SOFT ON ME, LIKE ALWAYS...
A WOMAN COULD NEVER UNDERSTAND.
HMPH! GRUMP.
HEY.
WHAT PART ARE YOU PLAYING TOMORROW?
BENTEN KOZO.
YOU'RE KIDDING! YOU? IN A GIRL'S KIMONO?
I SAID IT WAS TOO MUCH FOR ME, BUT A CERTAIN DUMMY WOULDN'T LISTEN.
YOU'RE GOING TO BE SO PRETTY!
I CAN'T WAIT!
Better ask for the day off.
SIGH
I'M NOT LOOKING FORWARD TO IT AT ALL.
DO YOU HAVE A MAKEUP ARTIST?
IT'S A SHOESTRING PRODUCTION. FUTATSUME ONLY.
WE HAD OUR HANDS FULL JUST FINDING COSTUMES AND SETS.

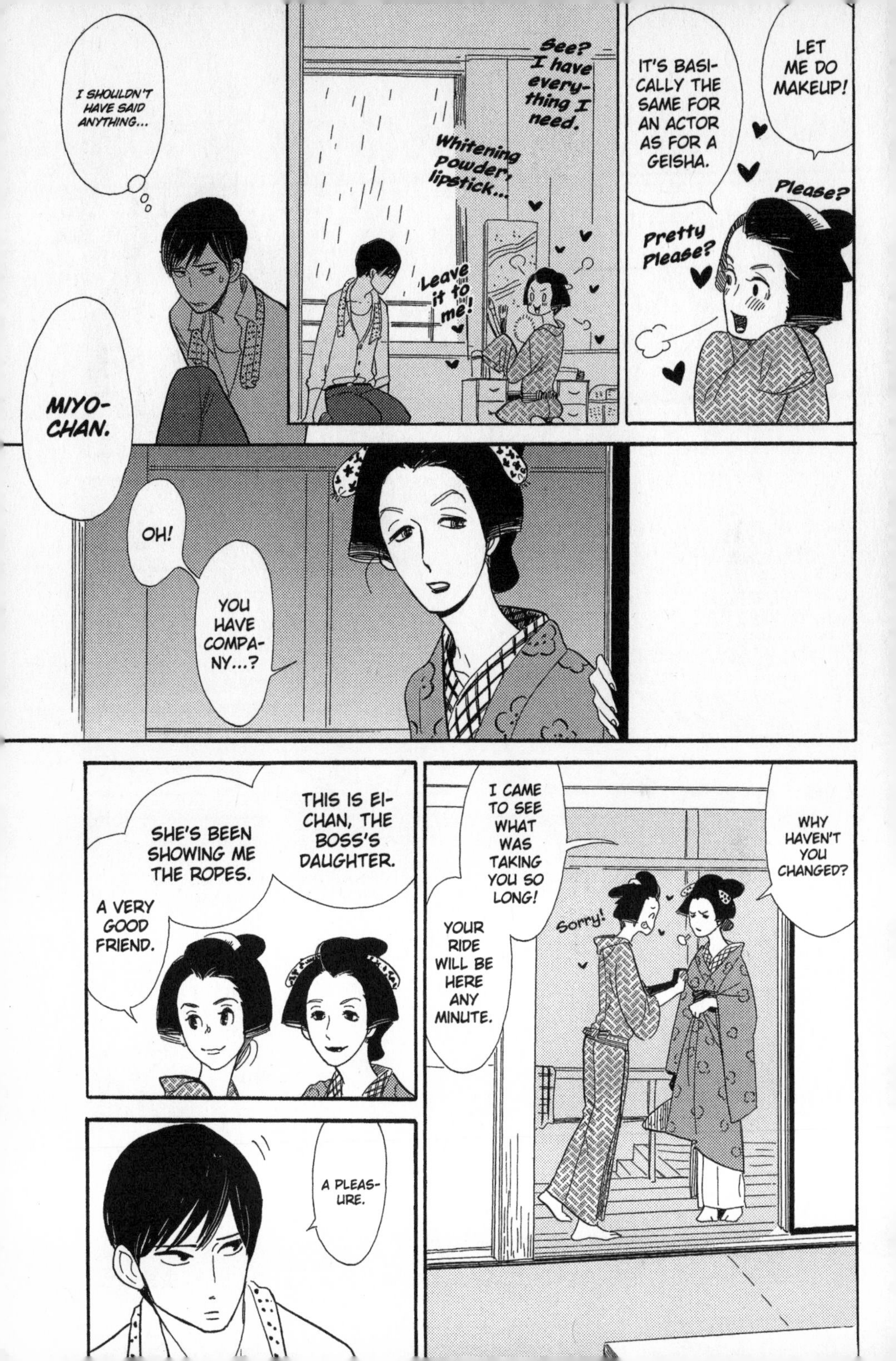
LET ME DO MAKEUP!
IT'S BASI-CALLY THE SAME FOR AN ACTOR AS FOR A GEISHA.
Please?
Pretty Please?
See? I have every-thing I need.
Whitening Powder, lipstick...
Leave it to me!
I SHOULDN'T HAVE SAID ANYTHING...
MIYO-CHAN.
OH!
YOU HAVE COMPA-NY...?
WHY HAVEN'T YOU CHANGED?
I CAME TO SEE WHAT WAS TAKING YOU SO LONG!
Sorry!
YOUR RIDE WILL BE HERE ANY MINUTE.
THIS IS EI-CHAN, THE BOSS'S DAUGHTER.
SHE'S BEEN SHOWING ME THE ROPES.
A VERY GOOD FRIEND.
A PLEAS-URE.

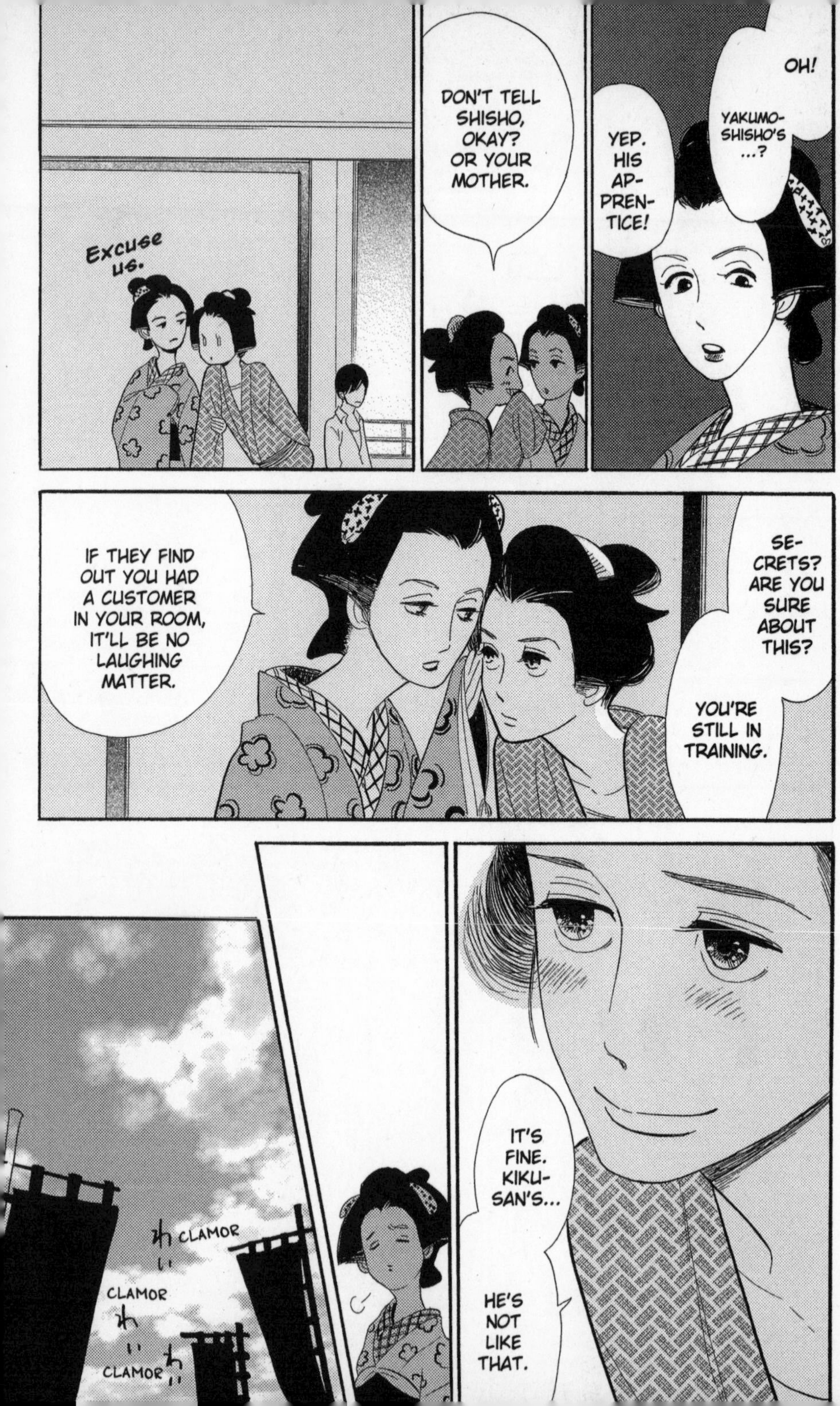
OH!
YAKUMO-SHISHO'S ...?
YEP. HIS AP-PREN-TICE!
DON'T TELL SHISHO, OKAY? OR YOUR MOTHER.
Excuse us.
SE-CRETS? ARE YOU SURE ABOUT THIS?
YOU'RE STILL IN TRAINING.
IF THEY FIND OUT YOU HAD A CUSTOMER IN YOUR ROOM, IT'LL BE NO LAUGHING MATTER.
IT'S FINE. KIKU-SAN'S...
HE'S NOT LIKE THAT.
CLAMOR
CLAMOR
CLAMOR

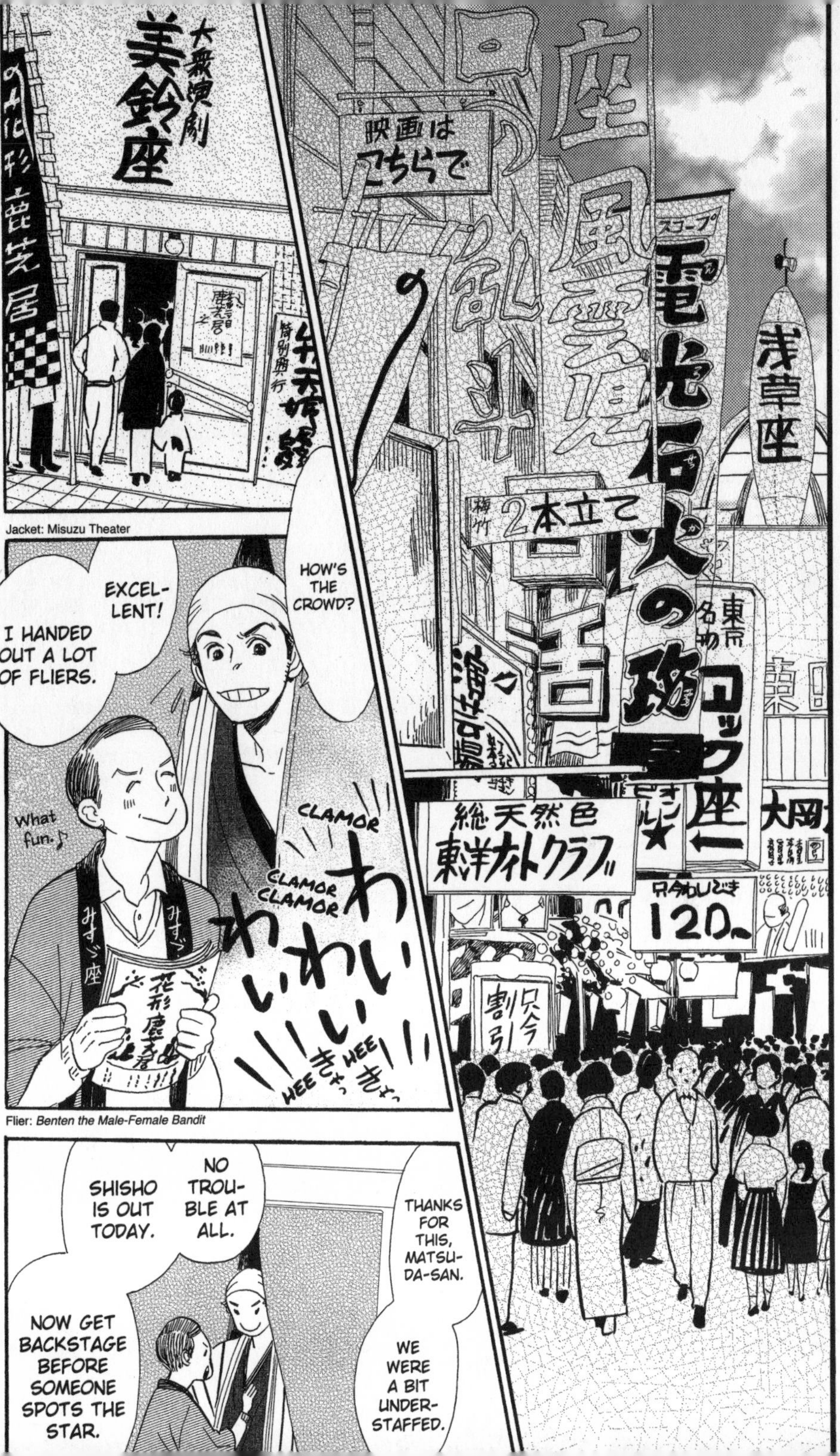

映画はこちらで
浅草座
2本立て
総天然色 東洋ナイトクラブ
ロック座
120
大衆演劇 美鈴座
Jacket: Misuzu Theater
HOW'S THE CROWD?
EXCEL-LENT!
I HANDED OUT A LOT OF FLIERS.
What fun.♪
CLAMOR
CLAMOR CLAMOR
わいわいい
HEE HEE
Flier: Benten the Male-Female Bandit
THANKS FOR THIS, MATSU-DA-SAN.
WE WERE A BIT UNDER-STAFFED.
NO TROU-BLE AT ALL.
SHISHO IS OUT TODAY.
NOW GET BACKSTAGE BEFORE SOMEONE SPOTS THE STAR.

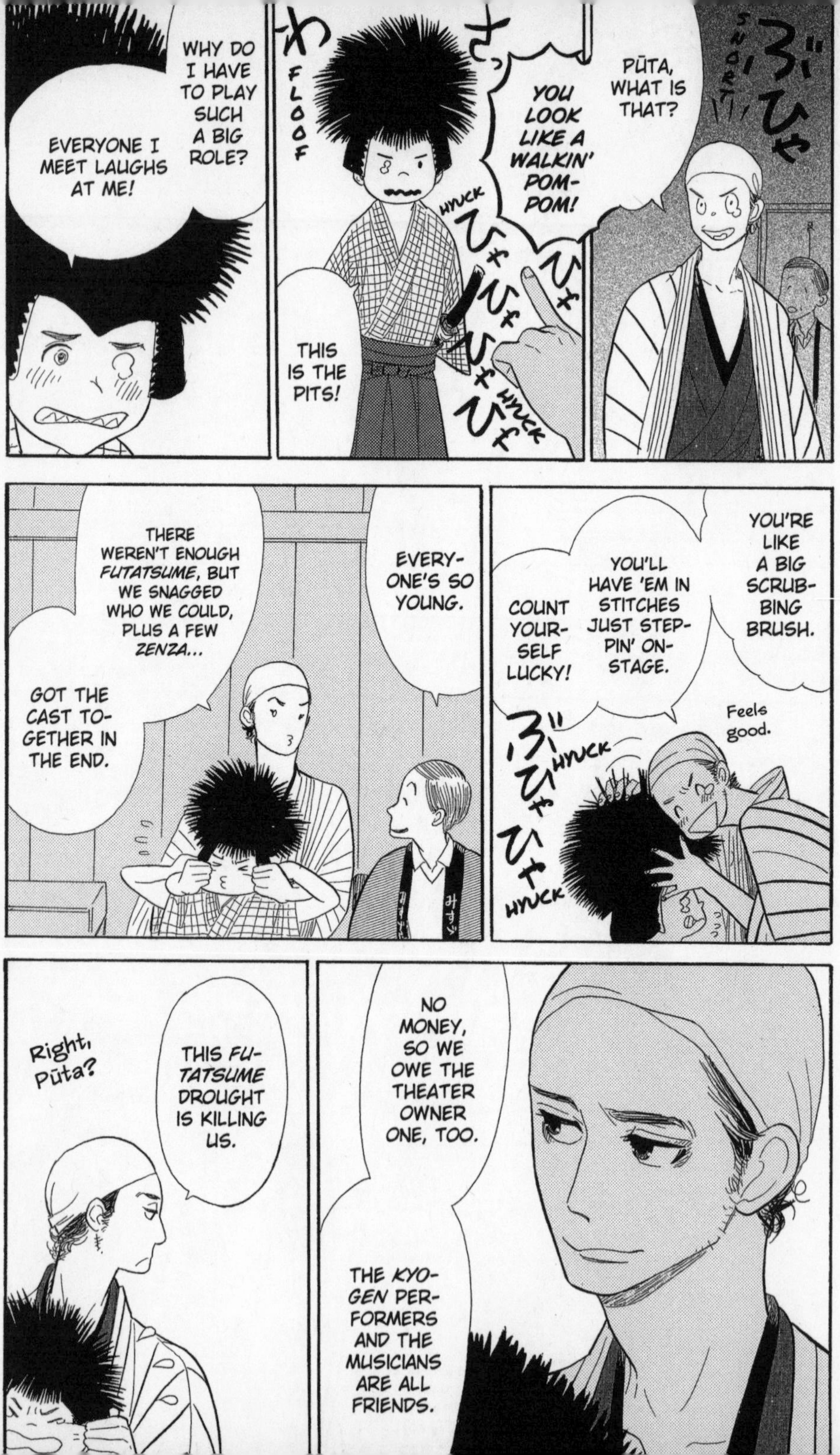

ぶひゃ
SNORT
PŪTA, WHAT IS THAT?
わさっ
FLOOOF
YOU LOOK LIKE A WALKIN' POM-POM!
ひゃひゃひゃひゃひゃ
HYUCK
HYUCK
THIS IS THE PITS!
WHY DO I HAVE TO PLAY SUCH A BIG ROLE?
EVERYONE I MEET LAUGHS AT ME!
YOU'RE LIKE A BIG SCRUBBING BRUSH.
YOU'LL HAVE 'EM IN STITCHES JUST STEPPIN' ONSTAGE.
COUNT YOURSELF LUCKY!
Feels good.
ぶひゃひゃ
HYUCK
HYUCK
EVERYONE'S SO YOUNG.
THERE WEREN'T ENOUGH *FUTATSUME*, BUT WE SNAGGED WHO WE COULD, PLUS A FEW *ZENZA*...
GOT THE CAST TOGETHER IN THE END.
NO MONEY, SO WE OWE THE THEATER OWNER ONE, TOO.
THE *KYOGEN* PERFORMERS AND THE MUSICIANS ARE ALL FRIENDS.
THIS *FUTATSUME* DROUGHT IS KILLING US.
Right, Pūta?

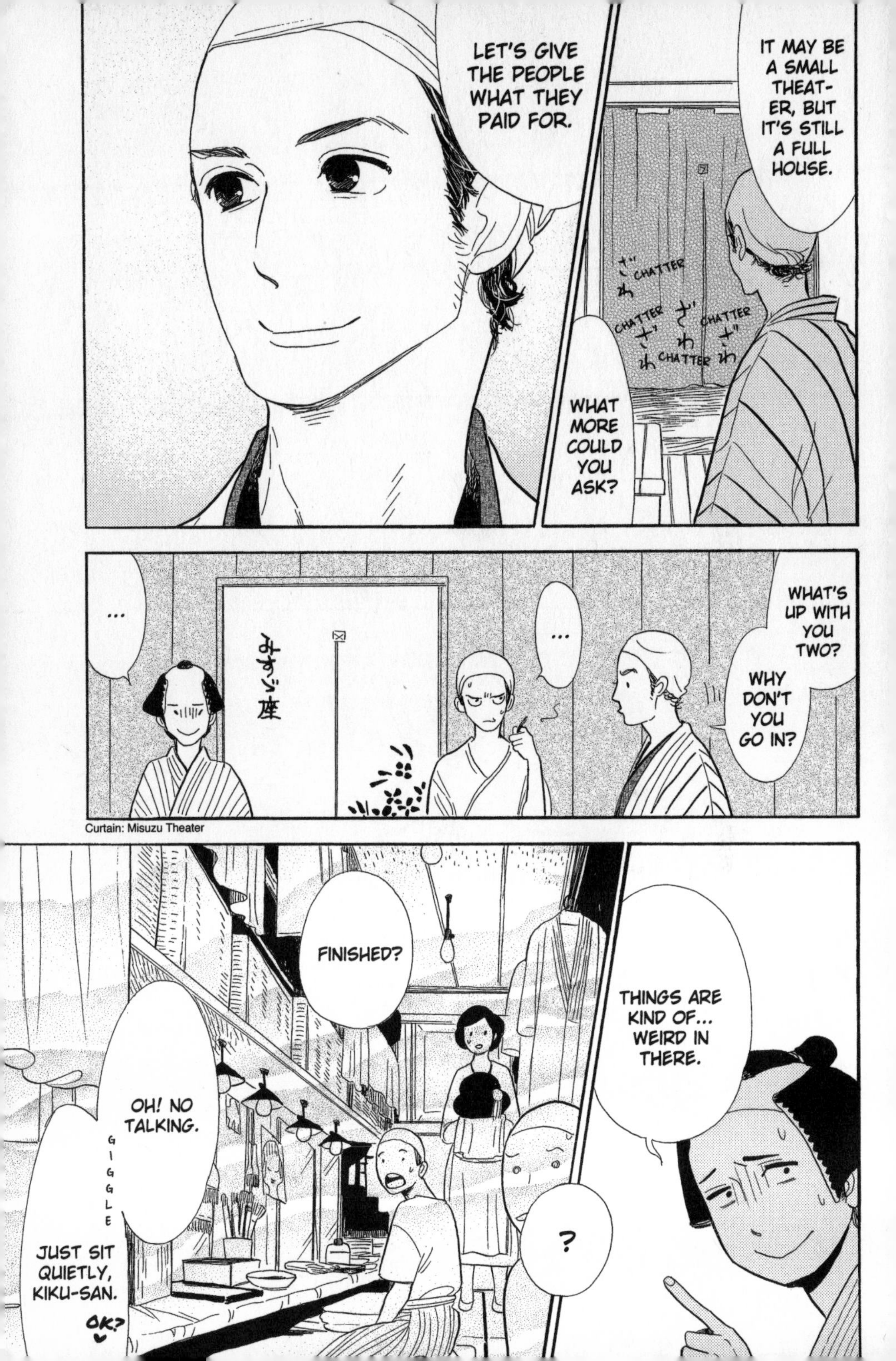
IT MAY BE A SMALL THEATER, BUT IT'S STILL A FULL HOUSE.
ざわ CHATTER
ざわ CHATTER
ざわ CHATTER
ざわ CHATTER
WHAT MORE COULD YOU ASK?
LET'S GIVE THE PEOPLE WHAT THEY PAID FOR.
WHAT'S UP WITH YOU TWO?
WHY DON'T YOU GO IN?
...
...
みすゞ座
Curtain: Misuzu Theater
THINGS ARE KIND OF... WEIRD IN THERE.
?
FINISHED?
OH! NO TALKING.
GIGGLE
JUST SIT QUIETLY, KIKU-SAN.
OK?

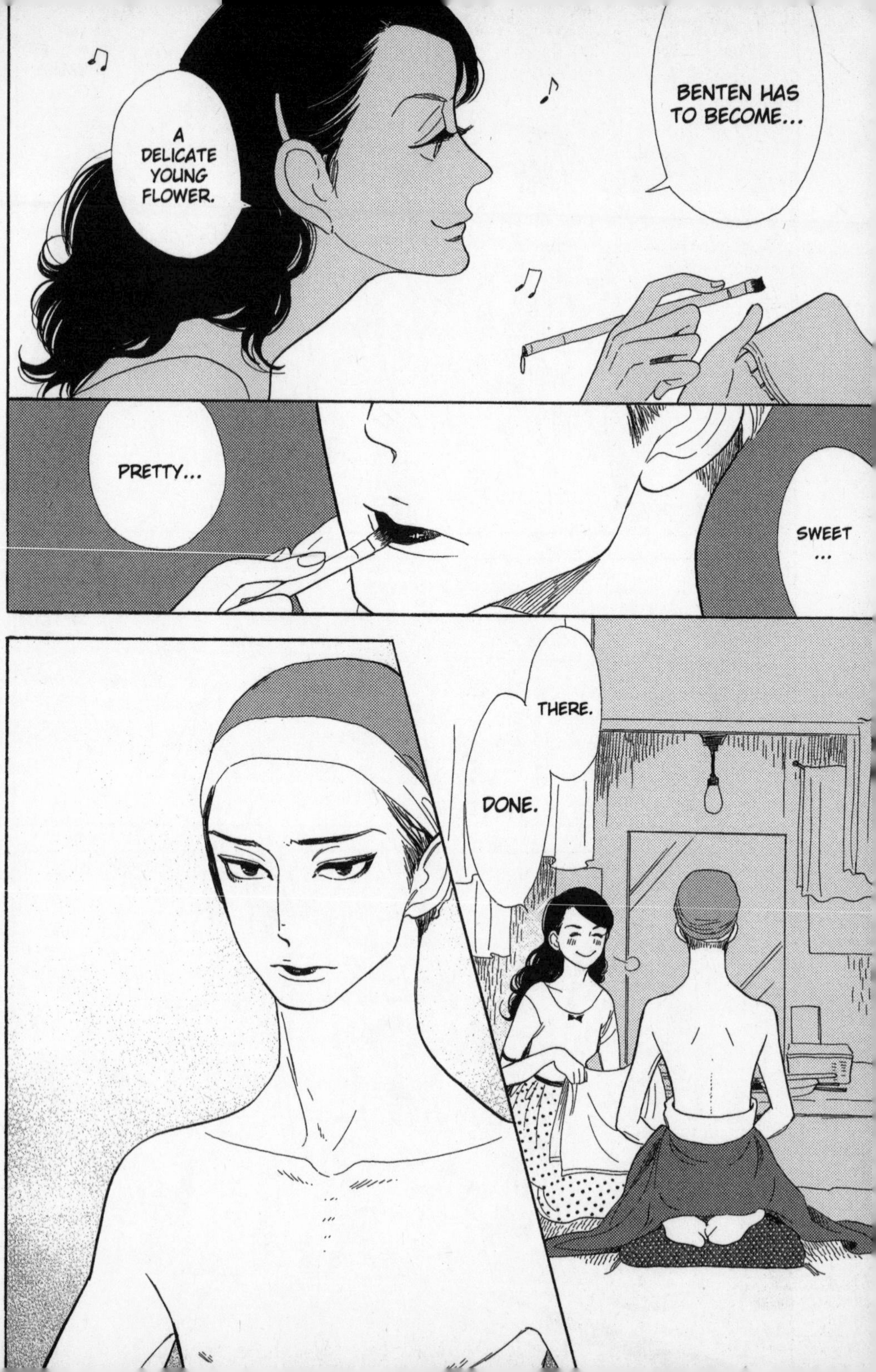
BENTEN HAS TO BECOME...
A DELICATE YOUNG FLOWER.
SWEET ...
PRETTY...
THERE.
DONE.

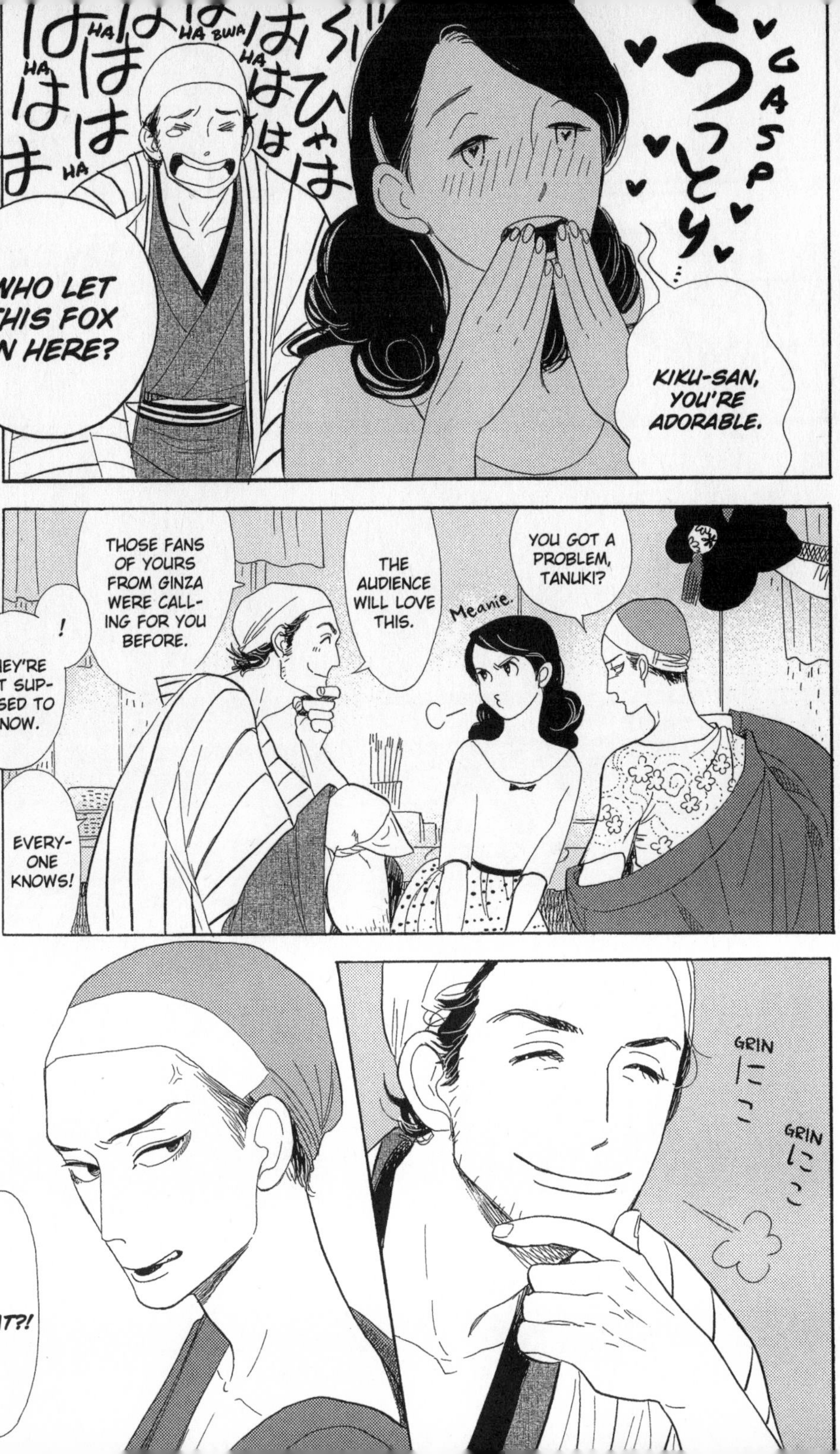
GASP
うっとり
KIKU-SAN, YOU'RE ADORABLE.
HA BWA HA HA HA HA
WHO LET THIS FOX IN HERE?
YOU GOT A PROBLEM, TANUKI?
Meanie.
THE AUDIENCE WILL LOVE THIS.
THOSE FANS OF YOURS FROM GINZA WERE CALLING FOR YOU BEFORE.
!
THEY'RE NOT SUPPOSED TO KNOW.
EVERYONE KNOWS!
GRIN にこ
GRIN にこ
WHAT?!

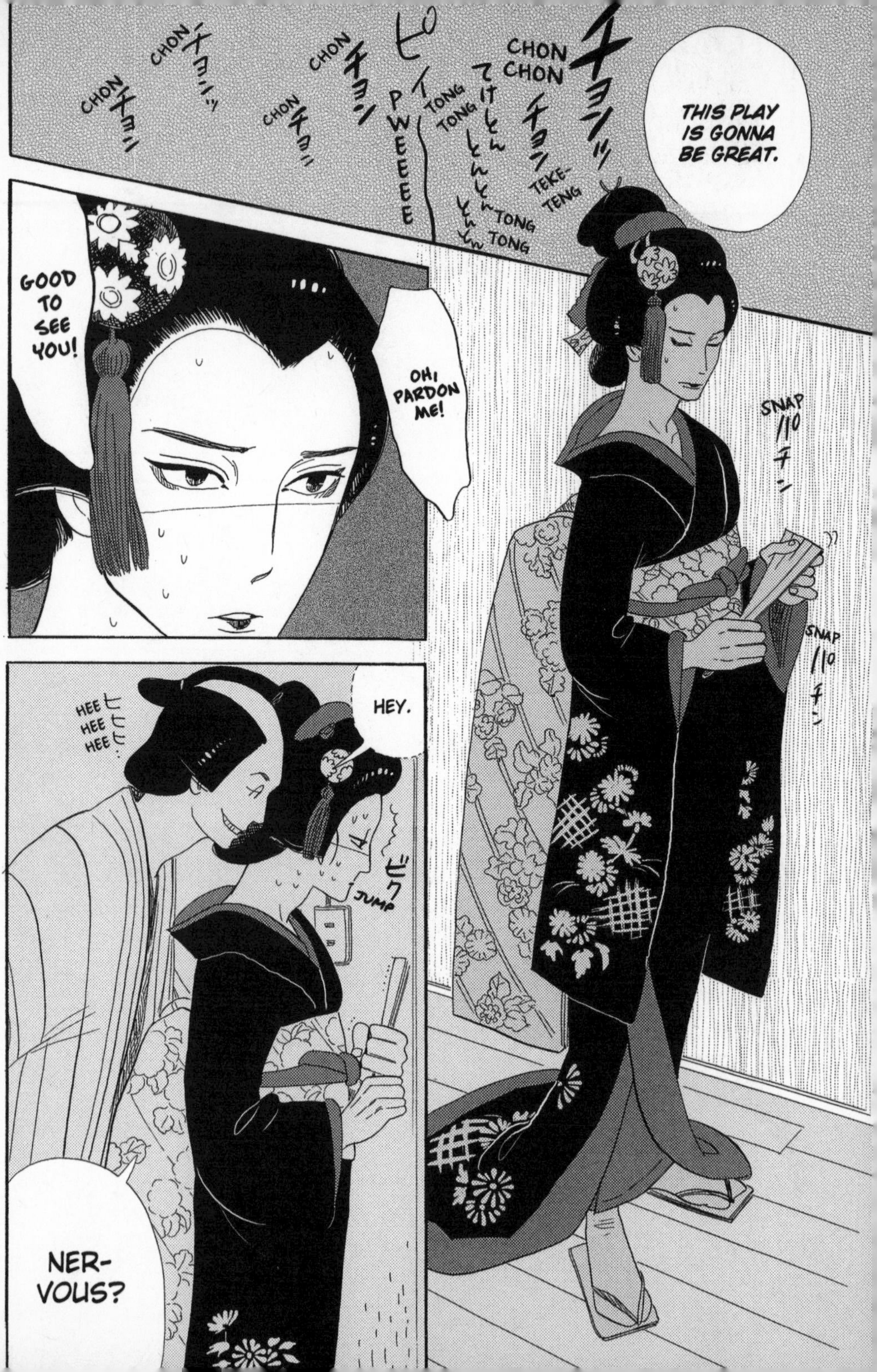
CHON CHON
TEKE-TENG
TONG TONG
TONG TONG
PWEEEE
CHON
CHON
CHON
CHON
THIS PLAY IS GONNA BE GREAT.
SNAP
SNAP
OH! PARDON ME!
GOOD TO SEE YOU!
HEY.
HEE HEE HEE
JUMP
NERVOUS?

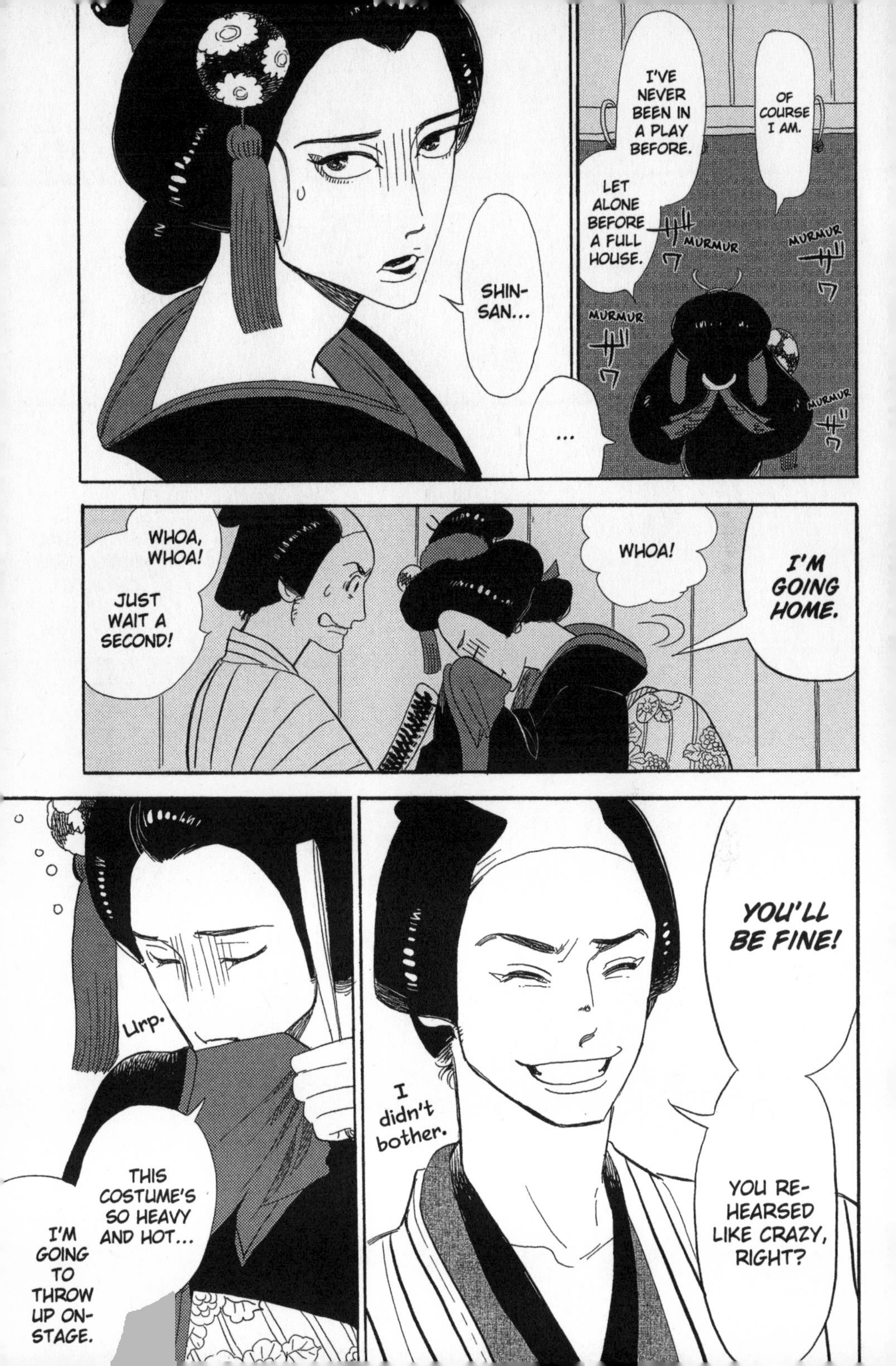
OF COURSE I AM.
I'VE NEVER BEEN IN A PLAY BEFORE.
LET ALONE BEFORE A FULL HOUSE.
MURMUR
MURMUR
MURMUR
MURMUR
SHIN-SAN...
...
I'M GOING HOME.
WHOA!
WHOA, WHOA!
JUST WAIT A SECOND!
YOU'LL BE FINE!
YOU RE-HEARSED LIKE CRAZY, RIGHT?
I didn't bother.
Urp.
THIS COSTUME'S SO HEAVY AND HOT...
I'M GOING TO THROW UP ON-STAGE.

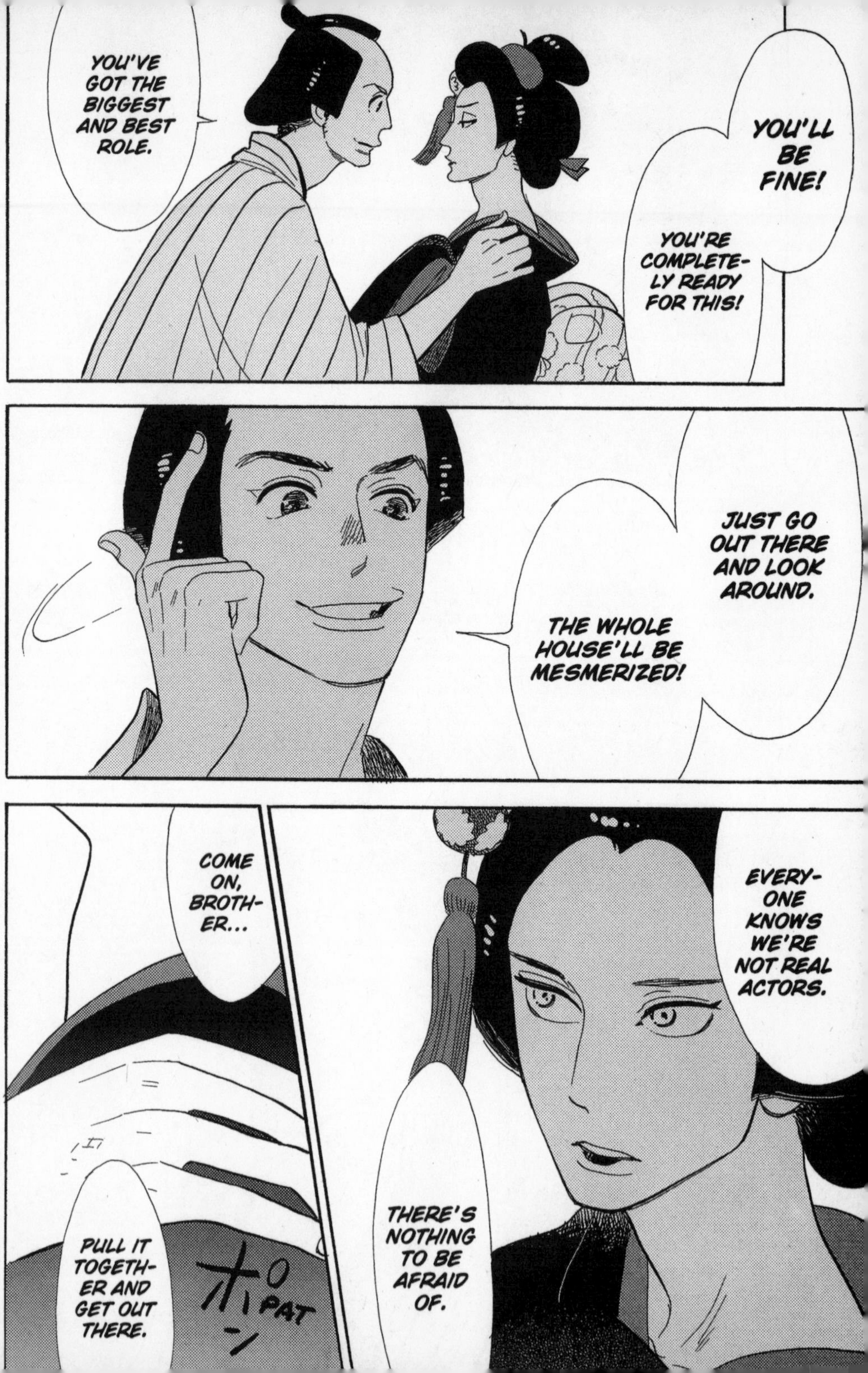

YOU'LL BE FINE!
YOU'RE COMPLETELY READY FOR THIS!
YOU'VE GOT THE BIGGEST AND BEST ROLE.
JUST GO OUT THERE AND LOOK AROUND.
THE WHOLE HOUSE'LL BE MESMERIZED!
EVERYONE KNOWS WE'RE NOT REAL ACTORS.
THERE'S NOTHING TO BE AFRAID OF.
COME ON, BROTHER...
PULL IT TOGETHER AND GET OUT THERE.
PAT

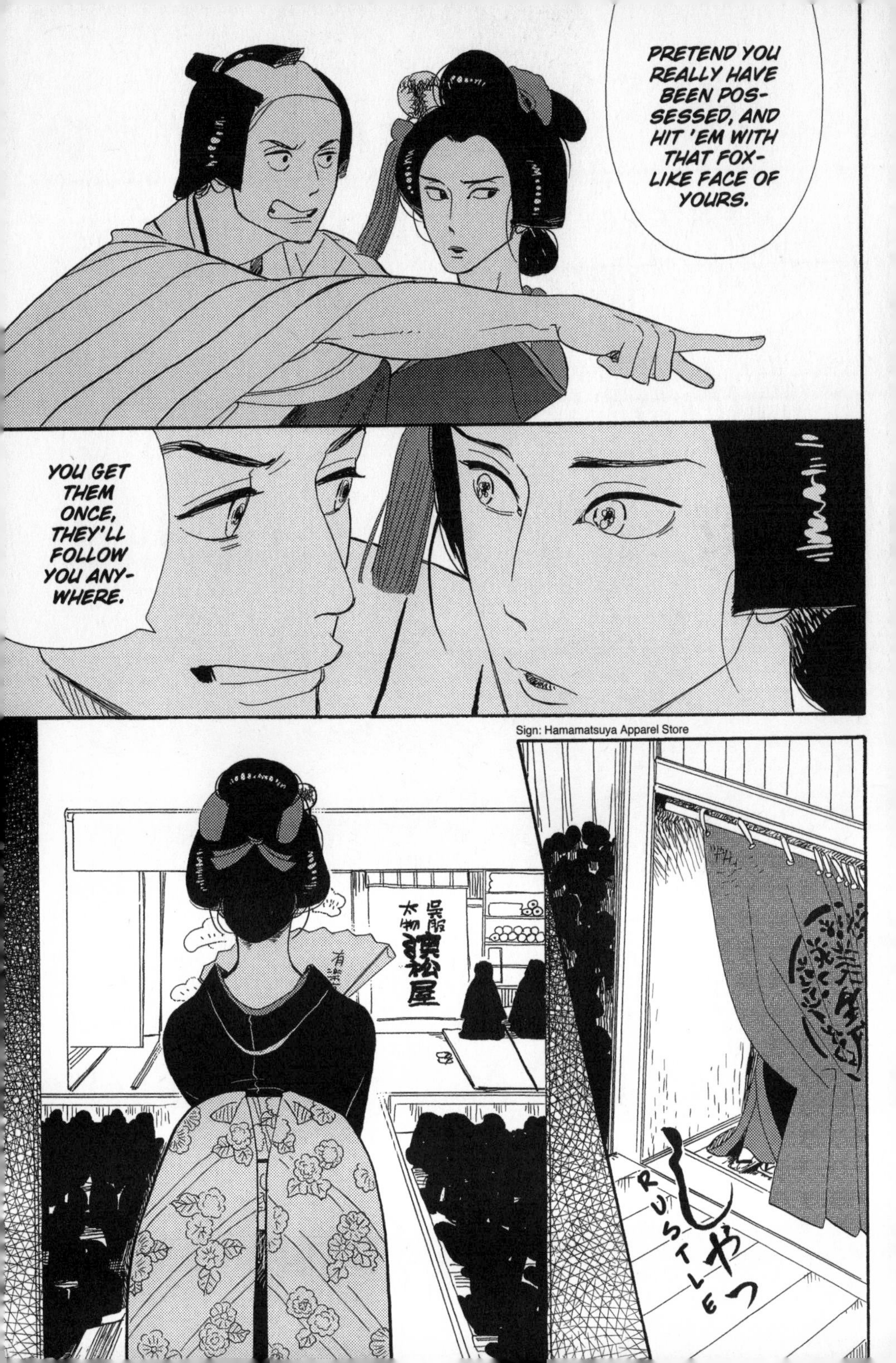
PRETEND YOU REALLY HAVE BEEN POSSESSED, AND HIT 'EM WITH THAT FOX-LIKE FACE OF YOURS.
YOU GET THEM ONCE, THEY'LL FOLLOW YOU ANYWHERE.
RUSTLE
Sign: Hamamatsuya Apparel Store

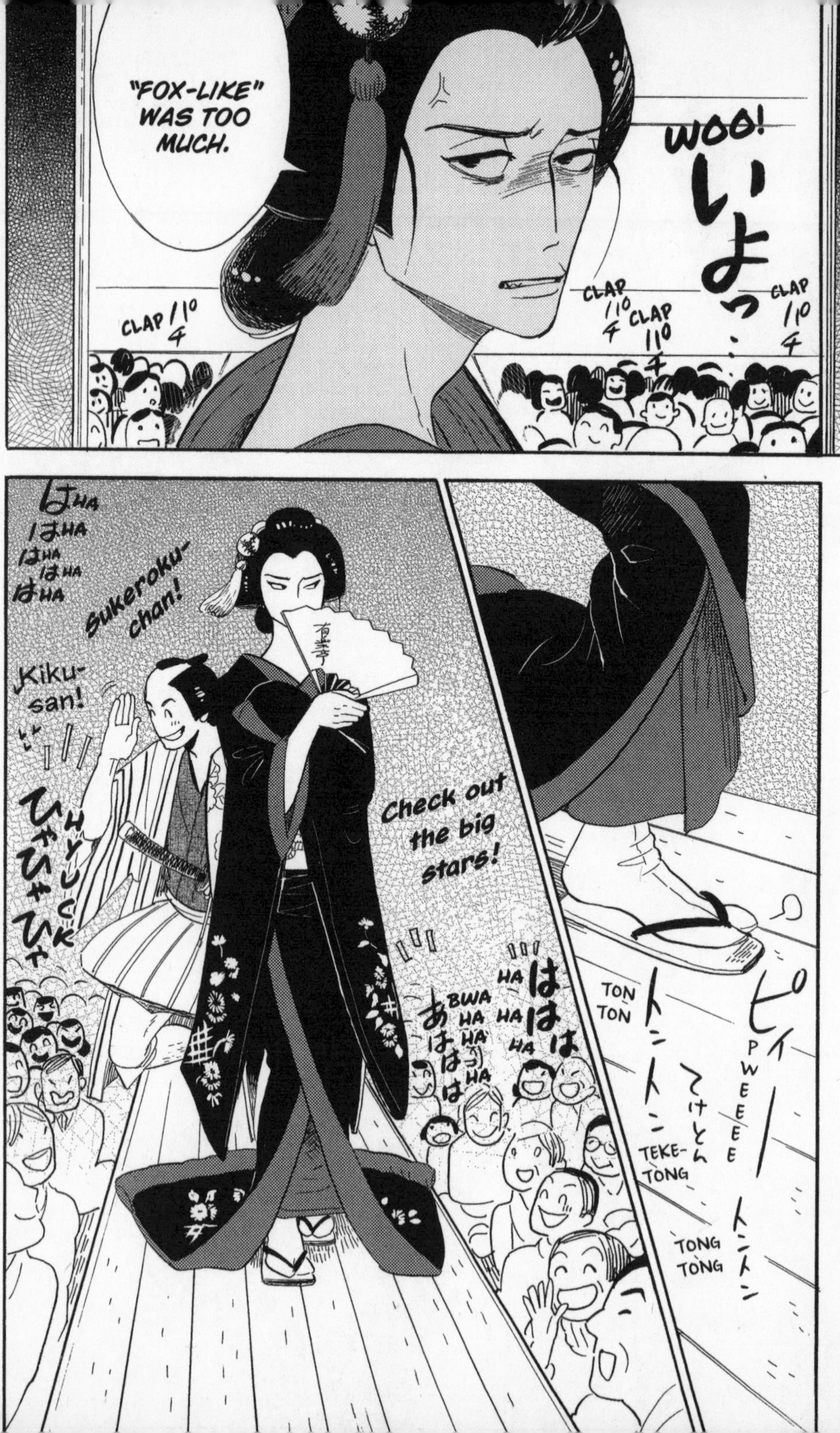

"FOX-LIKE" WAS TOO MUCH.
WOO! いよっ
CLAP パチ
CLAP パチ
CLAP パチ
CLAP パチ
ピィー PWEEEEE
トントン TON TON
てけとん TEKE-TONG
トントン TONG TONG
Check out the big stars!
ははは HA HA HA
あははは BWA HA HA HA
Sukeroku-chan!
Kiku-san!
ひゃひゃひゃ HYUCK
はははははは HA HA HA HA HA HA

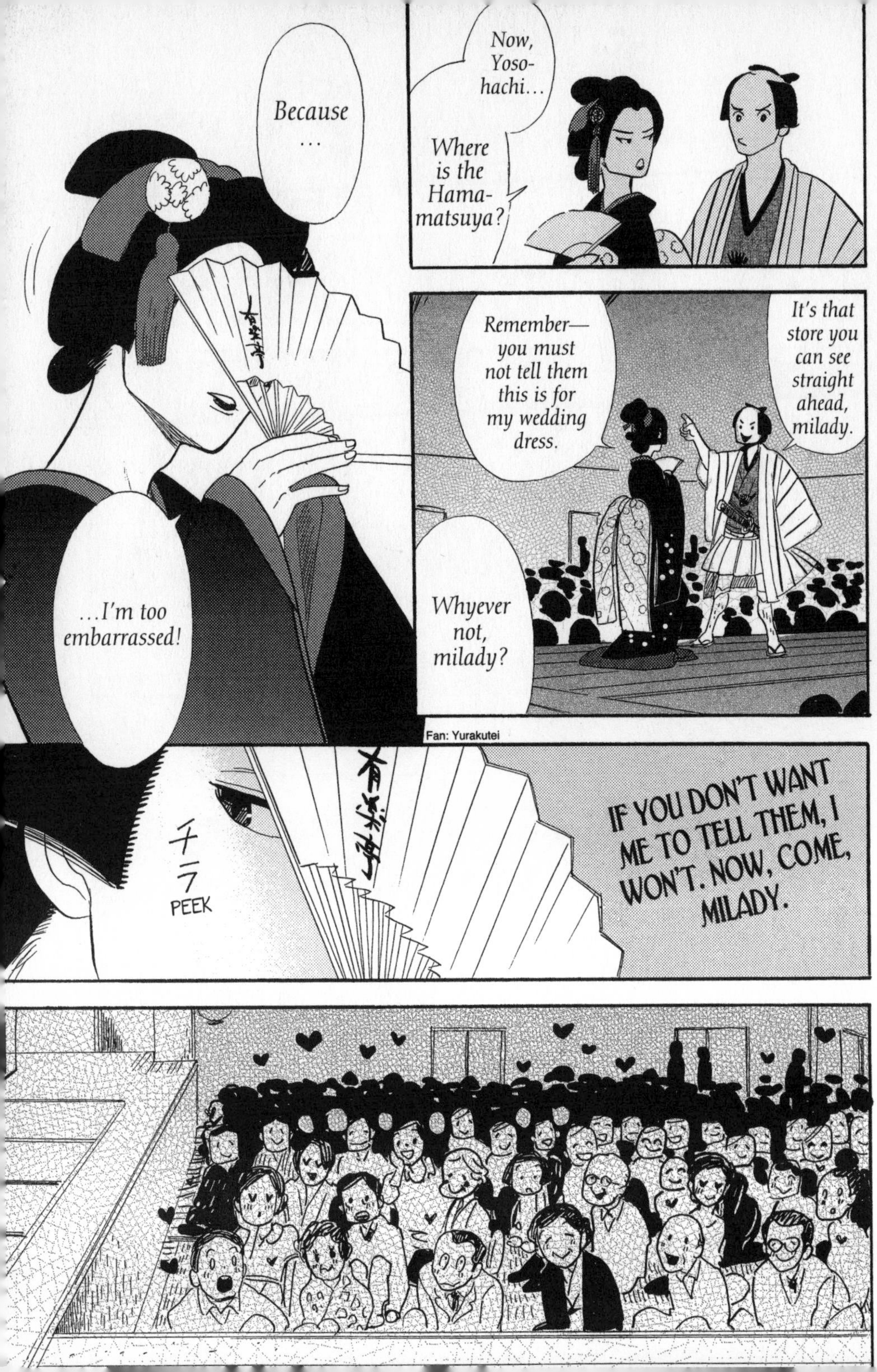
Now, Yoso-hachi…
Where is the Hama-matsuya?
It's that store you can see straight ahead, milady.
Remember—you must not tell them this is for my wedding dress.
Whyever not, milady?
Because…
…I'm too embarrassed!
Fan: Yurakutei
IF YOU DON'T WANT ME TO TELL THEM, I WON'T. NOW, COME, MILADY.
チラ
PEEK

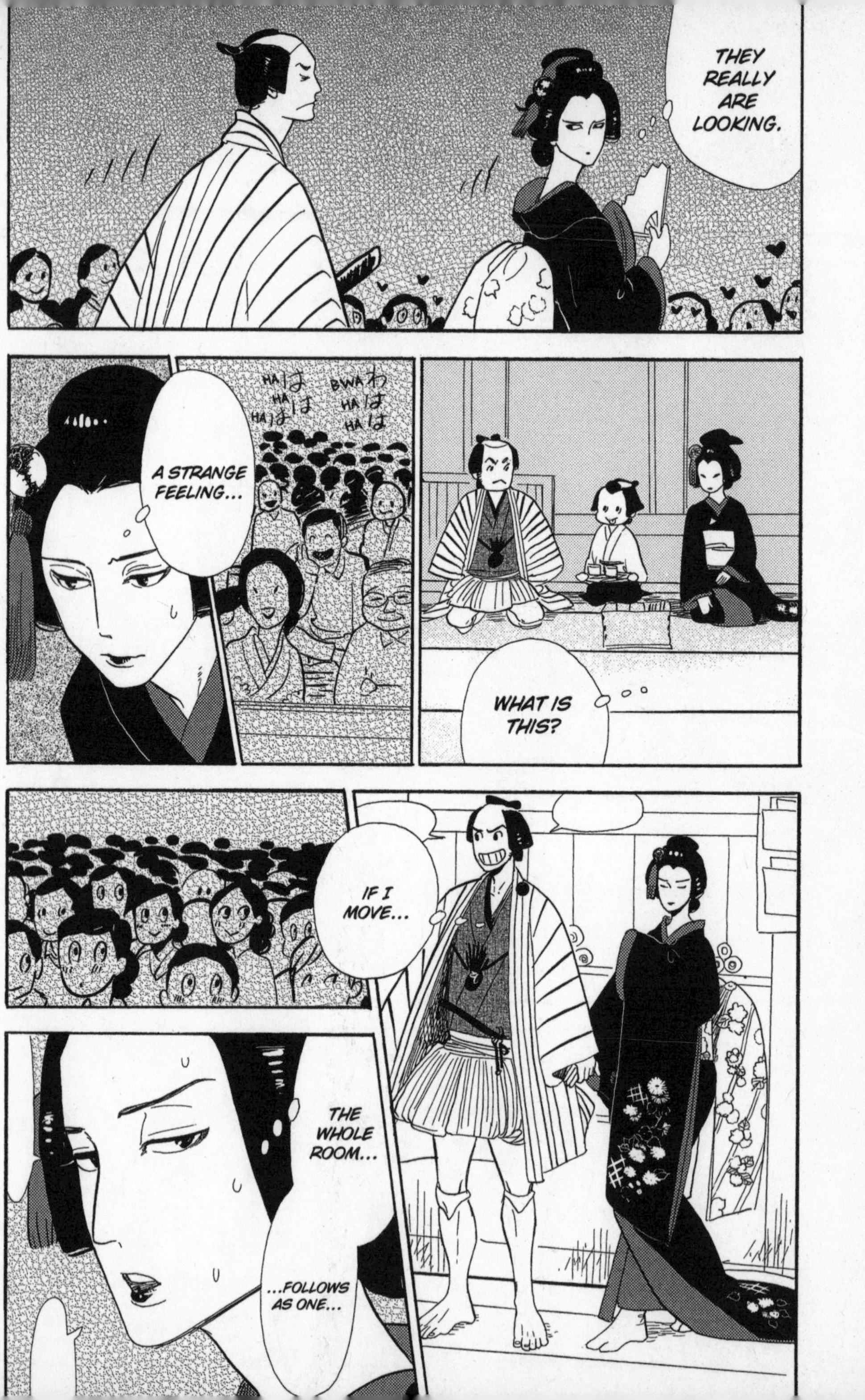
THEY REALLY ARE LOOKING.
WHAT IS THIS?
BWA HA HA
HA HA HA
A STRANGE FEELING...
IF I MOVE...
THE WHOLE ROOM...
...FOLLOWS AS ONE...

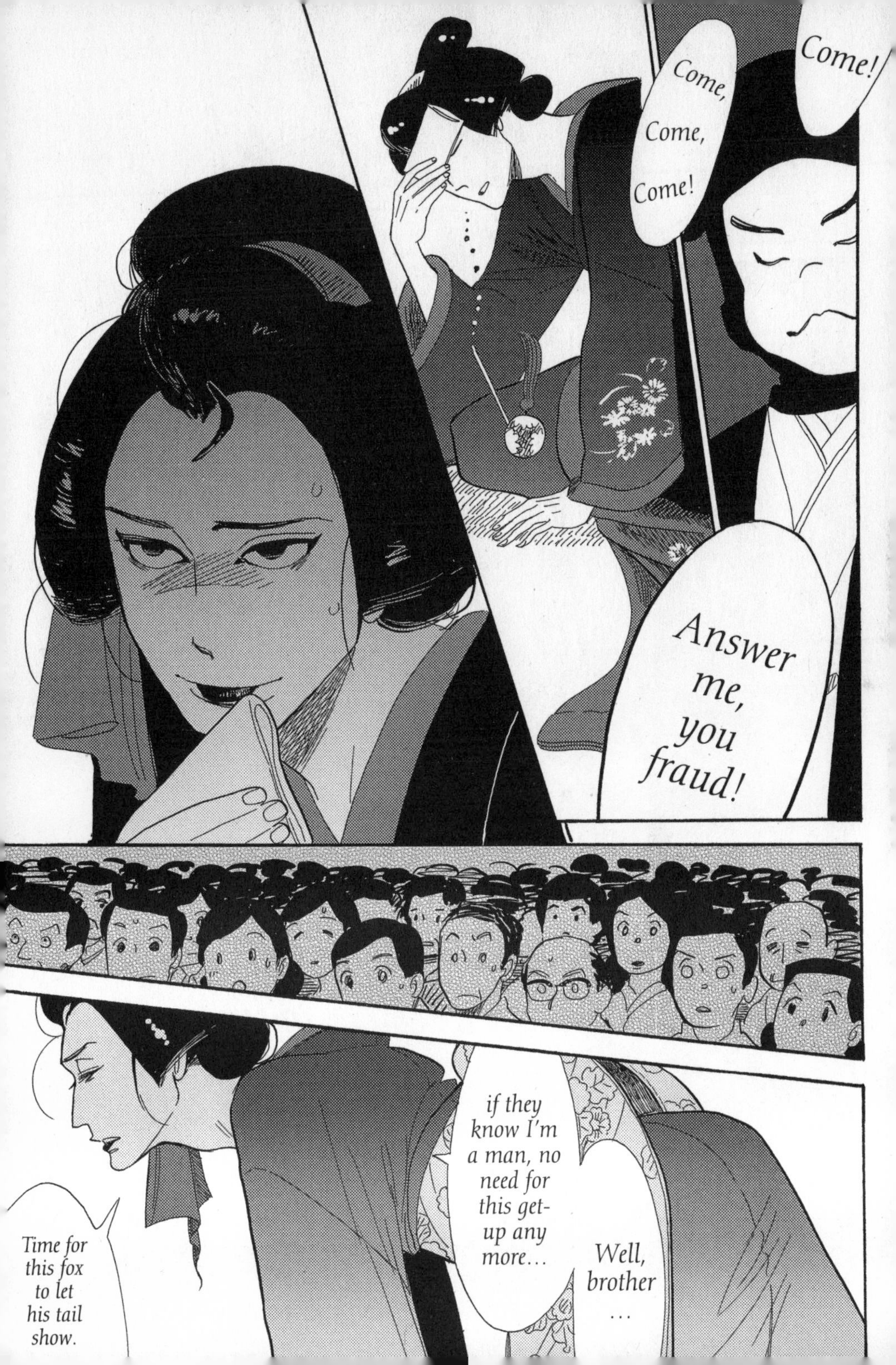
Come!
Come, Come, Come!
Answer me, you fraud!
Well, brother …
if they know I'm a man, no need for this get-up any more…
Time for this fox to let his tail show.

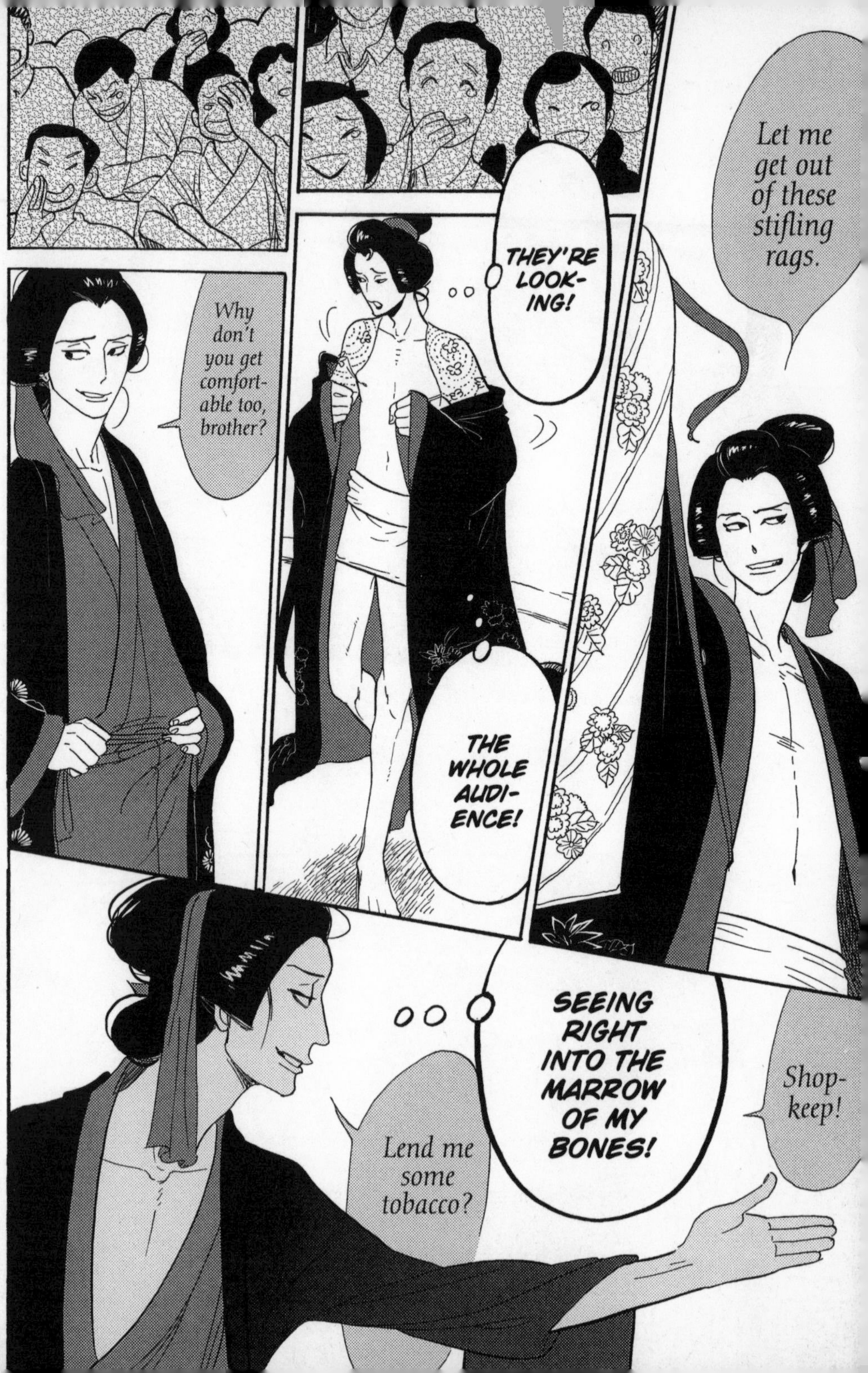
Let me get out of these stifling rags.
THEY'RE LOOKING!
THE WHOLE AUDIENCE!
Why don't you get comfortable too, brother?
Shop-keep!
SEEING RIGHT INTO THE MARROW OF MY BONES!
Lend me some tobacco?

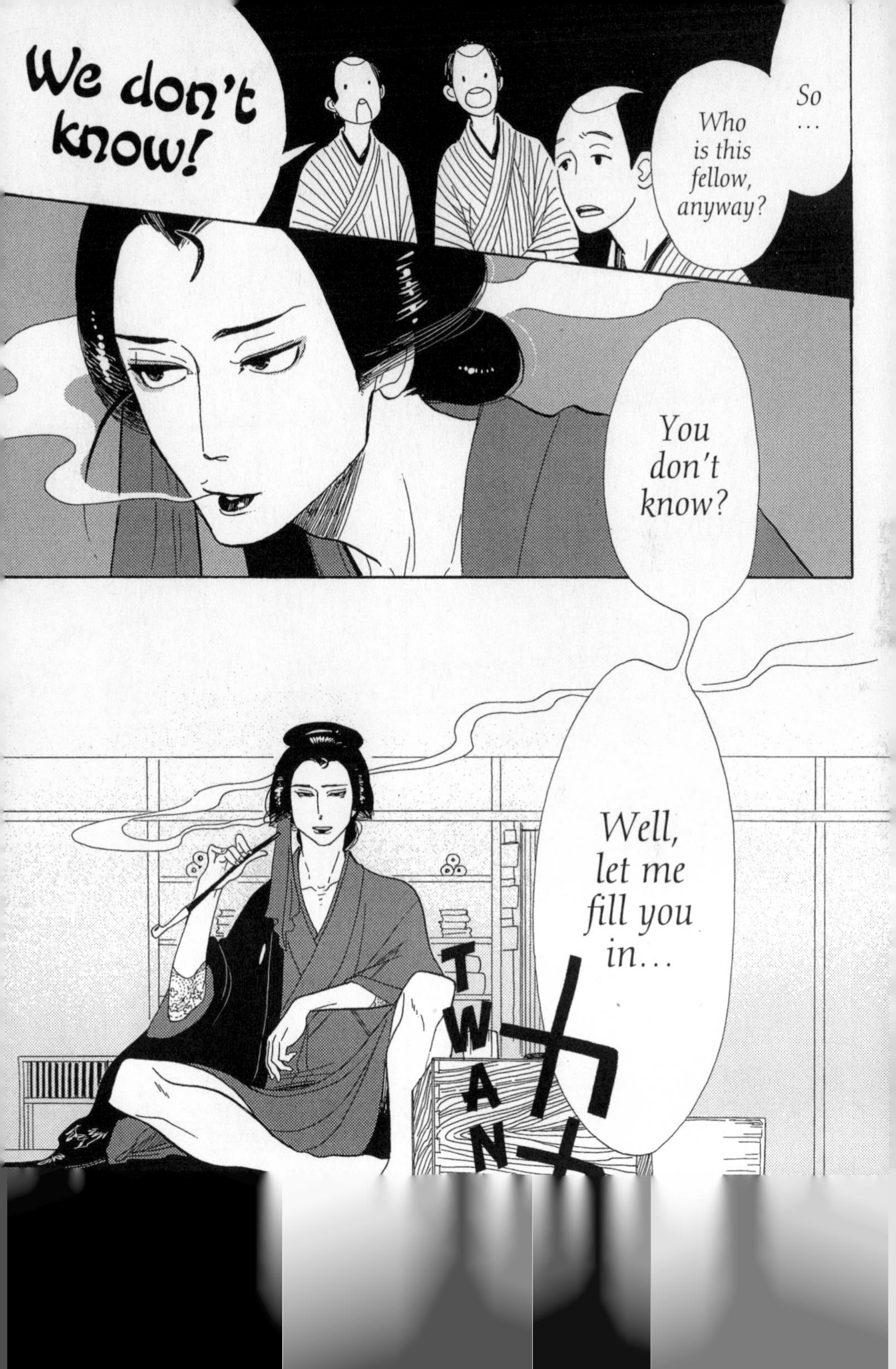
So…
Who is this fellow, anyway?
We don't know!
You don't know?
Well, let me fill you in…
TWAN

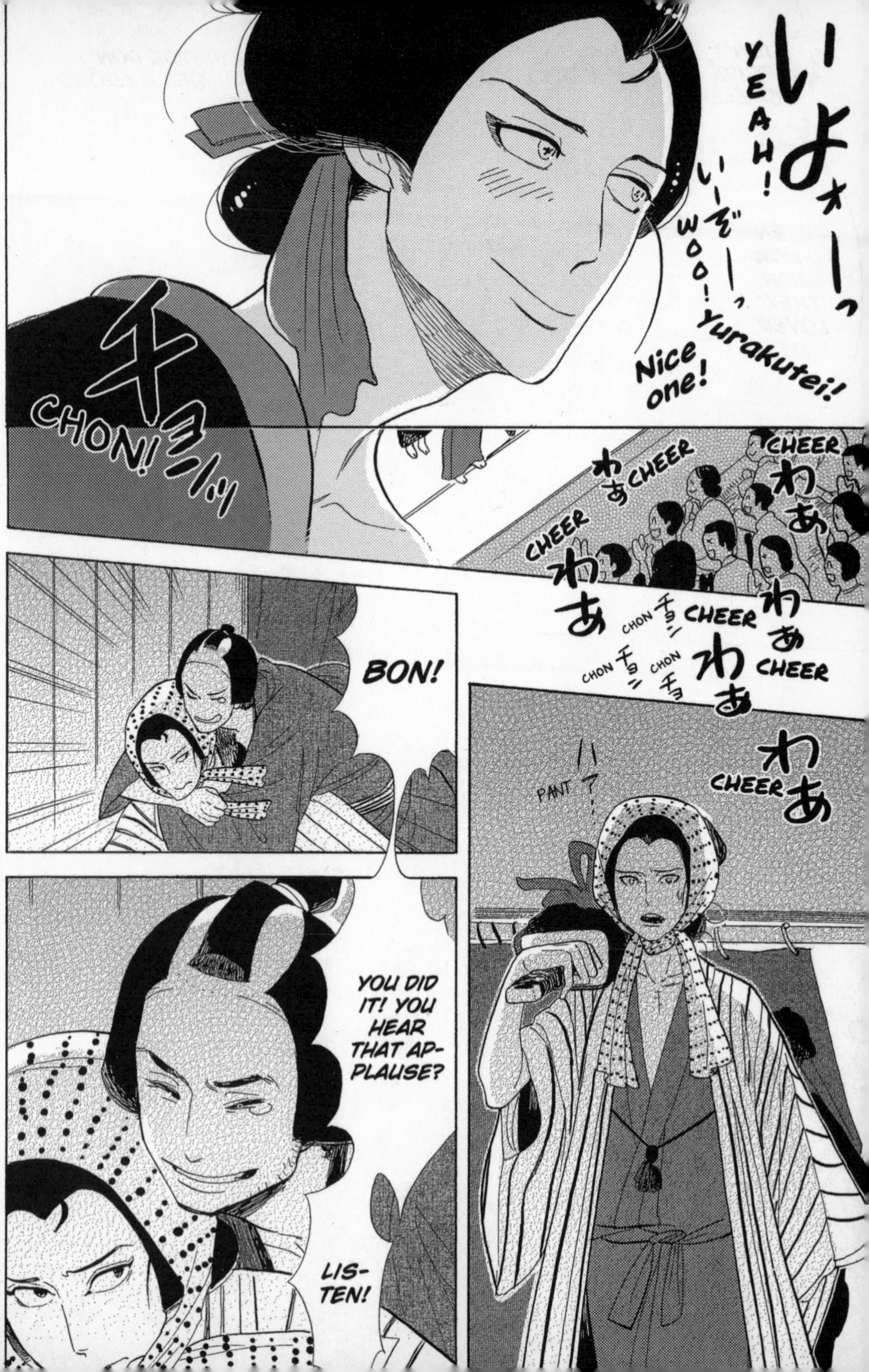
いよォー
YEAH!
いーぞー
WOO!
Yurakutei!
Nice one!
チョンッ
CHON!
わあ CHEER
CHEER わあ
CHEER わあ
わあ CHEER
CHON チョン
CHON チョン
CHON チョン
わあ CHEER
わあ CHEER
ハァ PANT
BON!
YOU DID IT! YOU HEAR THAT AP-PLAUSE?
LIS-TEN!

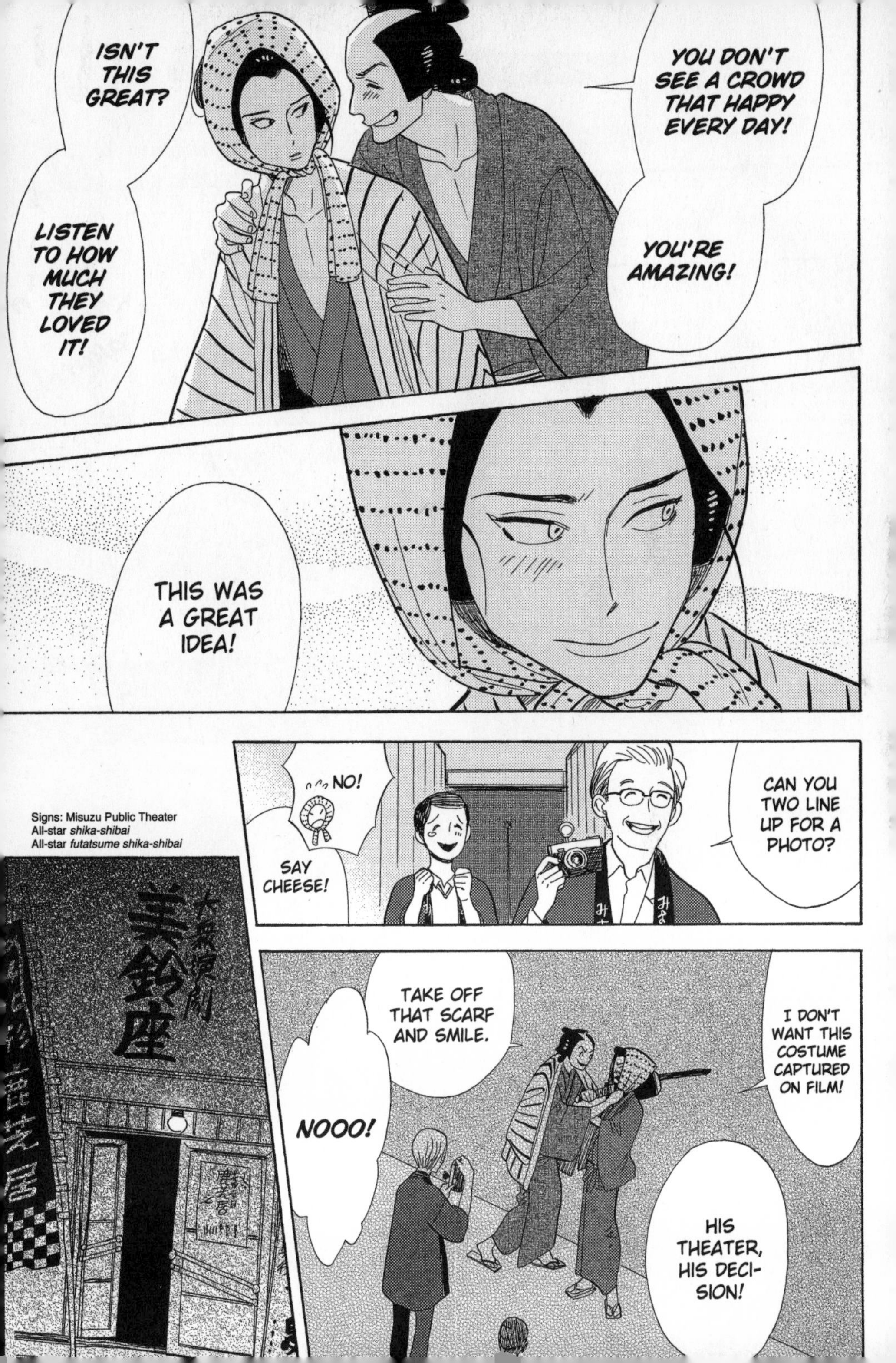
YOU DON'T SEE A CROWD THAT HAPPY EVERY DAY!
YOU'RE AMAZING!
ISN'T THIS GREAT?
LISTEN TO HOW MUCH THEY LOVED IT!
THIS WAS A GREAT IDEA!
CAN YOU TWO LINE UP FOR A PHOTO?
NO!
SAY CHEESE!
I DON'T WANT THIS COSTUME CAPTURED ON FILM!
TAKE OFF THAT SCARF AND SMILE.
HIS THEATER, HIS DECISION!
NOOO!
Signs: Misuzu Public Theater
All-star *shika-shibai*
All-star *futatsume shika-shibai*

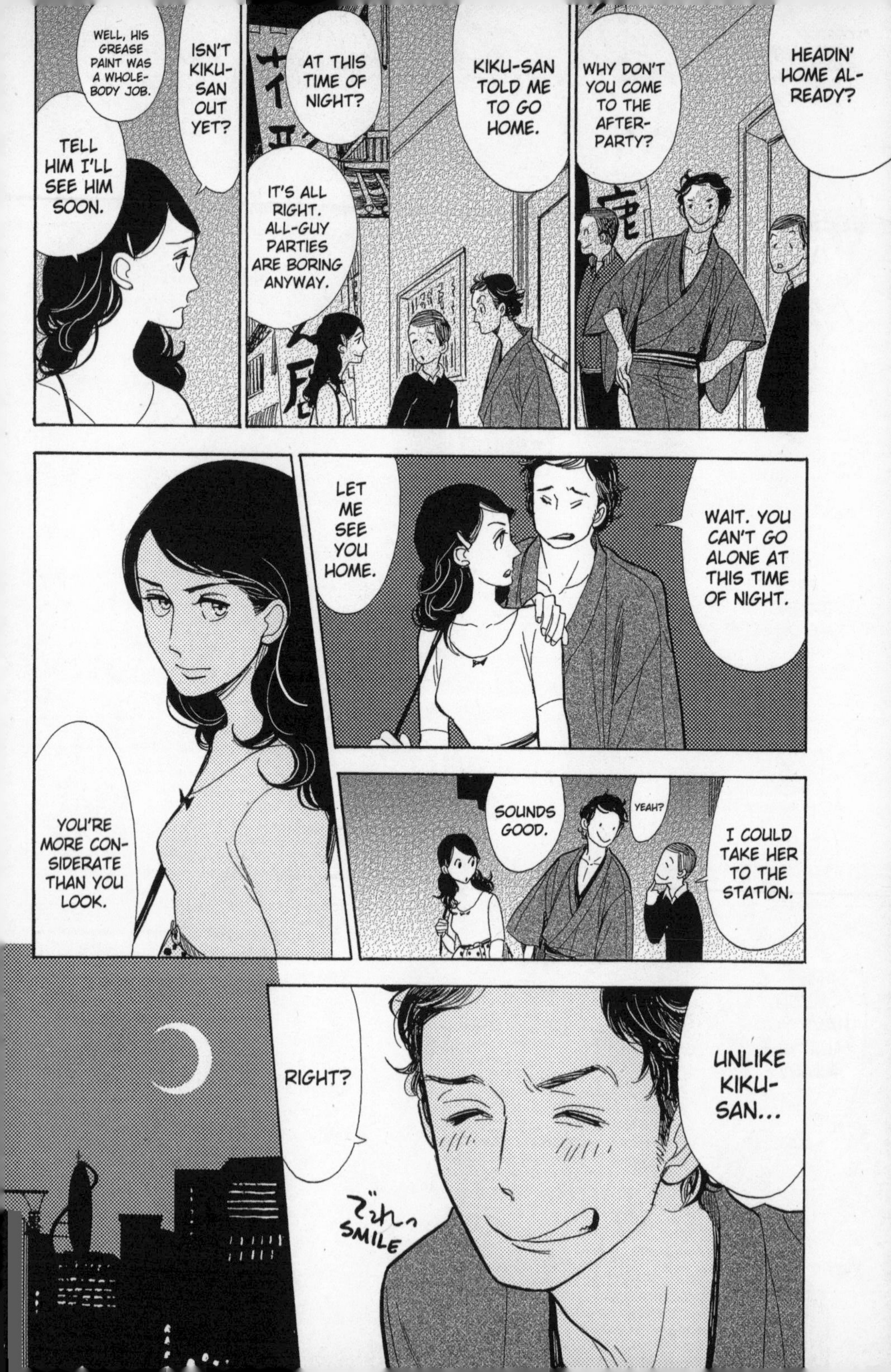
HEADIN' HOME AL-READY?
WHY DON'T YOU COME TO THE AFTER-PARTY?
KIKU-SAN TOLD ME TO GO HOME.
AT THIS TIME OF NIGHT?
IT'S ALL RIGHT. ALL-GUY PARTIES ARE BORING ANYWAY.
ISN'T KIKU-SAN OUT YET?
WELL, HIS GREASE PAINT WAS A WHOLE-BODY JOB.
TELL HIM I'LL SEE HIM SOON.
WAIT. YOU CAN'T GO ALONE AT THIS TIME OF NIGHT.
LET ME SEE YOU HOME.
I COULD TAKE HER TO THE STATION.
YEAH?
SOUNDS GOOD.
YOU'RE MORE CONSIDERATE THAN YOU LOOK.
UNLIKE KIKU-SAN...
RIGHT?
SMILE

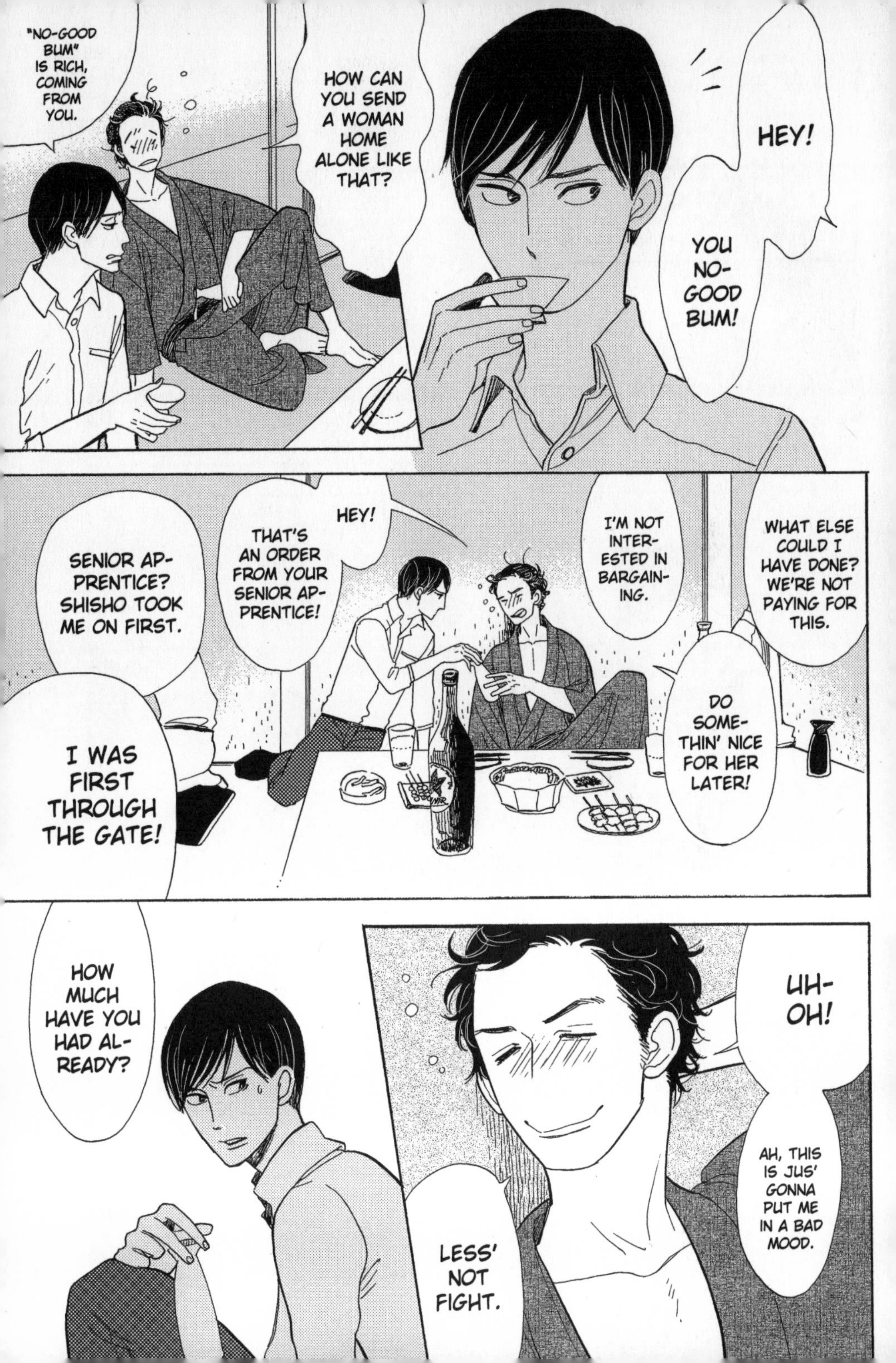

HEY!
YOU NO-GOOD BUM!
HOW CAN YOU SEND A WOMAN HOME ALONE LIKE THAT?
"NO-GOOD BUM" IS RICH, COMING FROM YOU.
WHAT ELSE COULD I HAVE DONE? WE'RE NOT PAYING FOR THIS.
I'M NOT INTERESTED IN BARGAINING.
DO SOMETHIN' NICE FOR HER LATER!
HEY!
THAT'S AN ORDER FROM YOUR SENIOR APPRENTICE!
SENIOR APPRENTICE? SHISHO TOOK ME ON FIRST.
I WAS FIRST THROUGH THE GATE!
UH-OH!
AH, THIS IS JUS' GONNA PUT ME IN A BAD MOOD.
LESS' NOT FIGHT.
HOW MUCH HAVE YOU HAD ALREADY?

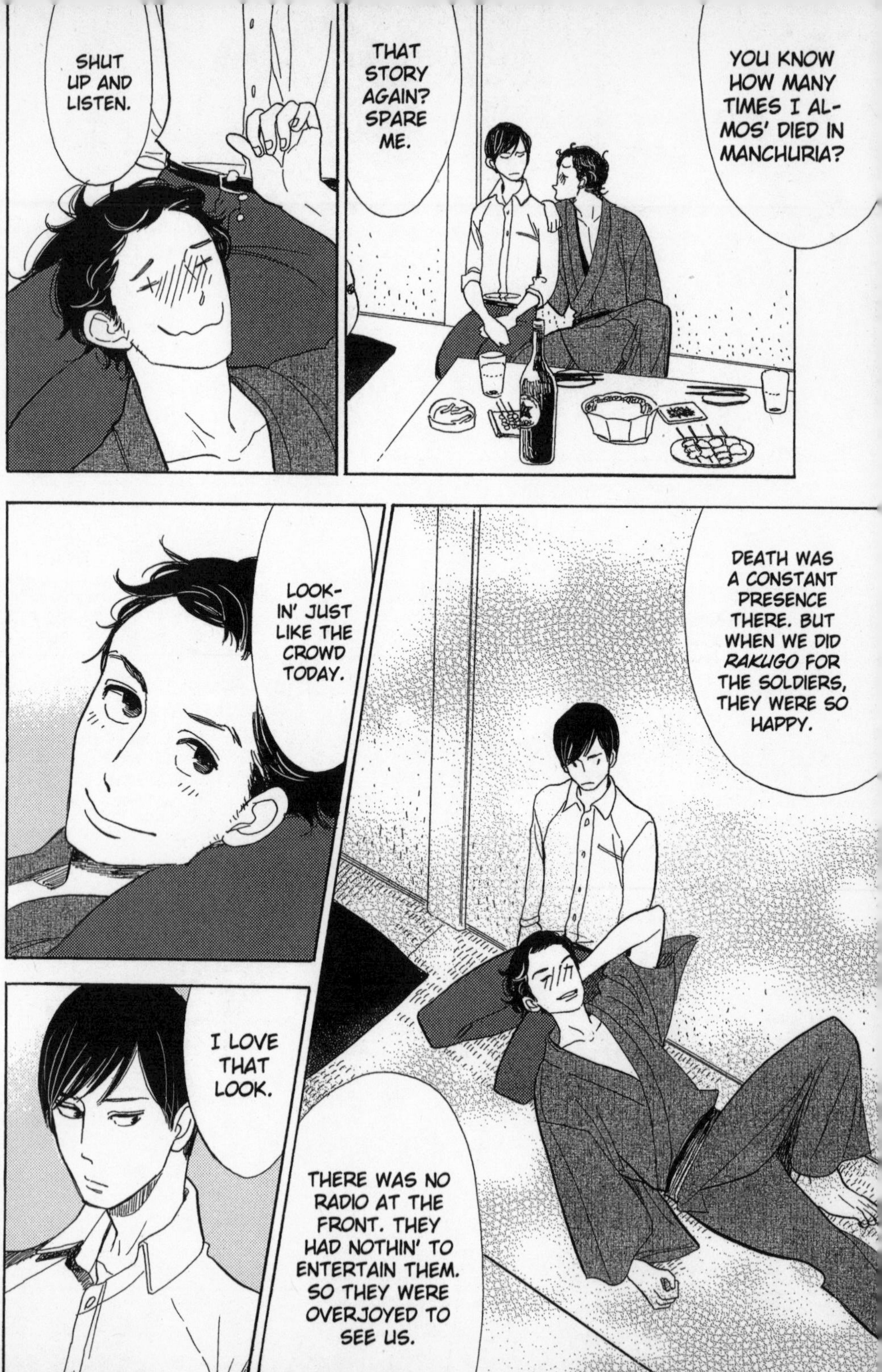
YOU KNOW HOW MANY TIMES I AL-MOS' DIED IN MANCHURIA?
THAT STORY AGAIN? SPARE ME.
SHUT UP AND LISTEN.
DEATH WAS A CONSTANT PRESENCE THERE. BUT WHEN WE DID *RAKUGO* FOR THE SOLDIERS, THEY WERE SO HAPPY.
THERE WAS NO RADIO AT THE FRONT. THEY HAD NOTHIN' TO ENTERTAIN THEM. SO THEY WERE OVERJOYED TO SEE US.
LOOK-IN' JUST LIKE THE CROWD TODAY.
I LOVE THAT LOOK.

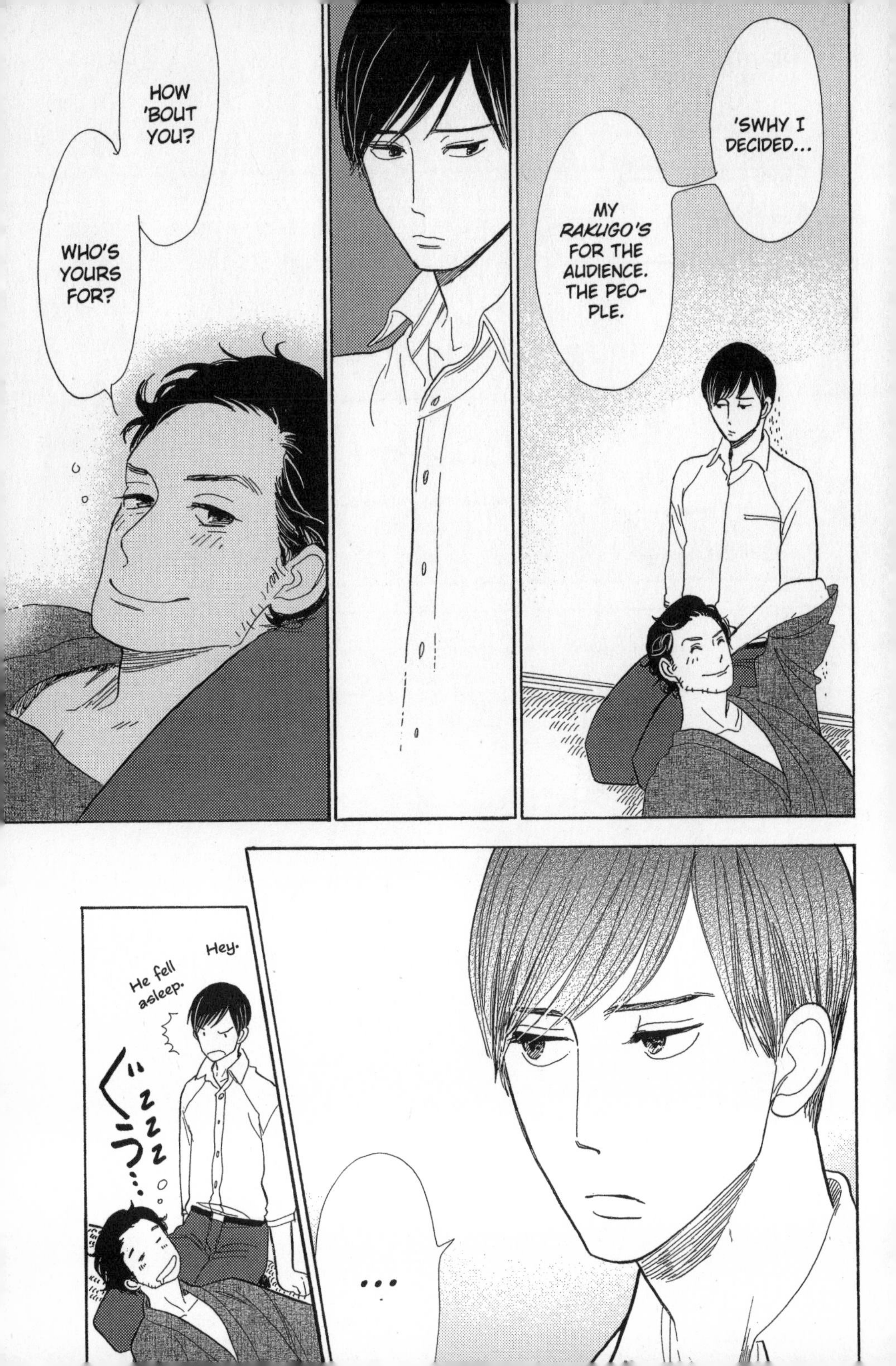
'SWHY I DECIDED...
MY *RAKUGO'S* FOR THE AUDIENCE. THE PEO-PLE.
HOW 'BOUT YOU?
WHO'S YOURS FOR?
...
Hey.
He fell asleep.
ぐぅ...
zzz

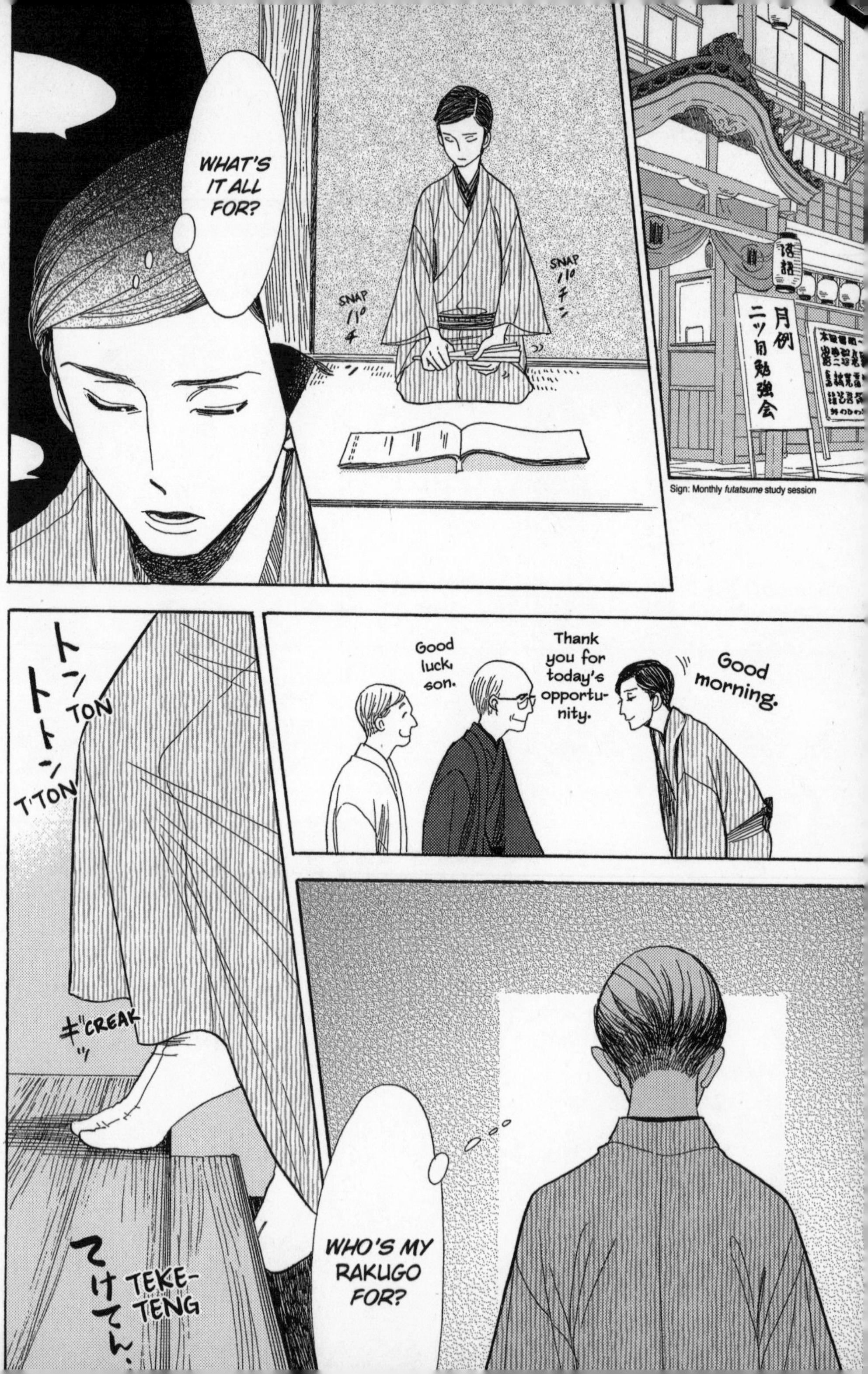
落語
月例 二ツ目勉強会
Sign: Monthly *futatsume* study session
SNAP
SNAP
WHAT'S IT ALL FOR?
Good morning.
Thank you for today's opportunity.
Good luck, son.
WHO'S MY RAKUGO FOR?
TON
T'TON
CREAK
TEKE-TENG

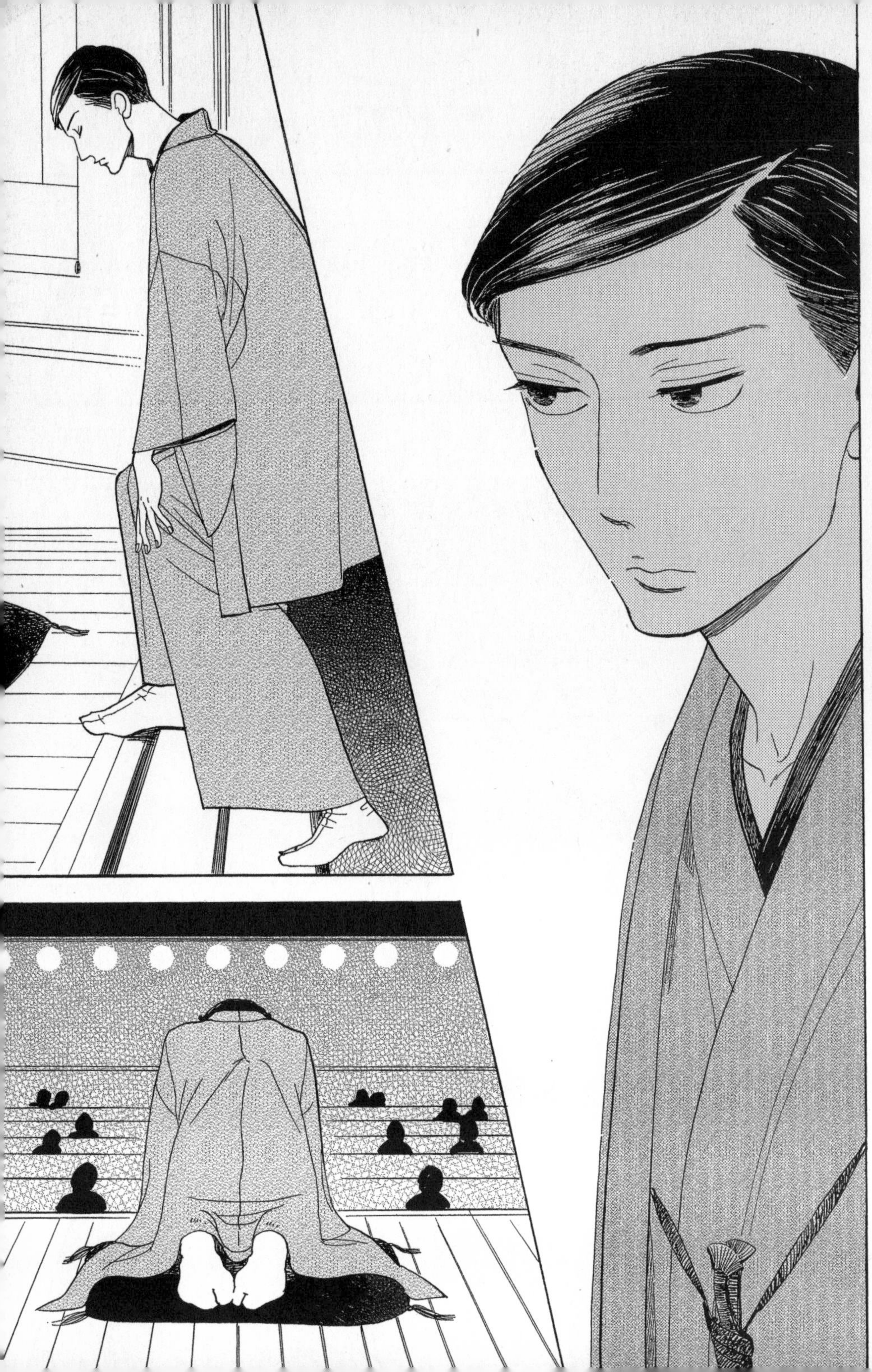

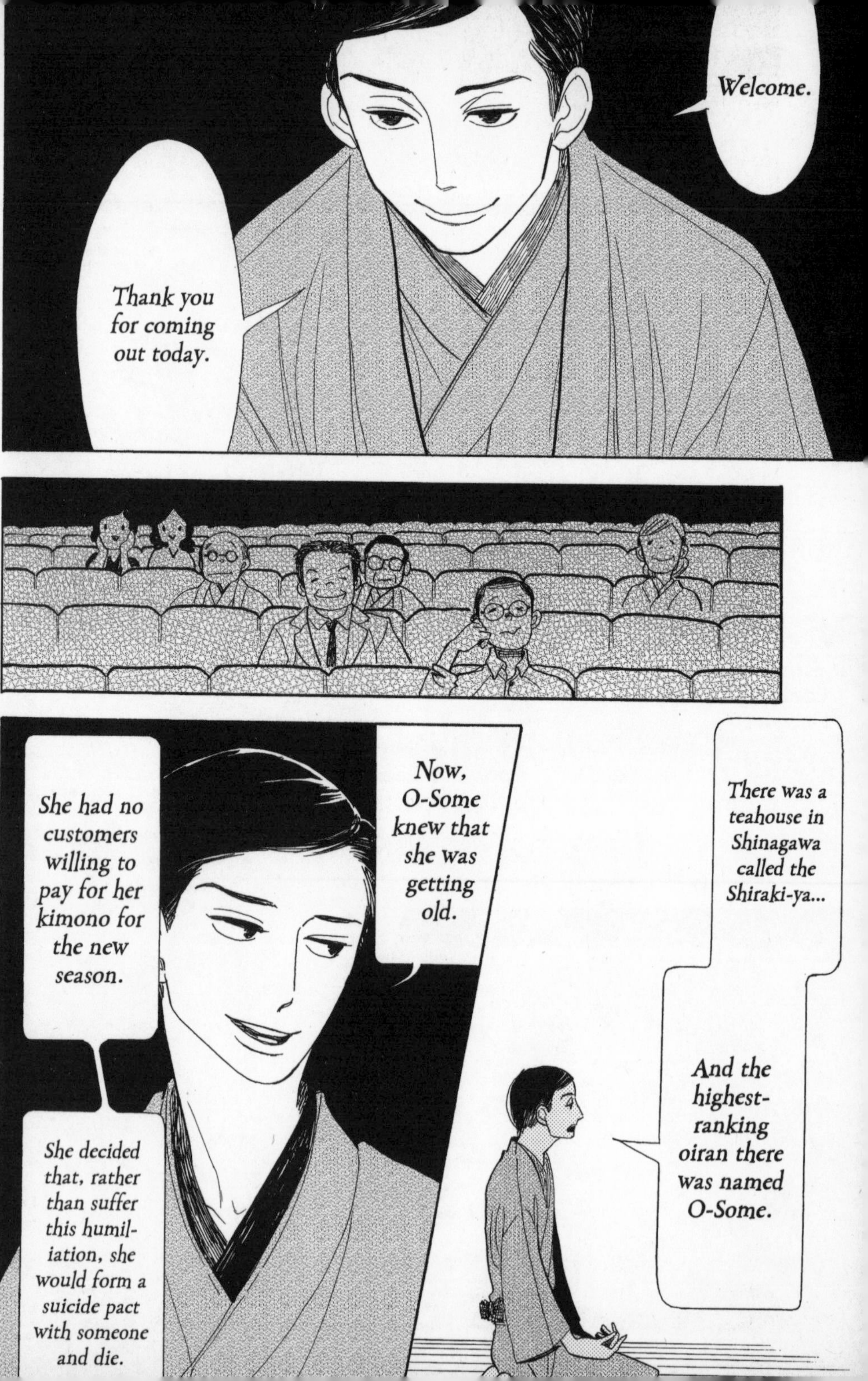
Welcome.
Thank you for coming out today.
There was a teahouse in Shinagawa called the Shiraki-ya...
And the highest-ranking oiran there was named O-Some.
Now, O-Some knew that she was getting old.
She had no customers willing to pay for her kimono for the new season.
She decided that, rather than suffer this humiliation, she would form a suicide pact with someone and die.

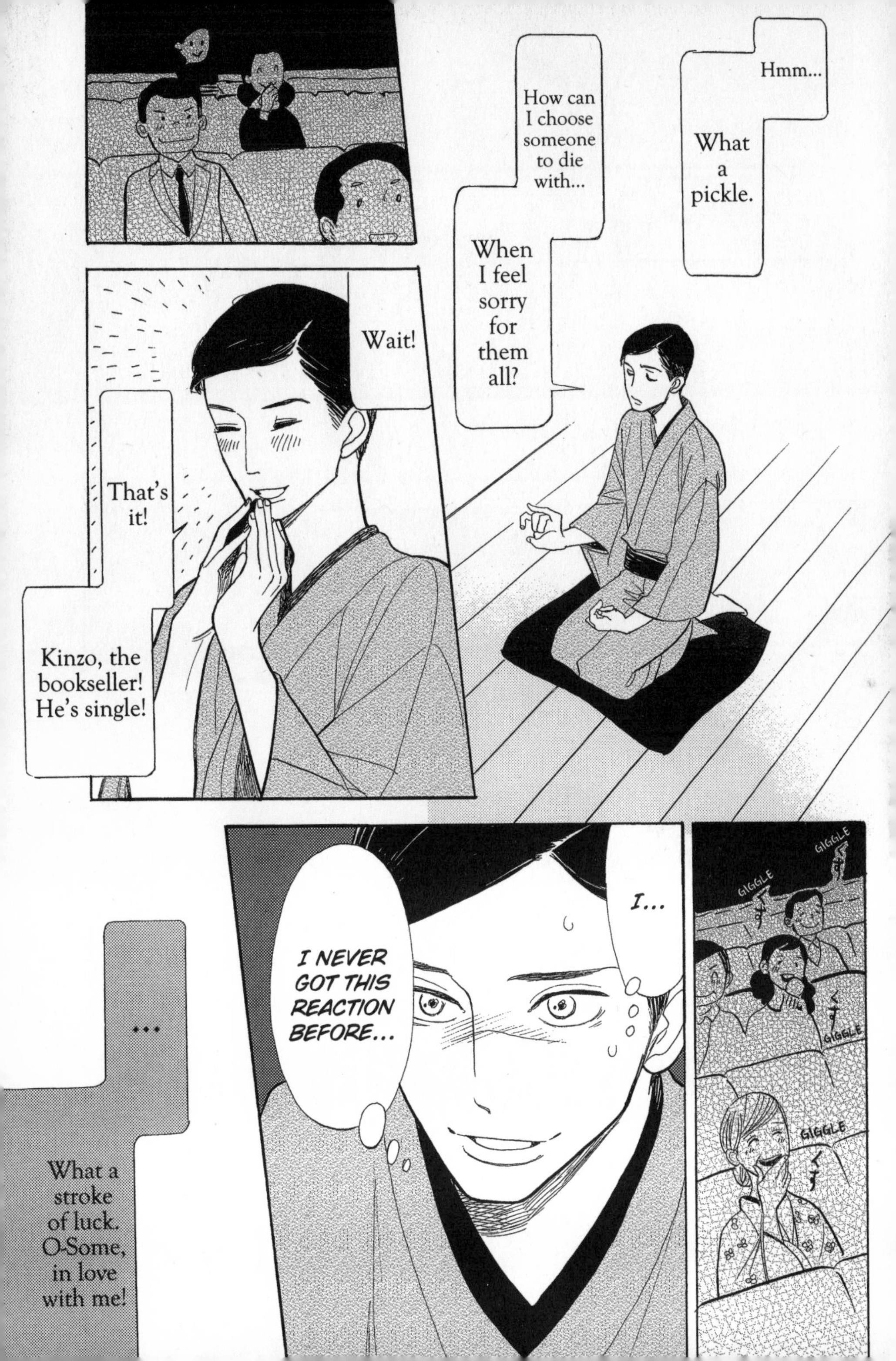
Hmm...
What a pickle.
How can I choose someone to die with...
When I feel sorry for them all?
Wait!
That's it!
Kinzo, the bookseller! He's single!
GIGGLE
GIGGLE
GIGGLE
GIGGLE
I...
I NEVER GOT THIS REACTION BEFORE...
...
What a stroke of luck. O-Some, in love with me!

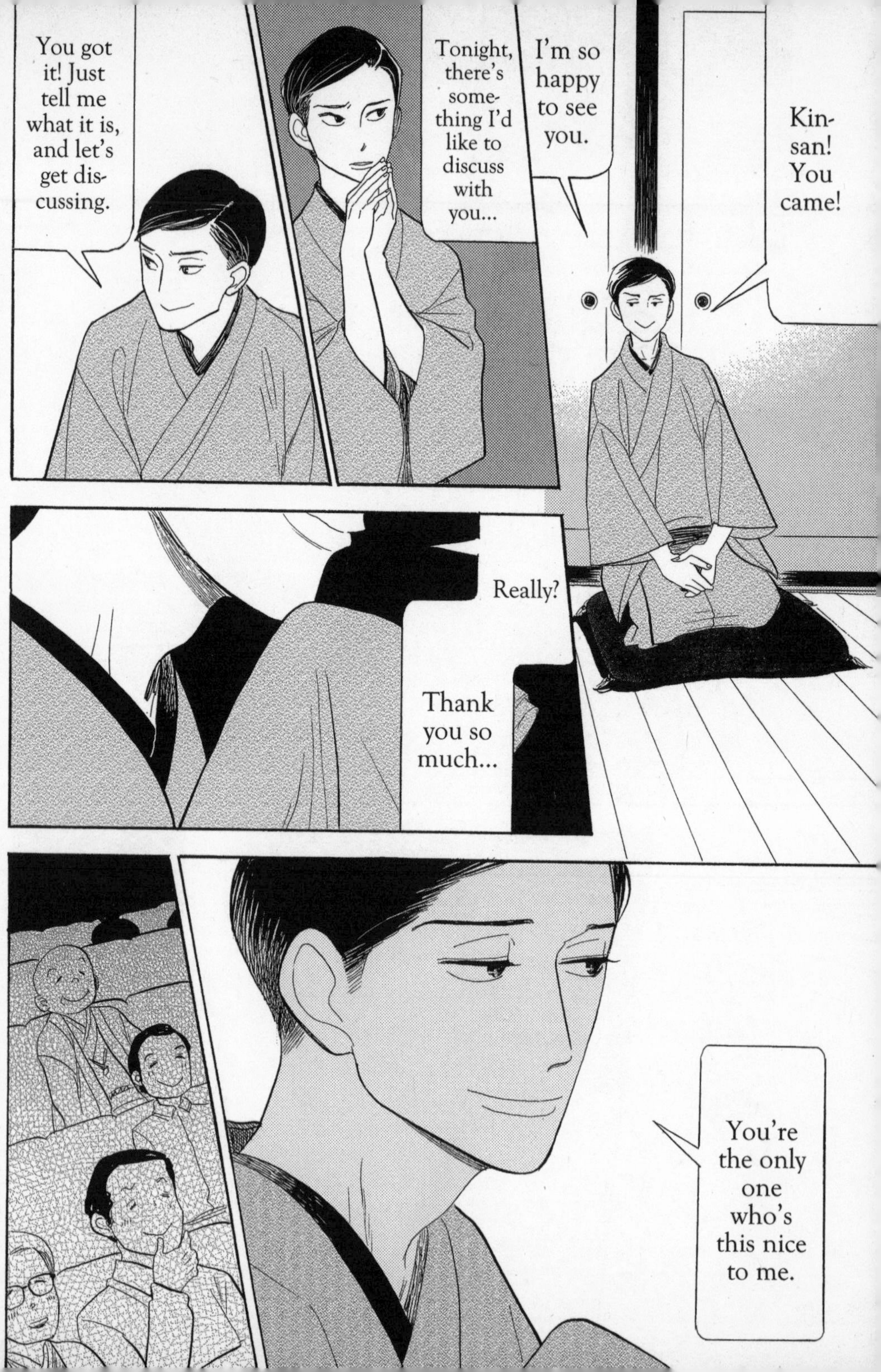

Kin-san! You came!
I'm so happy to see you.
Tonight, there's some-thing I'd like to discuss with you...
You got it! Just tell me what it is, and let's get dis-cussing.
Really?
Thank you so much...
You're the only one who's this nice to me.

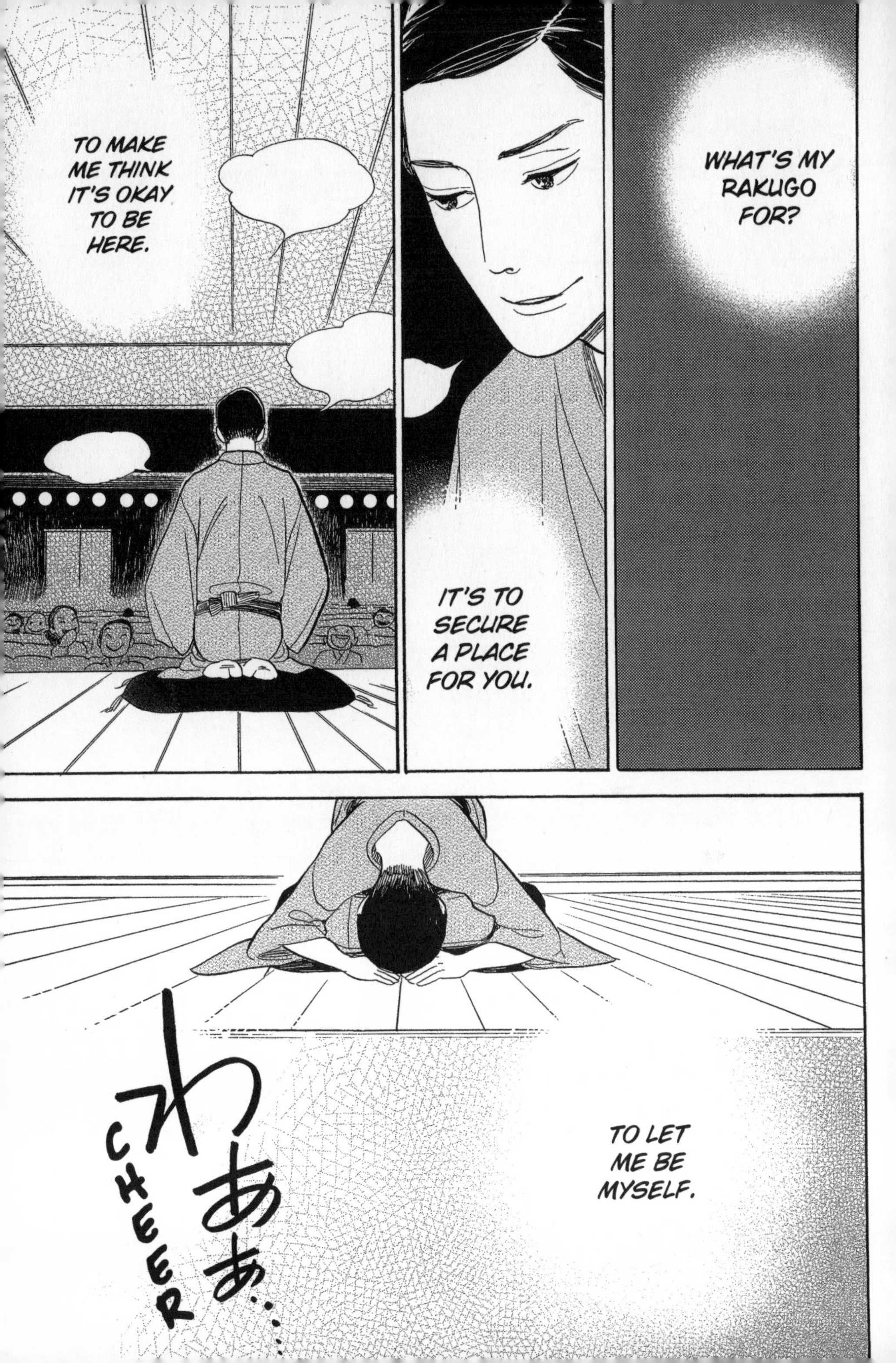
WHAT'S MY RAKUGO FOR?
IT'S TO SECURE A PLACE FOR YOU.
TO MAKE ME THINK IT'S OKAY TO BE HERE.
TO LET ME BE MYSELF.
わぁぁ…
CHEER

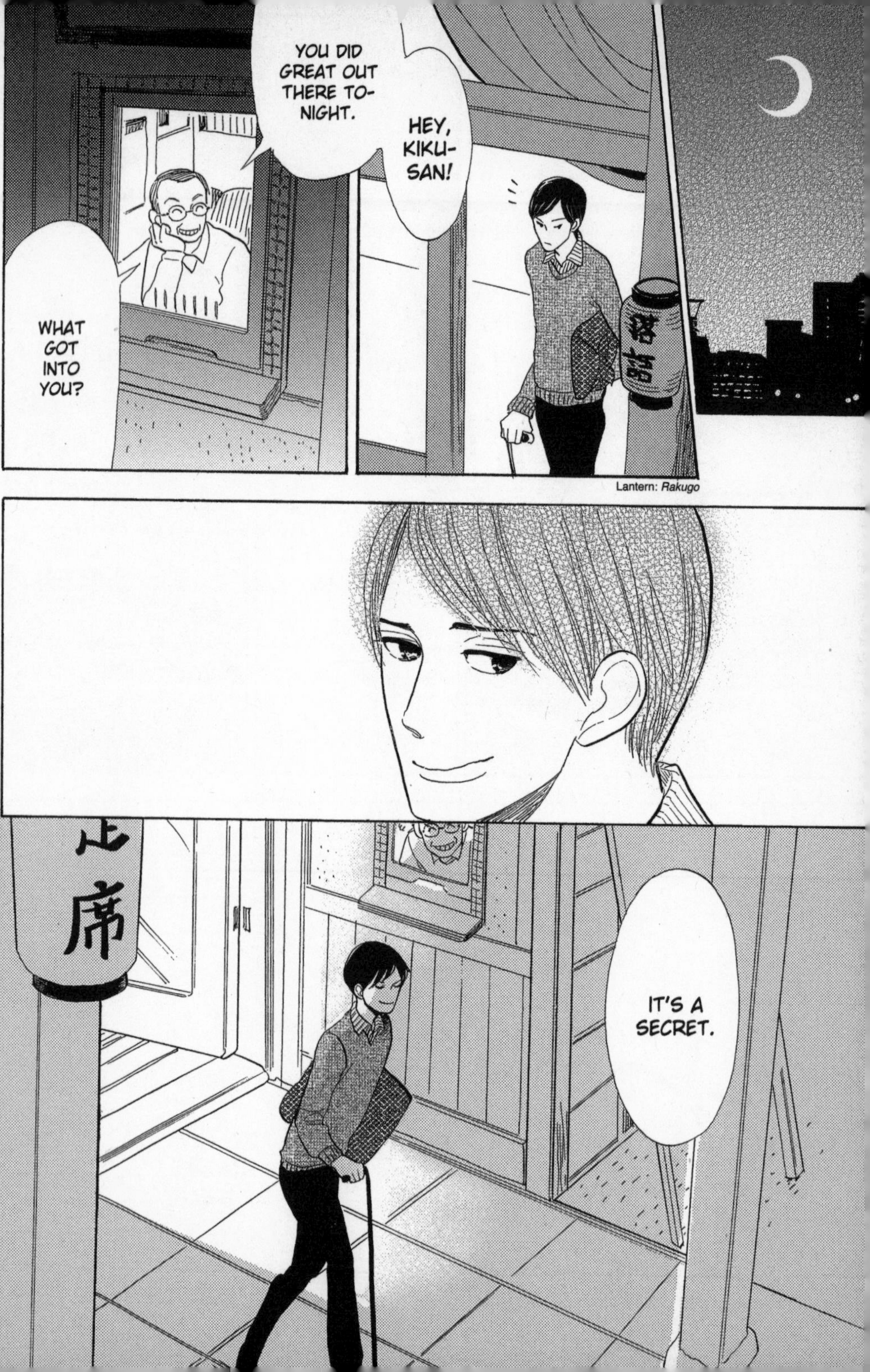
HEY, KIKU-SAN!
YOU DID GREAT OUT THERE TO-NIGHT.
WHAT GOT INTO YOU?
IT'S A SECRET.
Lantern: *Rakugo*

DESCENDING
STORIES

SHOWA
GENROKU
RAKUGO
SHINJU

HARUKO KUMOTA

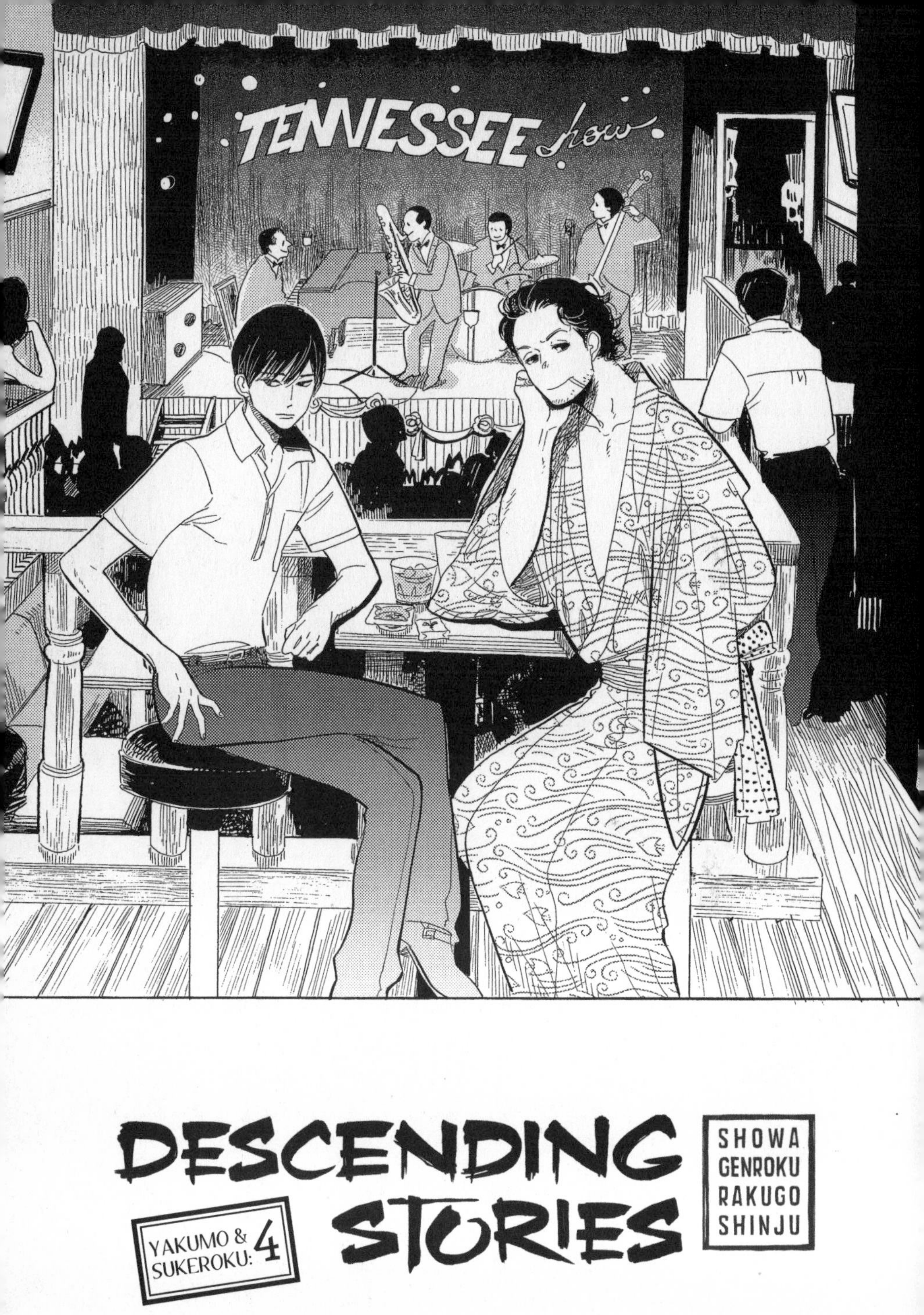
TENNESSEE show

DESCENDING STORIES

SHOWA GENROKU RAKUGO SHINJU

YAKUMO & SUKEROKU: 4

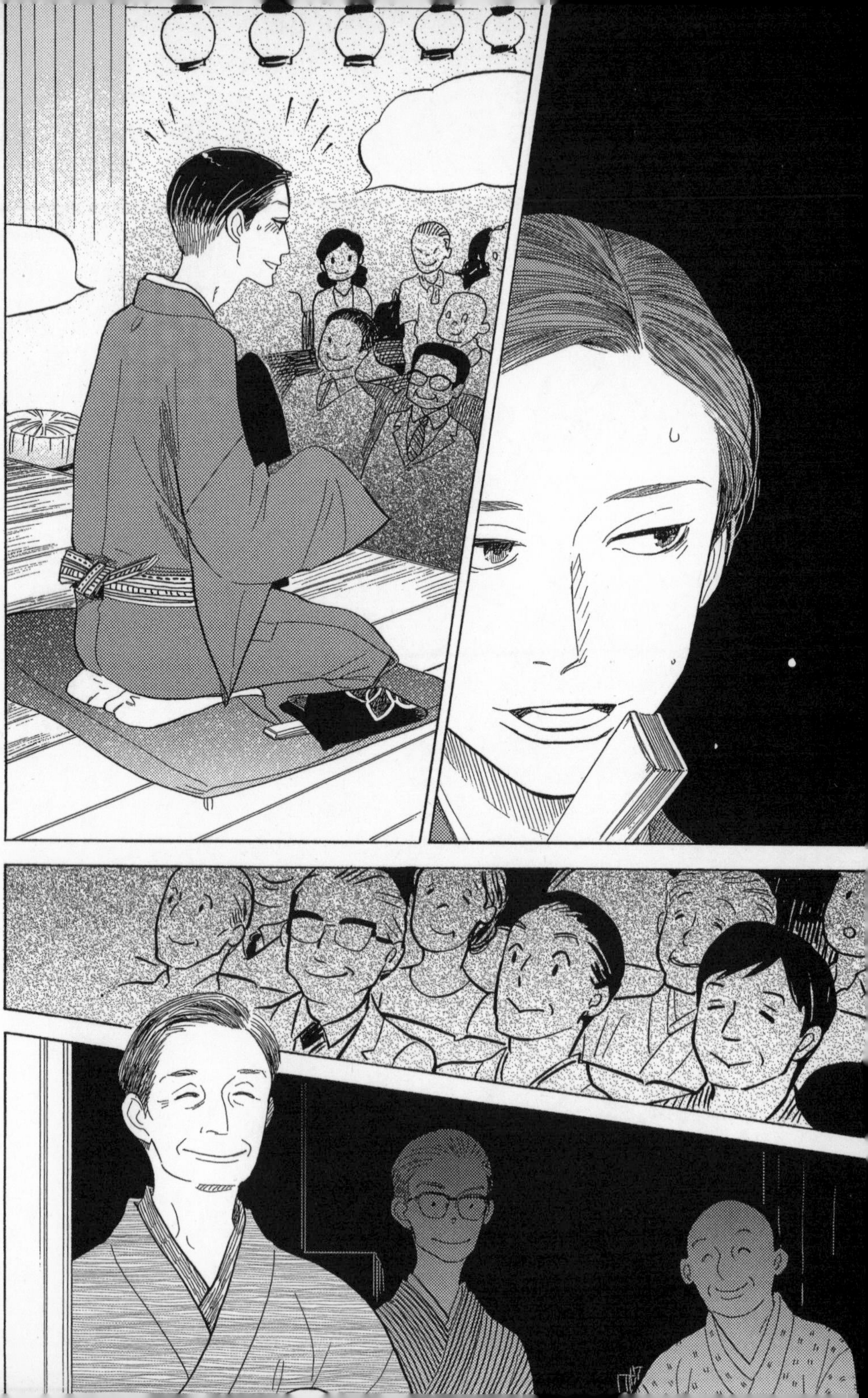

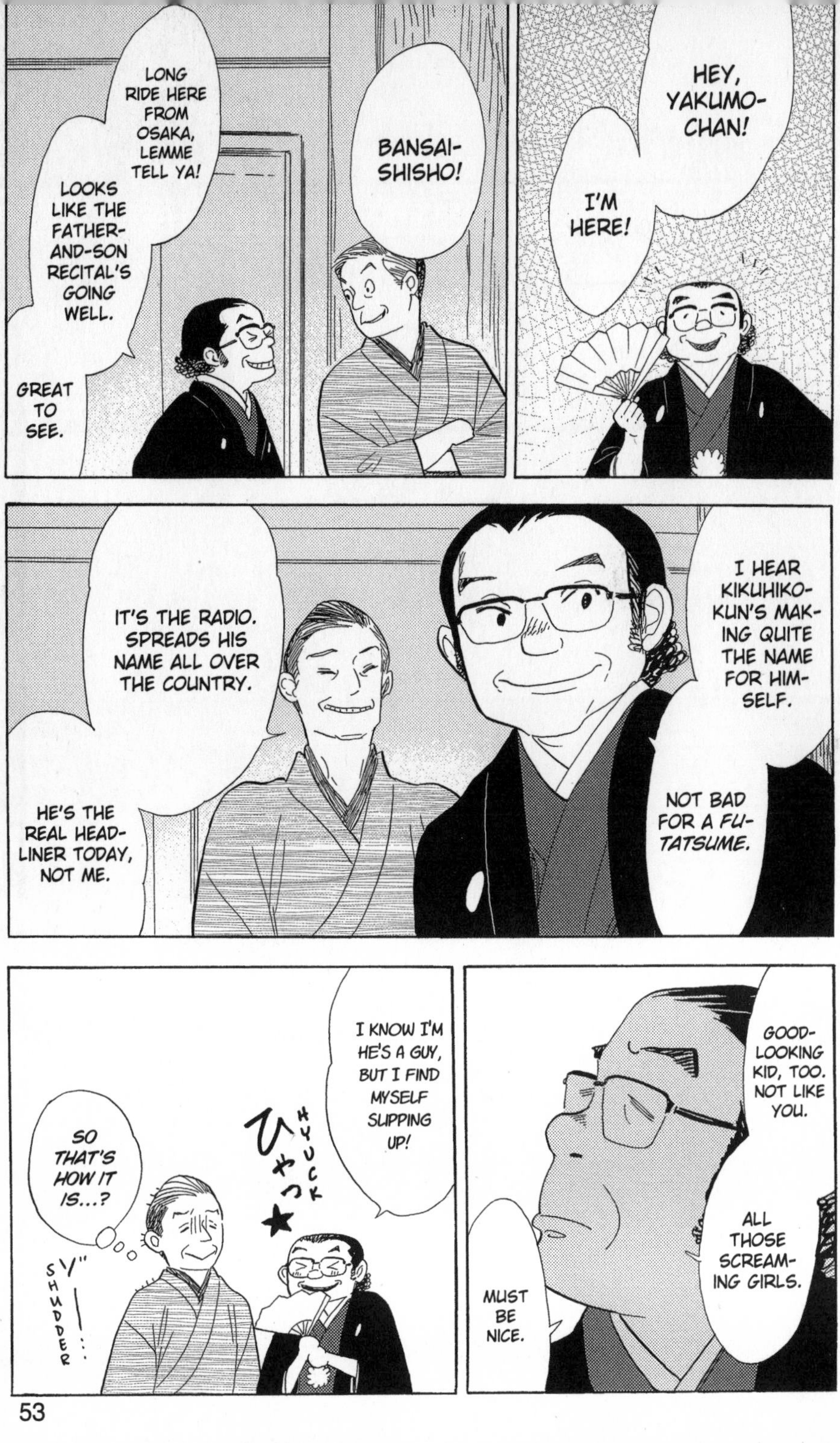
HEY, YAKUMO-CHAN!
I'M HERE!
BANSAI-SHISHO!
LONG RIDE HERE FROM OSAKA, LEMME TELL YA!
LOOKS LIKE THE FATHER-AND-SON RECITAL'S GOING WELL.
GREAT TO SEE.
I HEAR KIKUHIKO-KUN'S MAKING QUITE THE NAME FOR HIMSELF.
NOT BAD FOR A *FUTATSUME*.
IT'S THE RADIO. SPREADS HIS NAME ALL OVER THE COUNTRY.
HE'S THE REAL HEADLINER TODAY, NOT ME.
GOOD-LOOKING KID, TOO. NOT LIKE YOU.
ALL THOSE SCREAMING GIRLS.
MUST BE NICE.
I KNOW I'M HE'S A GUY, BUT I FIND MYSELF SLIPPING UP!
ひやっ HYUCK
SO THAT'S HOW IT IS...?
SHUDDER

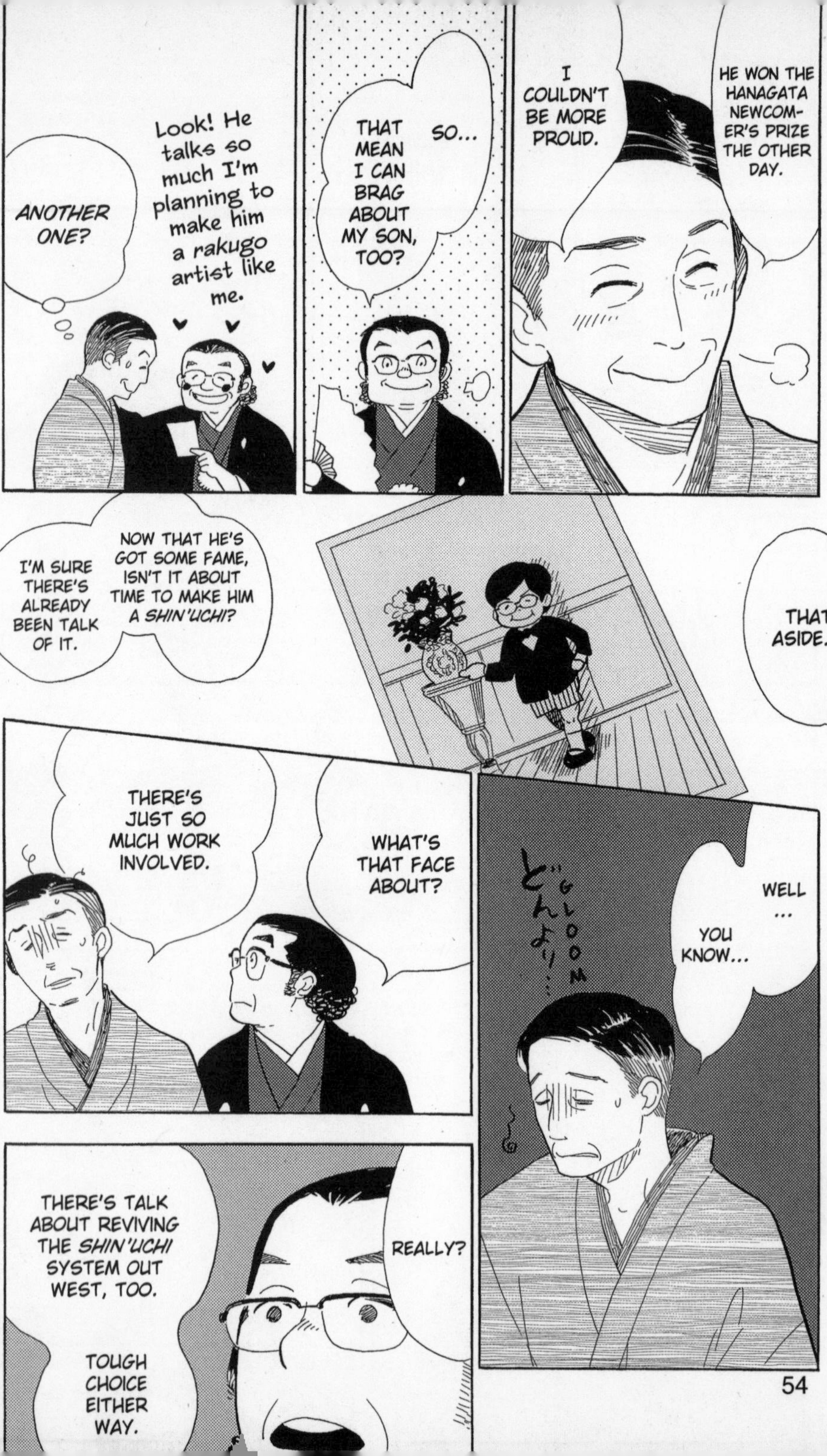
HE WON THE HANAGATA NEWCOMER'S PRIZE THE OTHER DAY.
I COULDN'T BE MORE PROUD.
SO...
THAT MEAN I CAN BRAG ABOUT MY SON, TOO?
Look! He talks so much I'm planning to make him a rakugo artist like me.
ANOTHER ONE?
THAT ASIDE...
NOW THAT HE'S GOT SOME FAME, ISN'T IT ABOUT TIME TO MAKE HIM A *SHIN'UCHI?*
I'M SURE THERE'S ALREADY BEEN TALK OF IT.
WELL...
YOU KNOW...
どんより…
GLOOM
WHAT'S THAT FACE ABOUT?
THERE'S JUST SO MUCH WORK INVOLVED.
REALLY?
THERE'S TALK ABOUT REVIVING THE *SHIN'UCHI* SYSTEM OUT WEST, TOO.
TOUGH CHOICE EITHER WAY.

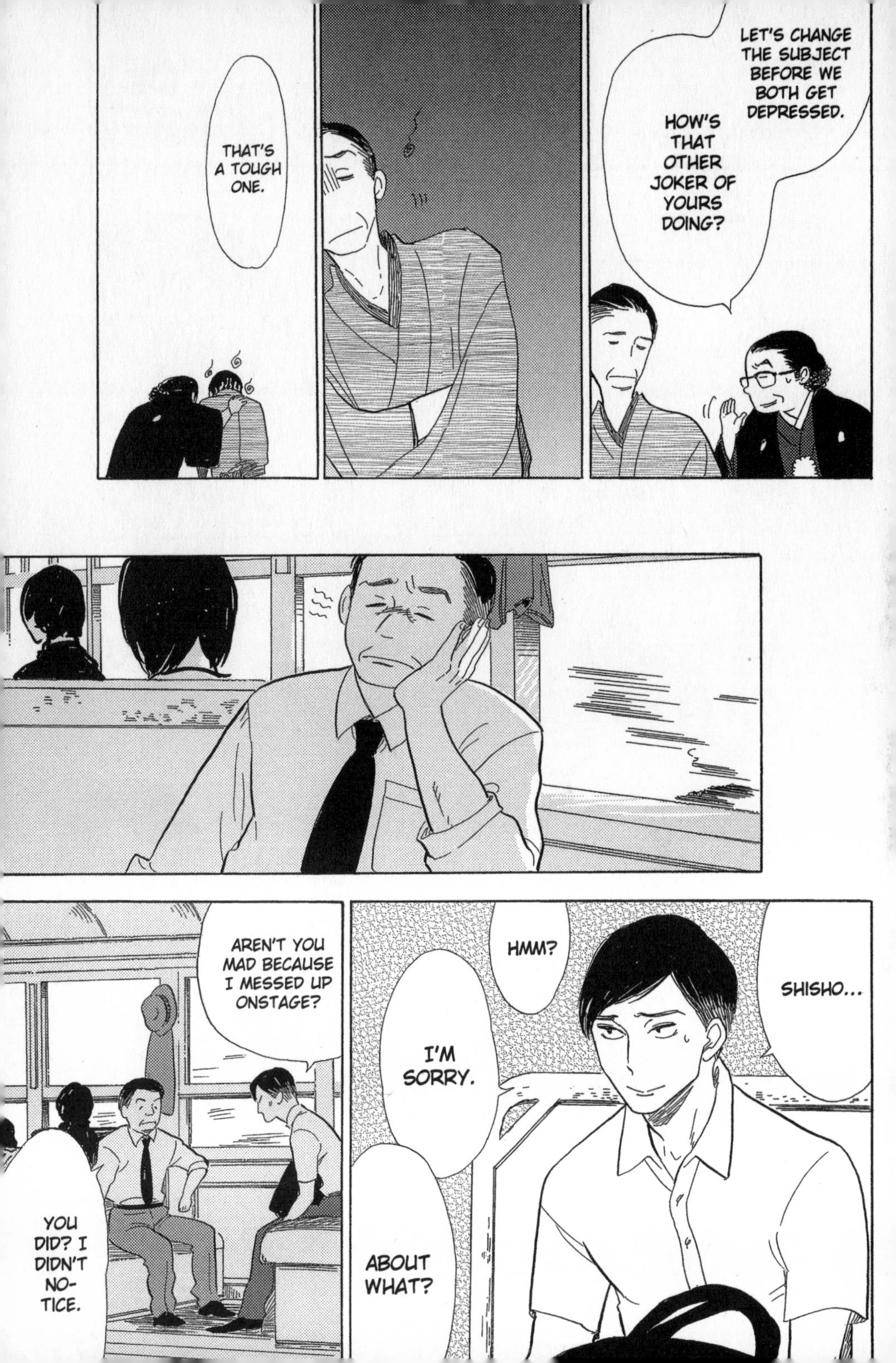
LET'S CHANGE THE SUBJECT BEFORE WE BOTH GET DEPRESSED.
HOW'S THAT OTHER JOKER OF YOURS DOING?
THAT'S A TOUGH ONE.
SHISHO...
HMM?
I'M SORRY.
ABOUT WHAT?
AREN'T YOU MAD BECAUSE I MESSED UP ONSTAGE?
YOU DID? I DIDN'T NO-TICE.

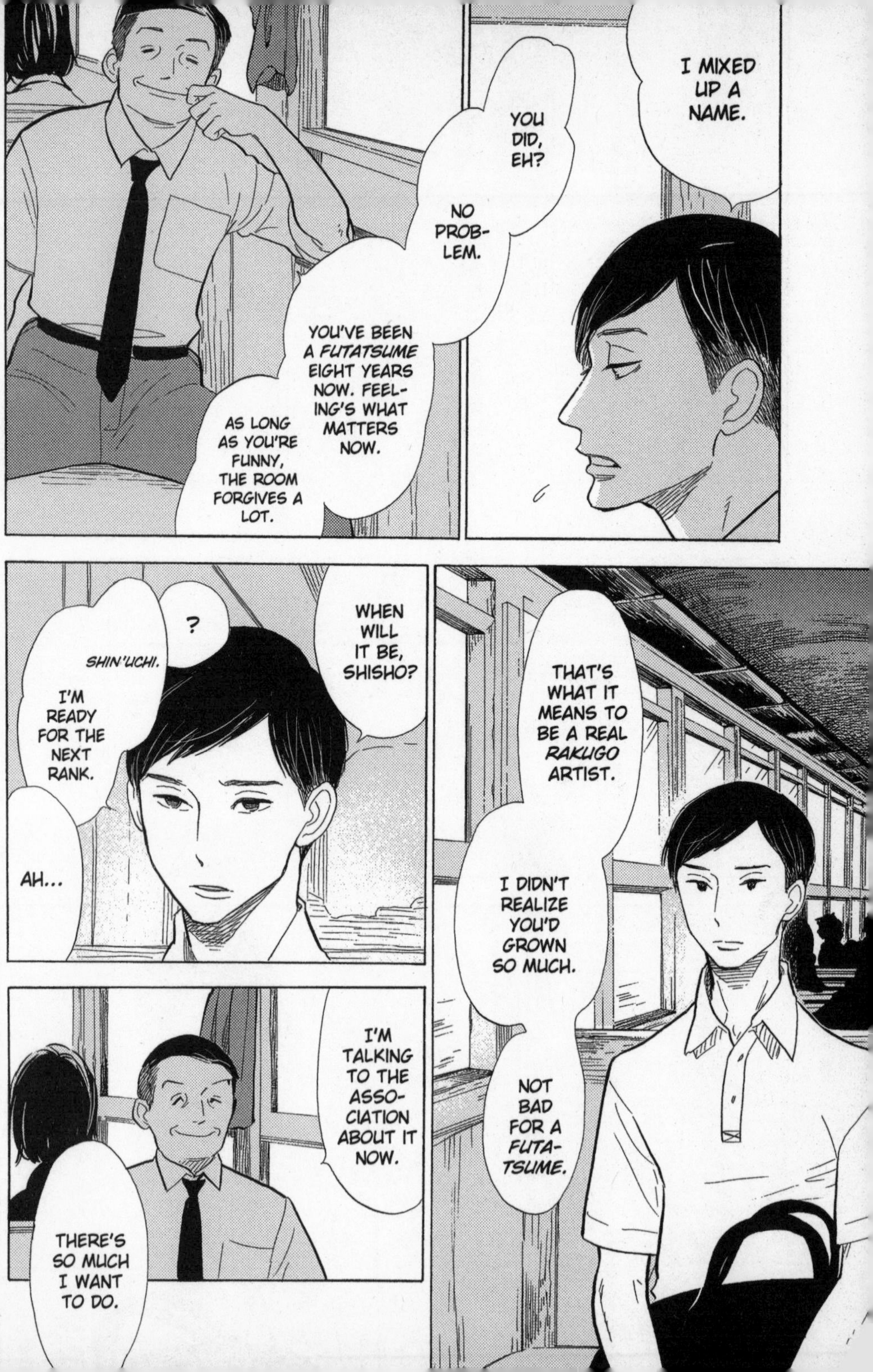

I MIXED UP A NAME.
YOU DID, EH?
NO PROBLEM.
YOU'VE BEEN A *FUTATSUME* EIGHT YEARS NOW. FEELING'S WHAT MATTERS NOW.
AS LONG AS YOU'RE FUNNY, THE ROOM FORGIVES A LOT.
THAT'S WHAT IT MEANS TO BE A REAL *RAKUGO* ARTIST.
I DIDN'T REALIZE YOU'D GROWN SO MUCH.
NOT BAD FOR A *FUTATSUME.*
WHEN WILL IT BE, SHISHO?
?
SHIN'UCHI.
I'M READY FOR THE NEXT RANK.
AH...
I'M TALKING TO THE ASSOCIATION ABOUT IT NOW.
THERE'S SO MUCH I WANT TO DO.

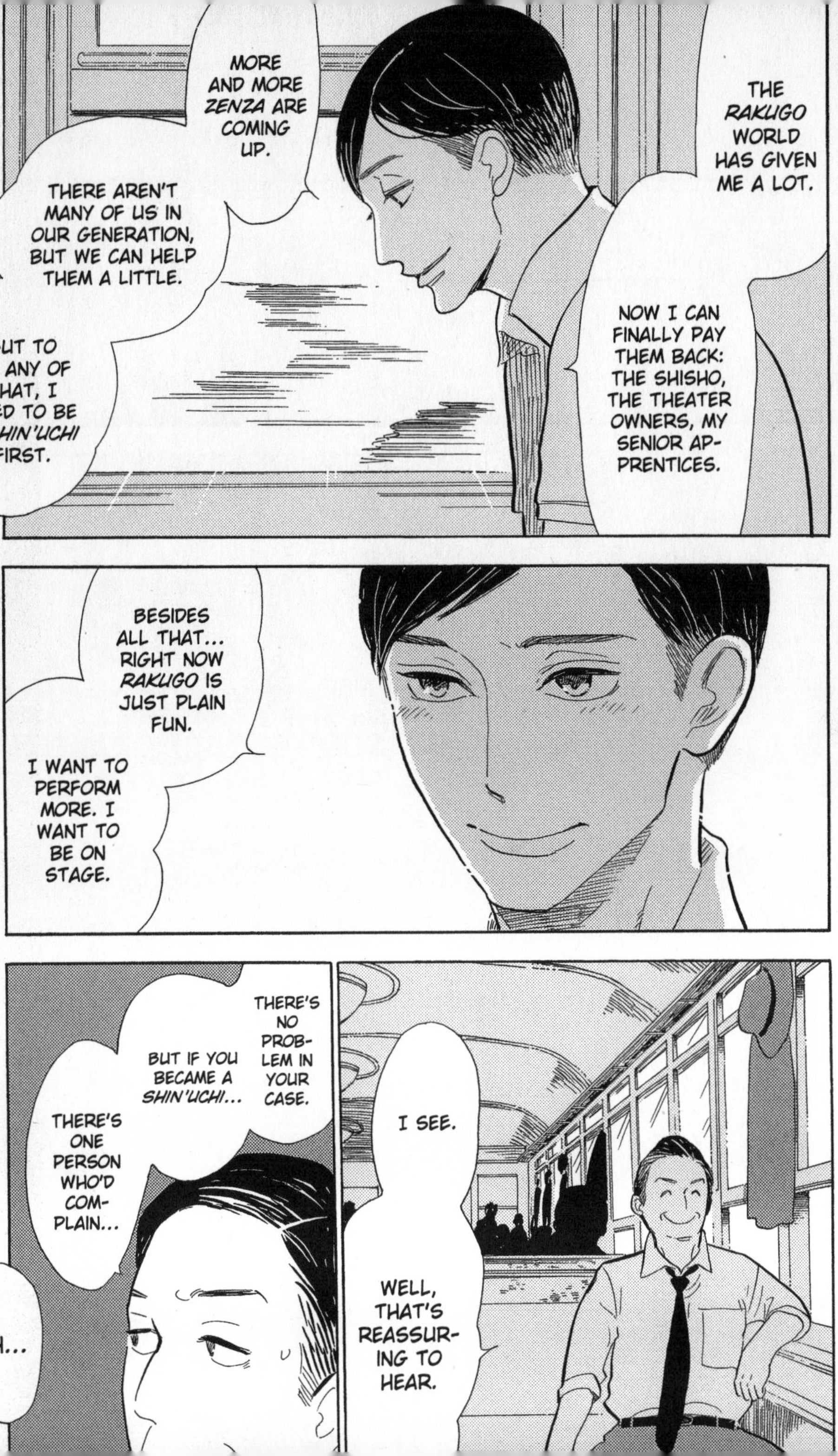
THE RAKUGO WORLD HAS GIVEN ME A LOT.
NOW I CAN FINALLY PAY THEM BACK: THE SHISHO, THE THEATER OWNERS, MY SENIOR APPRENTICES.
MORE AND MORE ZENZA ARE COMING UP.
THERE AREN'T MANY OF US IN OUR GENERATION, BUT WE CAN HELP THEM A LITTLE.
BUT TO DO ANY OF THAT, I NEED TO BE A SHIN'UCHI FIRST.
BESIDES ALL THAT... RIGHT NOW RAKUGO IS JUST PLAIN FUN.
I WANT TO PERFORM MORE. I WANT TO BE ON STAGE.
I SEE.
WELL, THAT'S REASSURING TO HEAR.
THERE'S NO PROBLEM IN YOUR CASE.
BUT IF YOU BECAME A SHIN'UCHI...
THERE'S ONE PERSON WHO'D COMPLAIN...
AH...

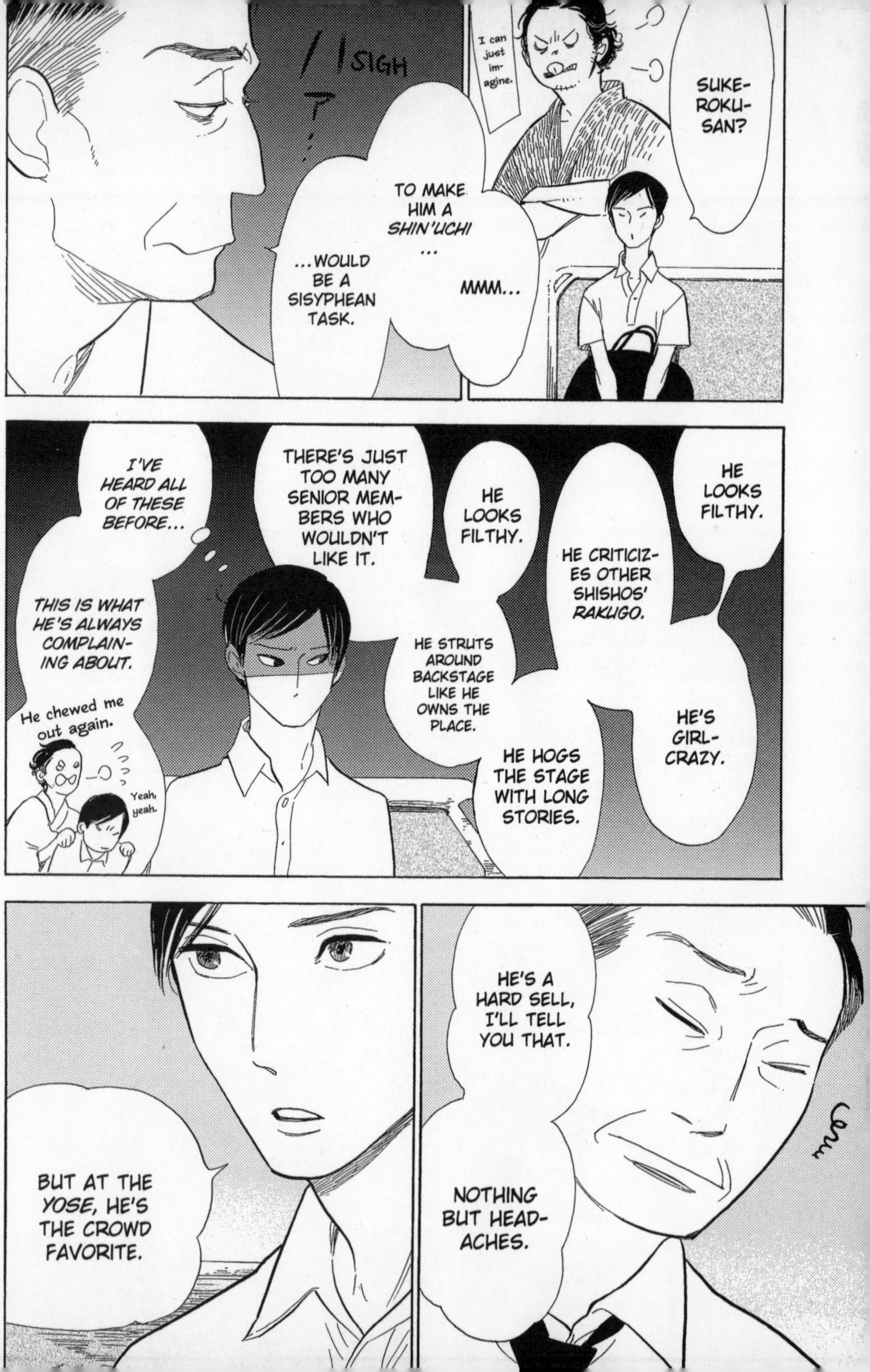
SUKE-ROKU-SAN?
I can just imagine.
SIGH
MMM...
TO MAKE HIM A SHIN'UCHI ...
...WOULD BE A SISYPHEAN TASK.
HE LOOKS FILTHY.
HE'S GIRL-CRAZY.
HE CRITICIZES OTHER SHISHOS' RAKUGO.
HE LOOKS FILTHY.
HE STRUTS AROUND BACKSTAGE LIKE HE OWNS THE PLACE.
HE HOGS THE STAGE WITH LONG STORIES.
THERE'S JUST TOO MANY SENIOR MEMBERS WHO WOULDN'T LIKE IT.
I'VE HEARD ALL OF THESE BEFORE...
THIS IS WHAT HE'S ALWAYS COMPLAINING ABOUT.
He chewed me out again.
Yeah, yeah.
HE'S A HARD SELL, I'LL TELL YOU THAT.
NOTHING BUT HEADACHES.
BUT AT THE YOSE, HE'S THE CROWD FAVORITE.

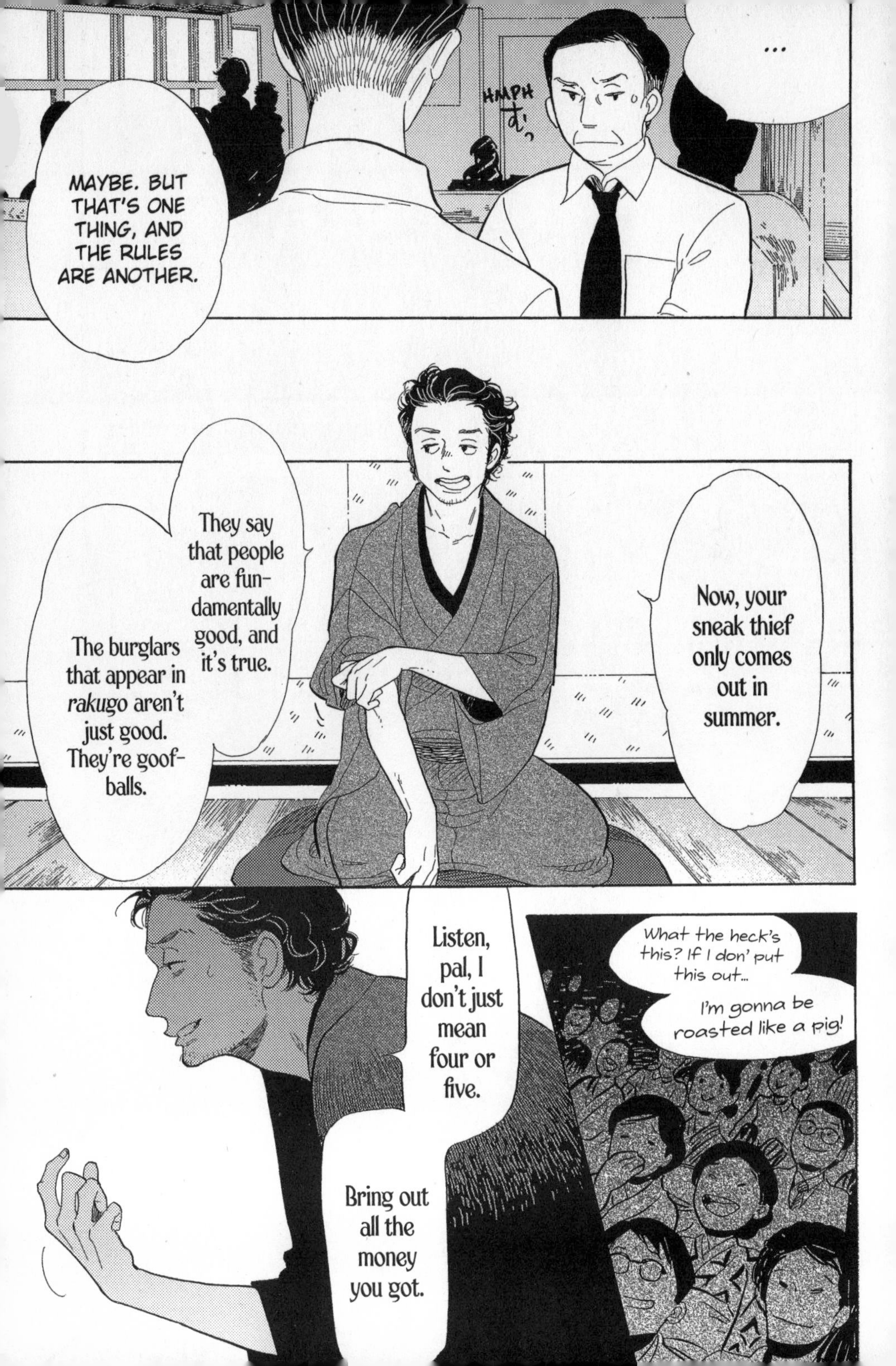
...
HMPH
MAYBE. BUT THAT'S ONE THING, AND THE RULES ARE ANOTHER.
Now, your sneak thief only comes out in summer.
They say that people are fun-damentally good, and it's true.
The burglars that appear in *rakugo* aren't just good. They're goof-balls.
What the heck's this? If I don' put this out...
I'm gonna be roasted like a pig!
Listen, pal, I don't just mean four or five.
Bring out all the money you got.

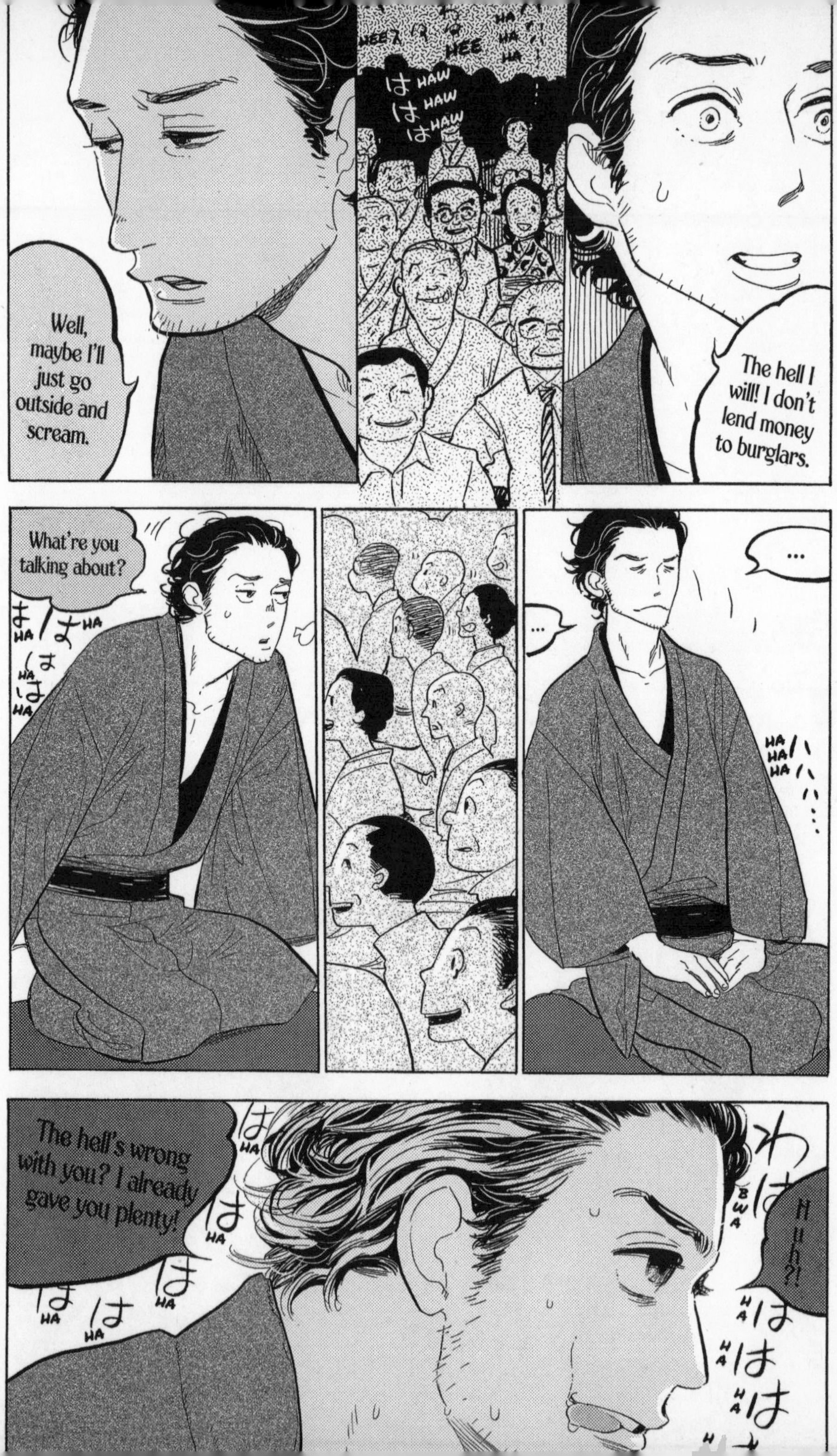
The hell I will! I don't lend money to burglars.
HEE HEE HA HA HA
は HAW は HAW は HAW
Well, maybe I'll just go outside and scream.
...
...
HA HA HA
What're you talking about?
HA HA HA HA
Huh?!
BWA HA HA HA
The hell's wrong with you? I already gave you plenty!
HA HA HA HA HA

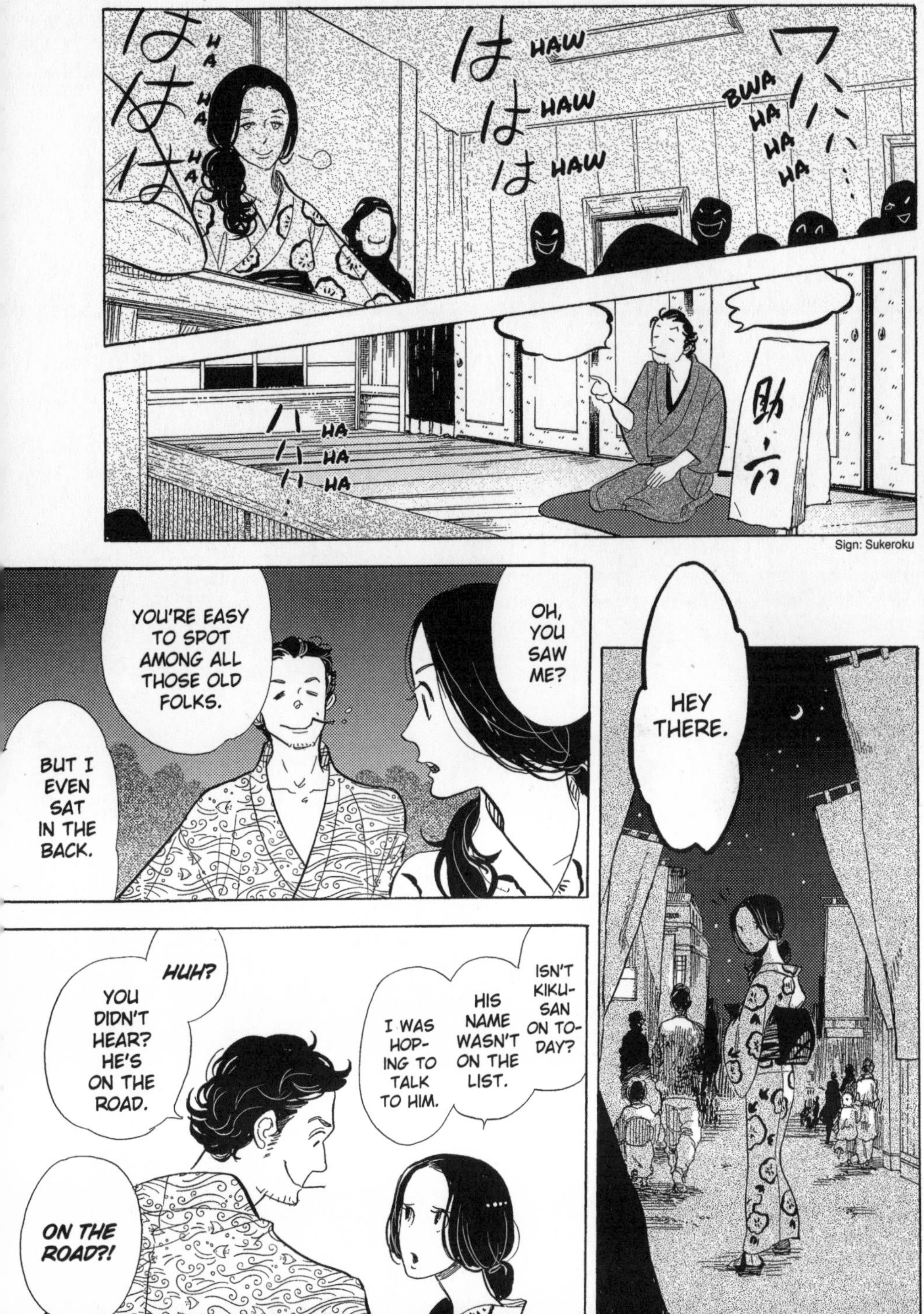
ワハハ…
BWA HA HA HA
ははは
HAW HAW HAW
ははは
HA HA HA HA
ハハハ
HA HA HA
助六
Sign: Sukeroku
HEY THERE.
OH, YOU SAW ME?
YOU'RE EASY TO SPOT AMONG ALL THOSE OLD FOLKS.
BUT I EVEN SAT IN THE BACK.
ISN'T KIKU-SAN ON TO-DAY?
HIS NAME WASN'T ON THE LIST.
I WAS HOP-ING TO TALK TO HIM.
HUH?
YOU DIDN'T HEAR? HE'S ON THE ROAD.
ON THE ROAD?!

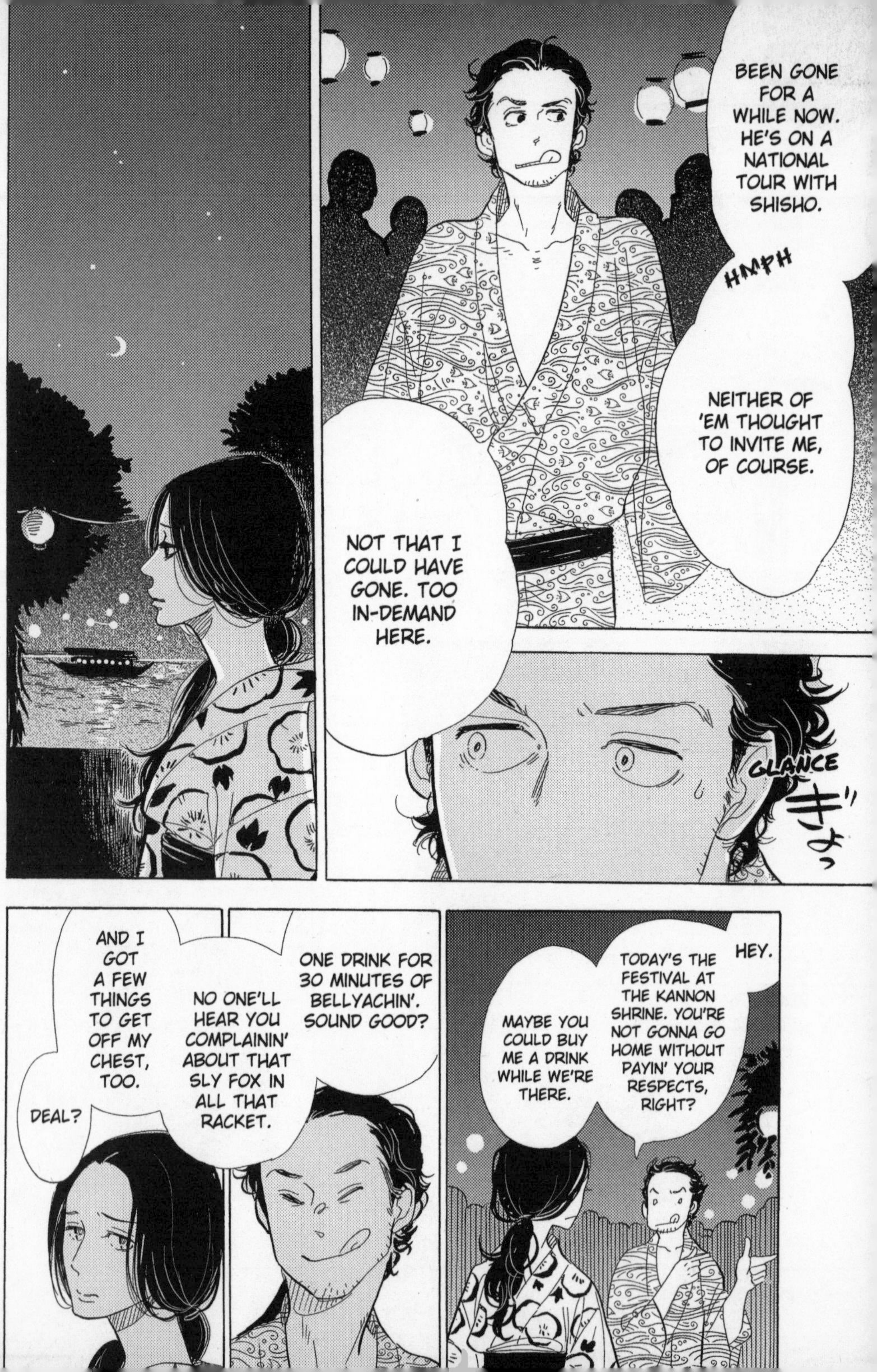
BEEN GONE FOR A WHILE NOW. HE'S ON A NATIONAL TOUR WITH SHISHO.
HMPH
NEITHER OF 'EM THOUGHT TO INVITE ME, OF COURSE.
NOT THAT I COULD HAVE GONE. TOO IN-DEMAND HERE.
GLANCE
ぎょっ
HEY.
TODAY'S THE FESTIVAL AT THE KANNON SHRINE. YOU'RE NOT GONNA GO HOME WITHOUT PAYIN' YOUR RESPECTS, RIGHT?
MAYBE YOU COULD BUY ME A DRINK WHILE WE'RE THERE.
ONE DRINK FOR 30 MINUTES OF BELLYACHIN'. SOUND GOOD?
NO ONE'LL HEAR YOU COMPLAININ' ABOUT THAT SLY FOX IN ALL THAT RACKET.
AND I GOT A FEW THINGS TO GET OFF MY CHEST, TOO.
DEAL?

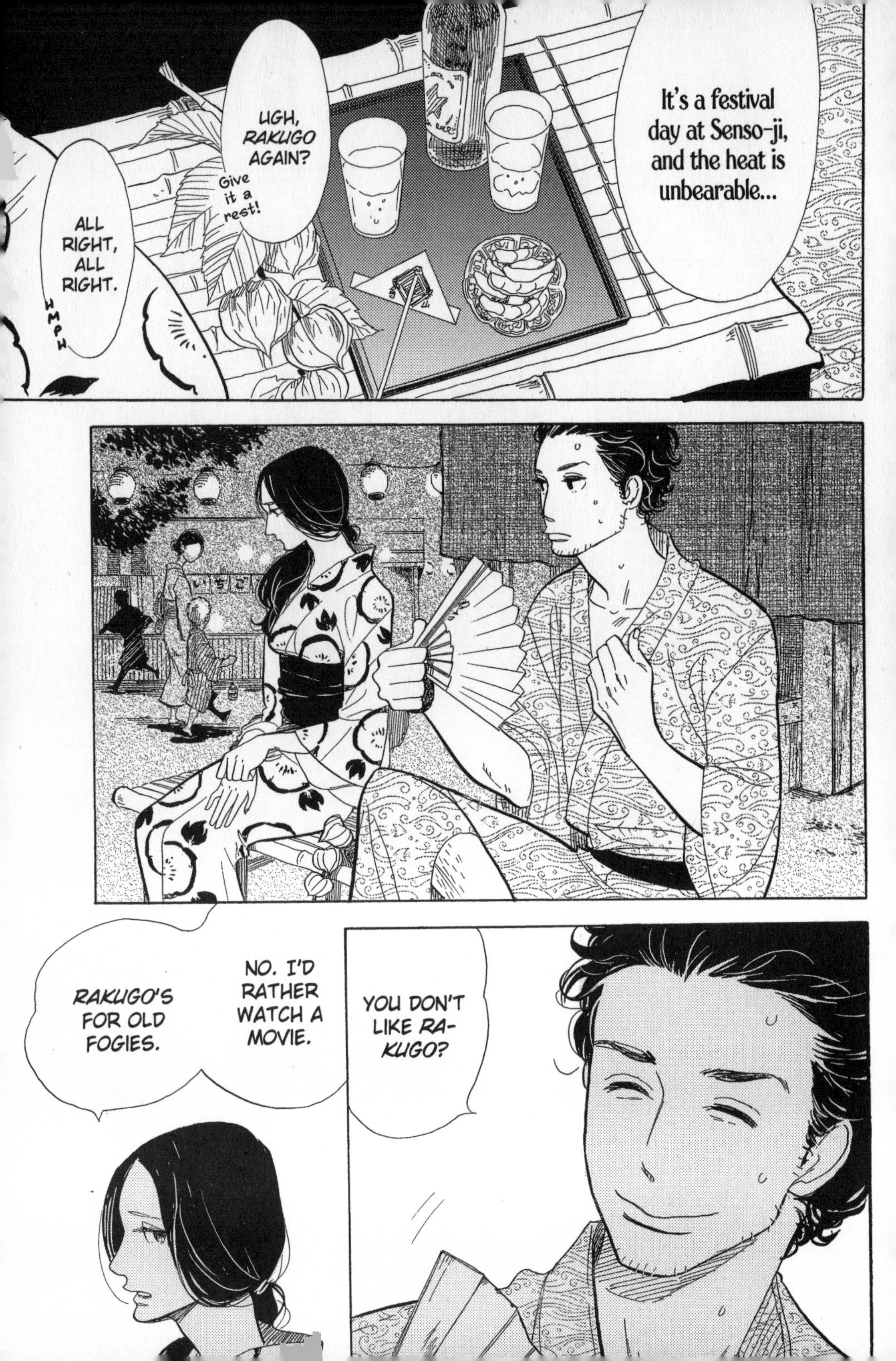
It's a festival day at Senso-ji, and the heat is unbearable...
UGH, *RAKUGO* AGAIN?
Give it a rest!
ALL RIGHT, ALL RIGHT.
HMPH
YOU DON'T LIKE *RA-KUGO*?
NO. I'D RATHER WATCH A MOVIE.
RAKUGO'S FOR OLD FOGIES.

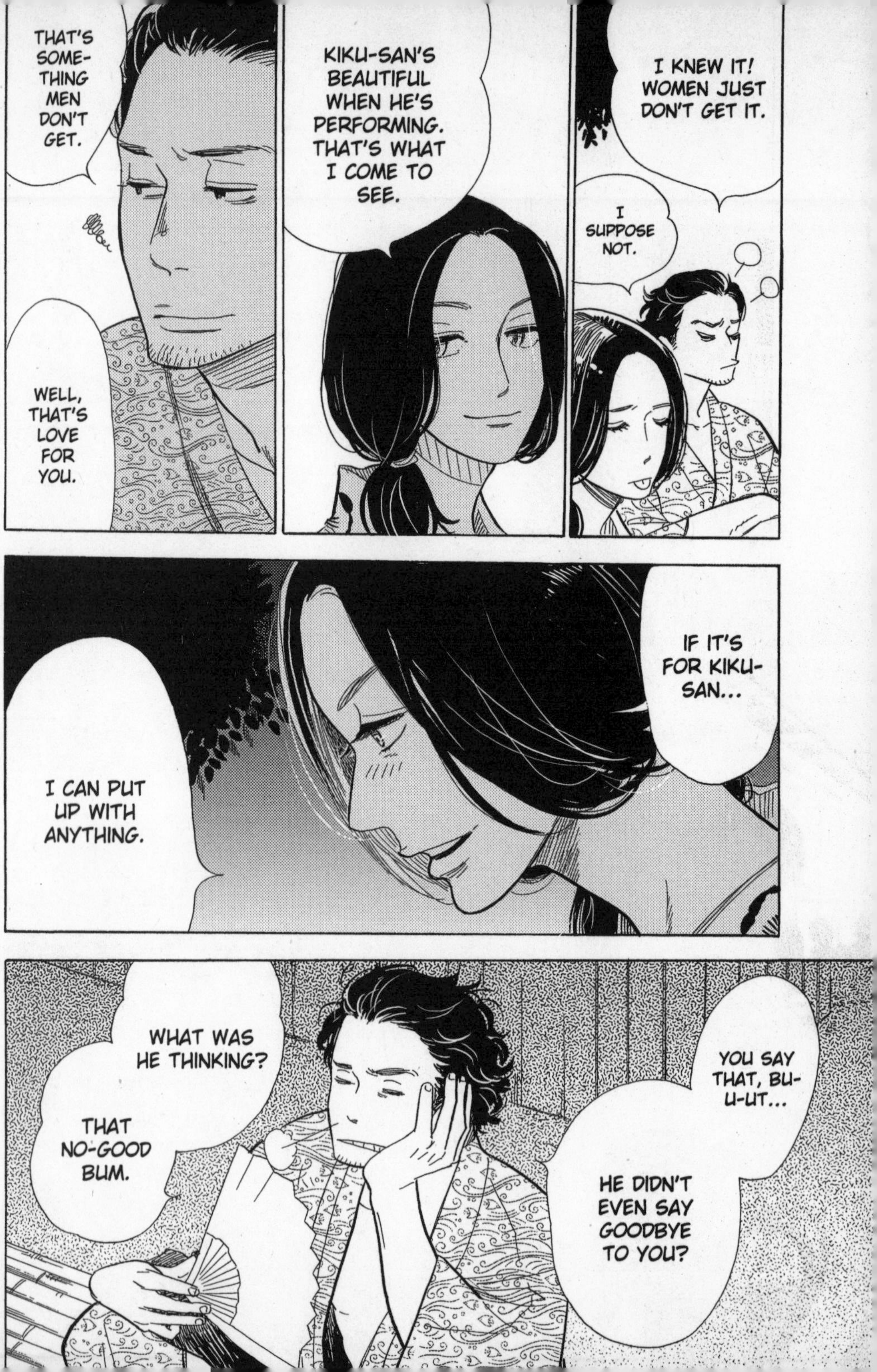
I KNEW IT! WOMEN JUST DON'T GET IT.
I SUPPOSE NOT.
KIKU-SAN'S BEAUTIFUL WHEN HE'S PERFORMING. THAT'S WHAT I COME TO SEE.
THAT'S SOME-THING MEN DON'T GET.
WELL, THAT'S LOVE FOR YOU.
IF IT'S FOR KIKU-SAN...
I CAN PUT UP WITH ANYTHING.
YOU SAY THAT, BU-U-UT...
HE DIDN'T EVEN SAY GOODBYE TO YOU?
WHAT WAS HE THINKING?
THAT NO-GOOD BUM.

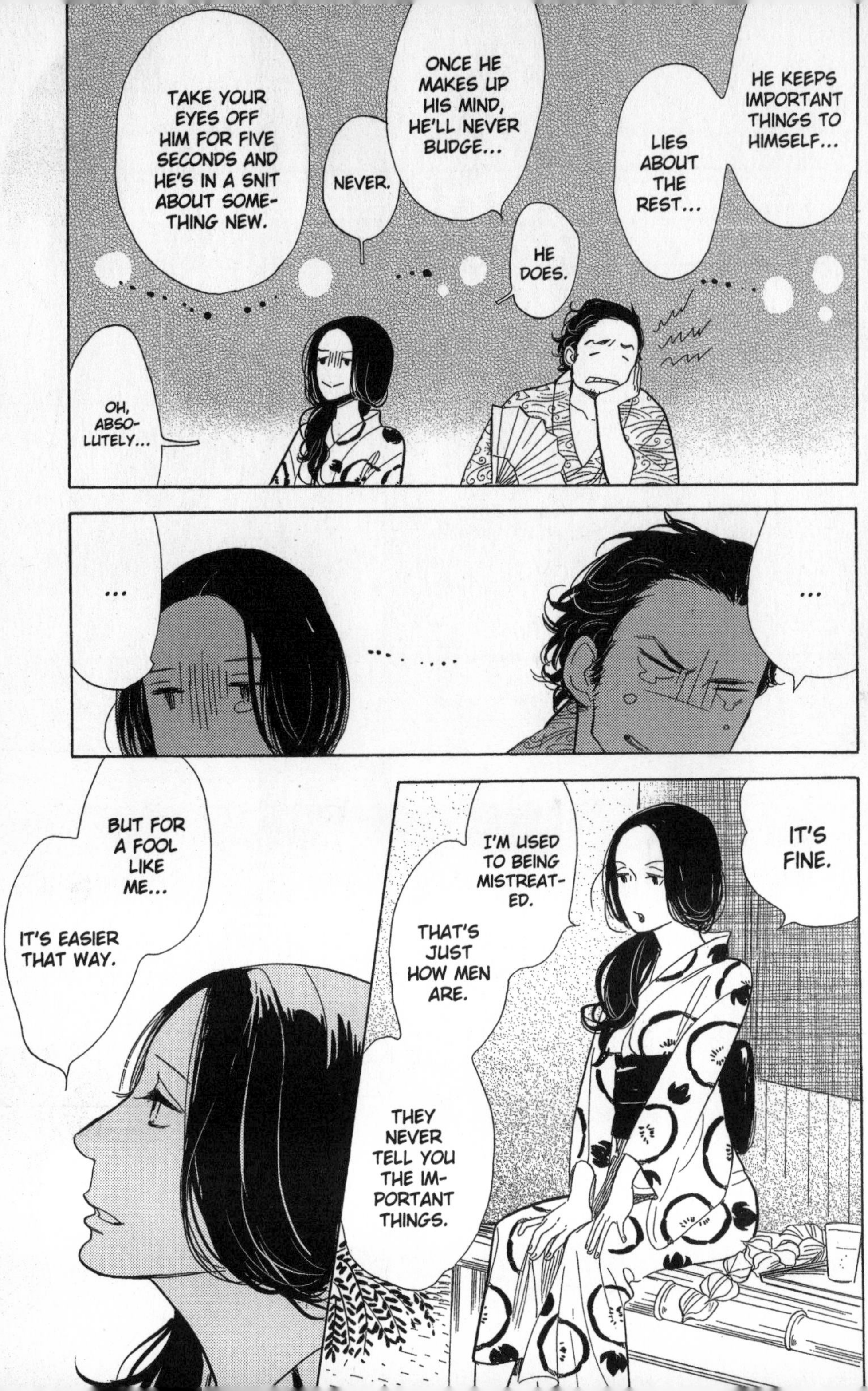
HE KEEPS IMPORTANT THINGS TO HIMSELF...
LIES ABOUT THE REST...
HE DOES.
ONCE HE MAKES UP HIS MIND, HE'LL NEVER BUDGE...
NEVER.
TAKE YOUR EYES OFF HIM FOR FIVE SECONDS AND HE'S IN A SNIT ABOUT SOME-THING NEW.
OH, ABSO-LUTELY...
...
...
IT'S FINE.
I'M USED TO BEING MISTREAT-ED.
THAT'S JUST HOW MEN ARE.
THEY NEVER TELL YOU THE IM-PORTANT THINGS.
BUT FOR A FOOL LIKE ME...
IT'S EASIER THAT WAY.

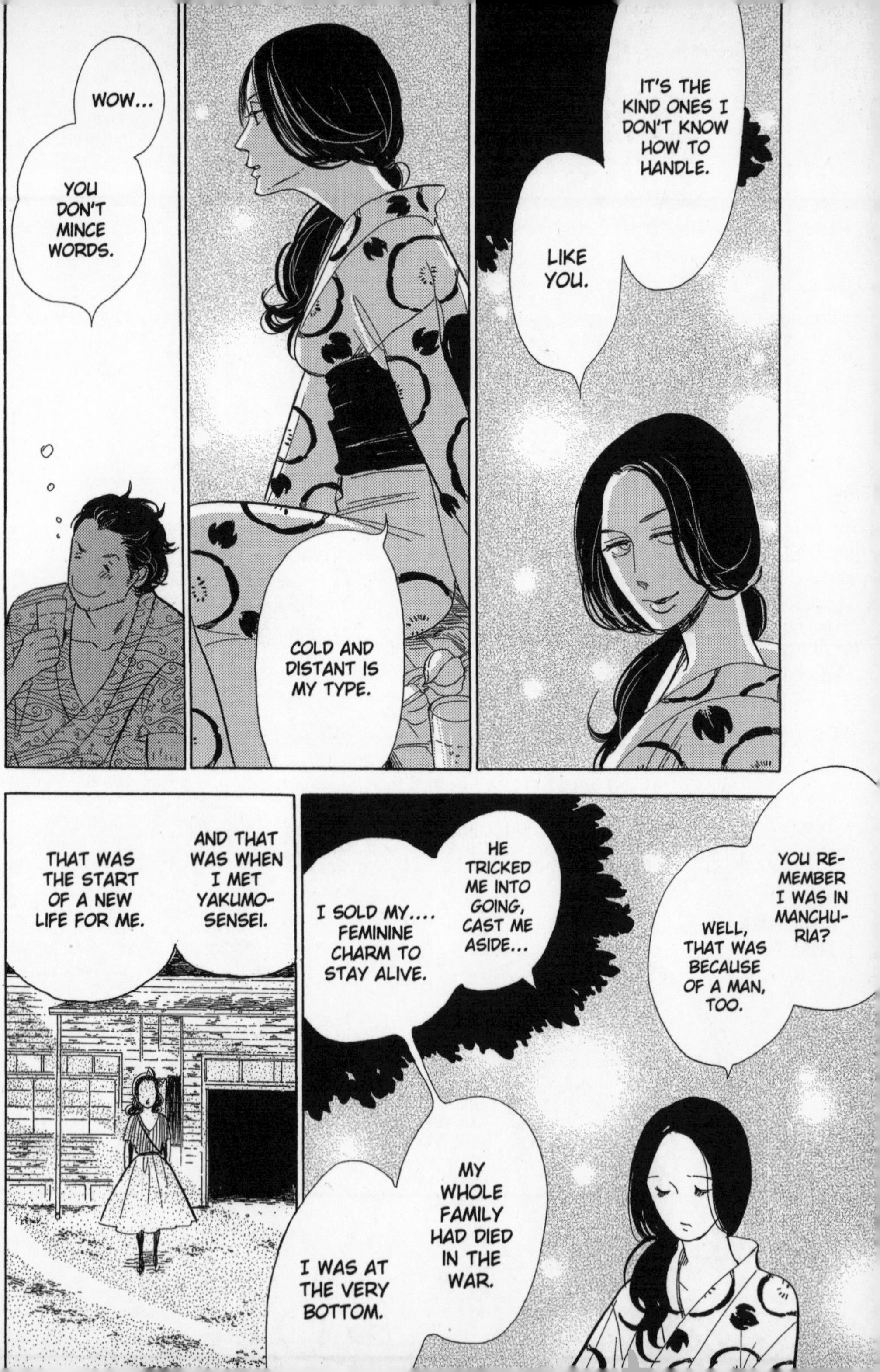
IT'S THE KIND ONES I DON'T KNOW HOW TO HANDLE.
LIKE YOU.
COLD AND DISTANT IS MY TYPE.
WOW...
YOU DON'T MINCE WORDS.
YOU RE-MEMBER I WAS IN MANCHU-RIA?
WELL, THAT WAS BECAUSE OF A MAN, TOO.
HE TRICKED ME INTO GOING, CAST ME ASIDE...
I SOLD MY.... FEMININE CHARM TO STAY ALIVE.
MY WHOLE FAMILY HAD DIED IN THE WAR.
I WAS AT THE VERY BOTTOM.
AND THAT WAS WHEN I MET YAKUMO-SENSEI.
THAT WAS THE START OF A NEW LIFE FOR ME.

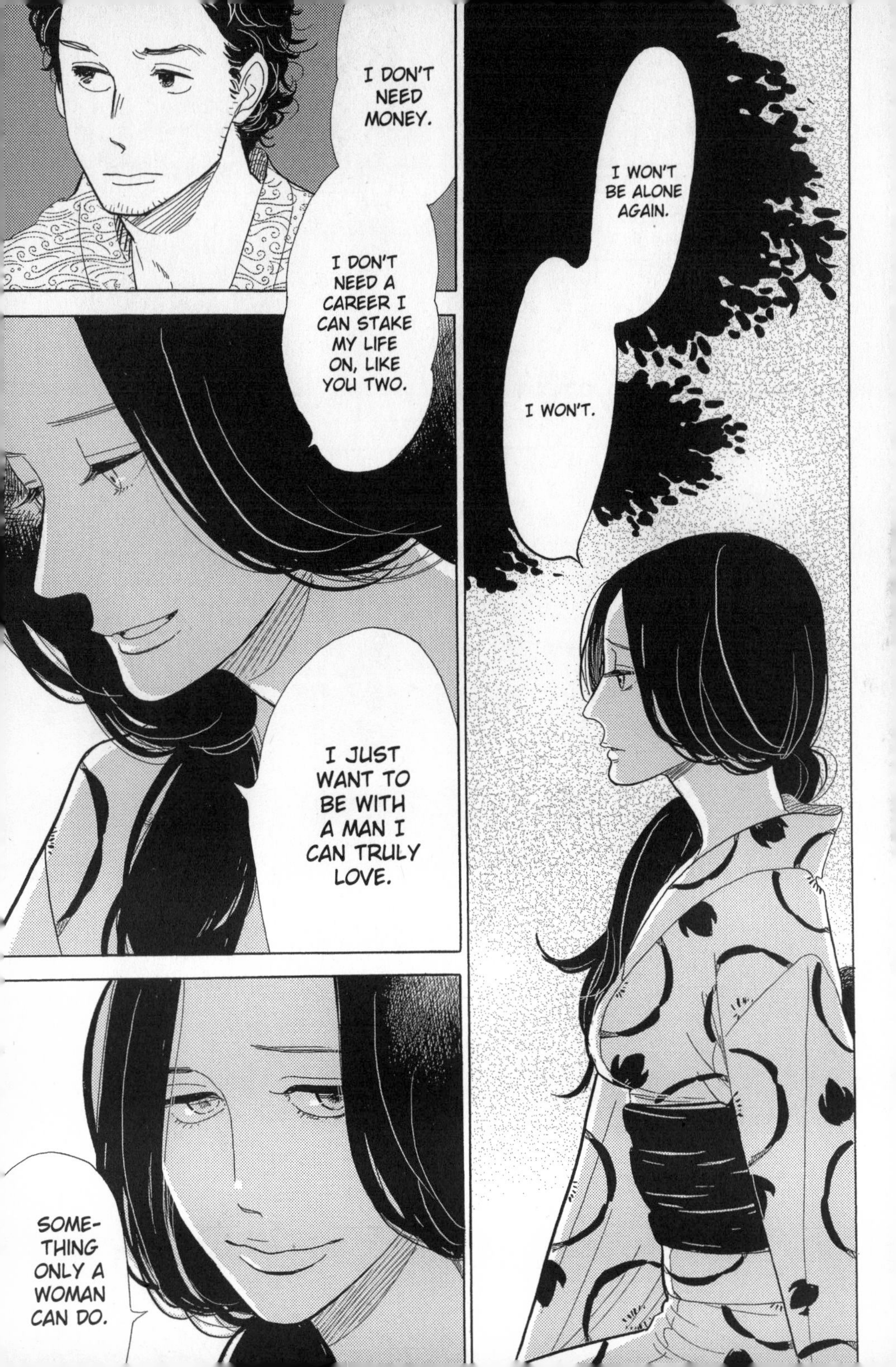
I WON'T BE ALONE AGAIN.
I WON'T.
I DON'T NEED MONEY.
I DON'T NEED A CAREER I CAN STAKE MY LIFE ON, LIKE YOU TWO.
I JUST WANT TO BE WITH A MAN I CAN TRULY LOVE.
SOME-THING ONLY A WOMAN CAN DO.

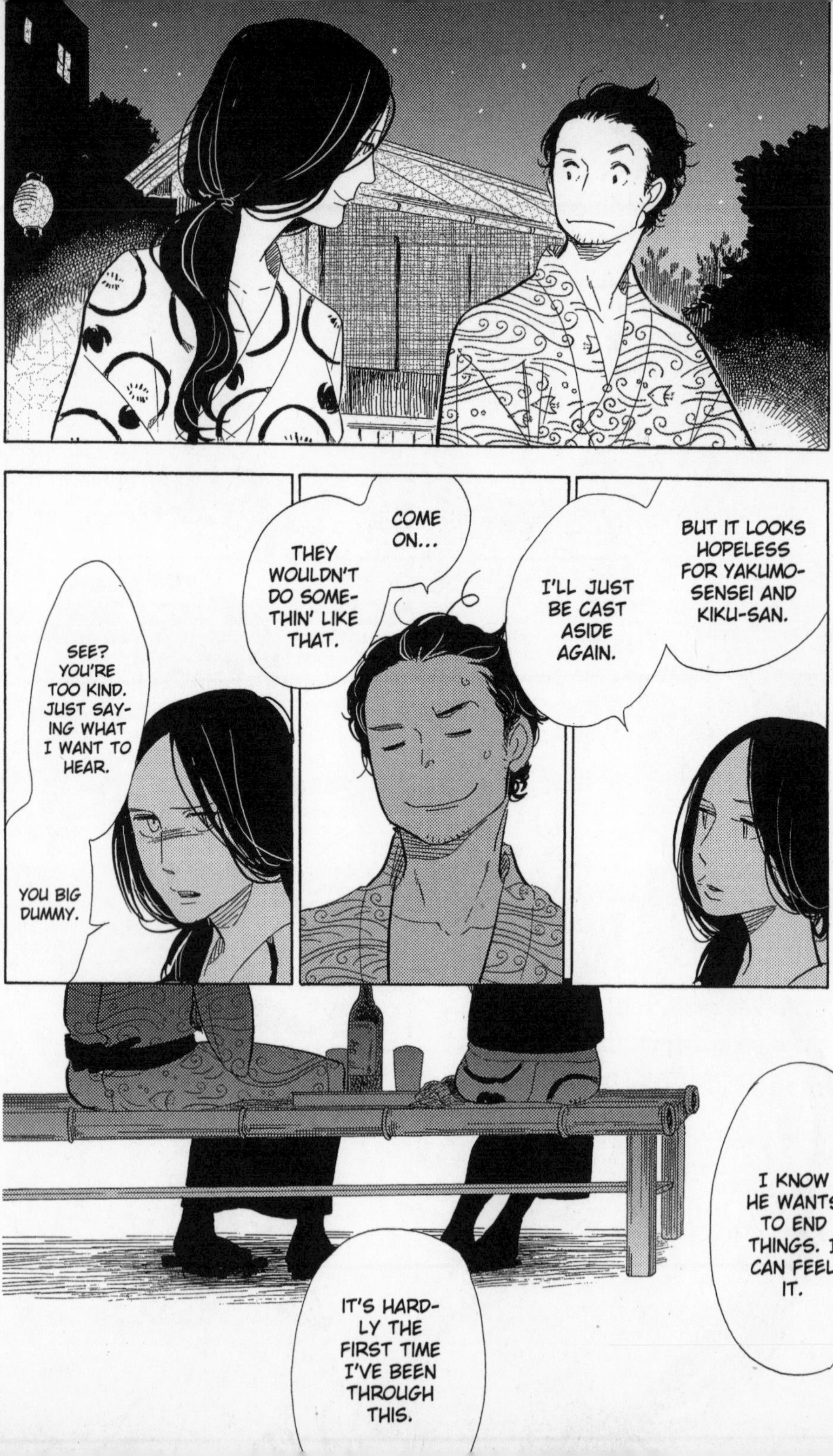
BUT IT LOOKS HOPELESS FOR YAKUMO-SENSEI AND KIKU-SAN.
I'LL JUST BE CAST ASIDE AGAIN.
COME ON...
THEY WOULDN'T DO SOMETHIN' LIKE THAT.
SEE? YOU'RE TOO KIND. JUST SAYING WHAT I WANT TO HEAR.
YOU BIG DUMMY.
I KNOW HE WANTS TO END THINGS. I CAN FEEL IT.
IT'S HARDLY THE FIRST TIME I'VE BEEN THROUGH THIS.

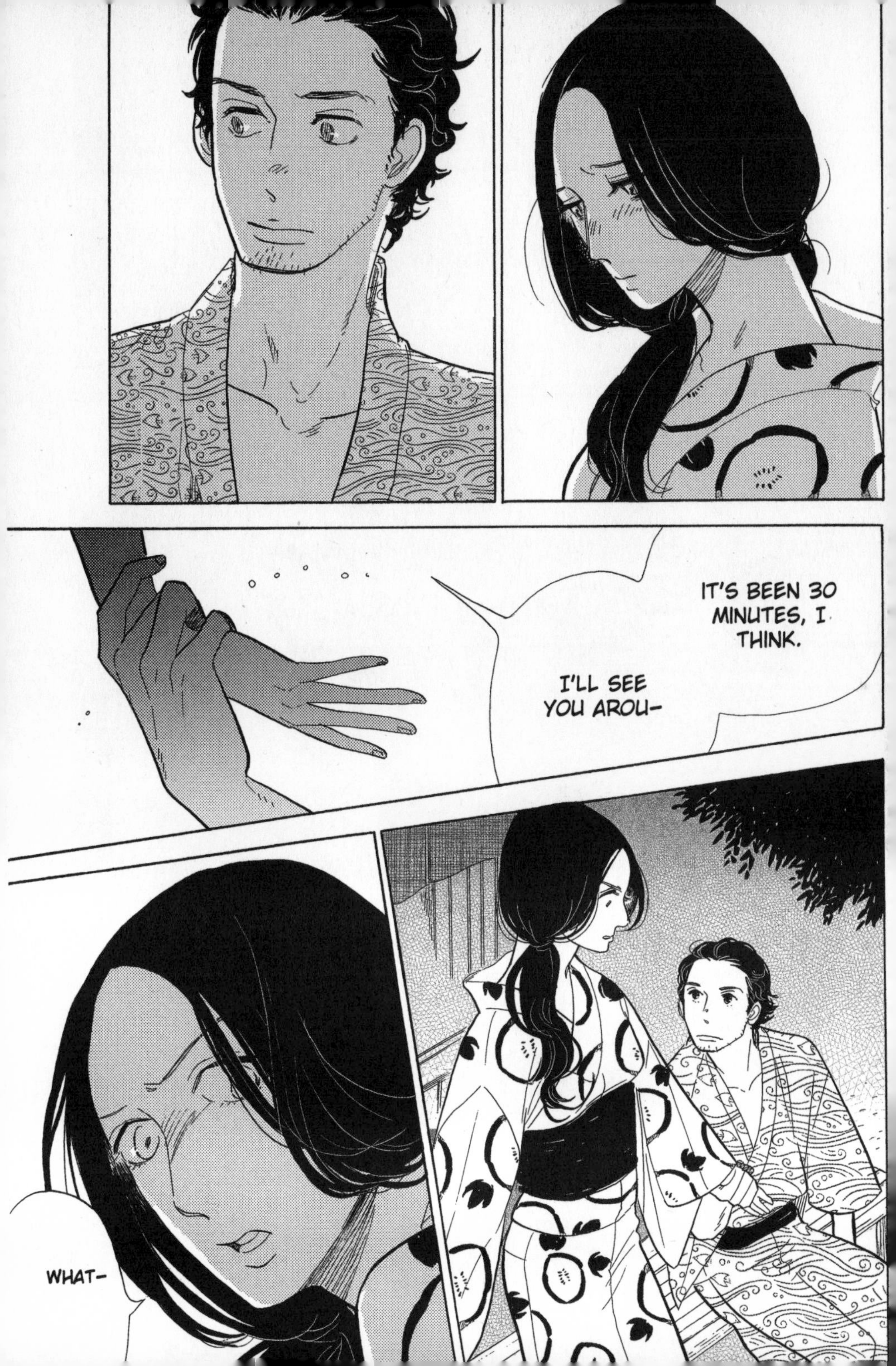
IT'S BEEN 30 MINUTES, I THINK.
I'LL SEE YOU AROU-
WHAT-

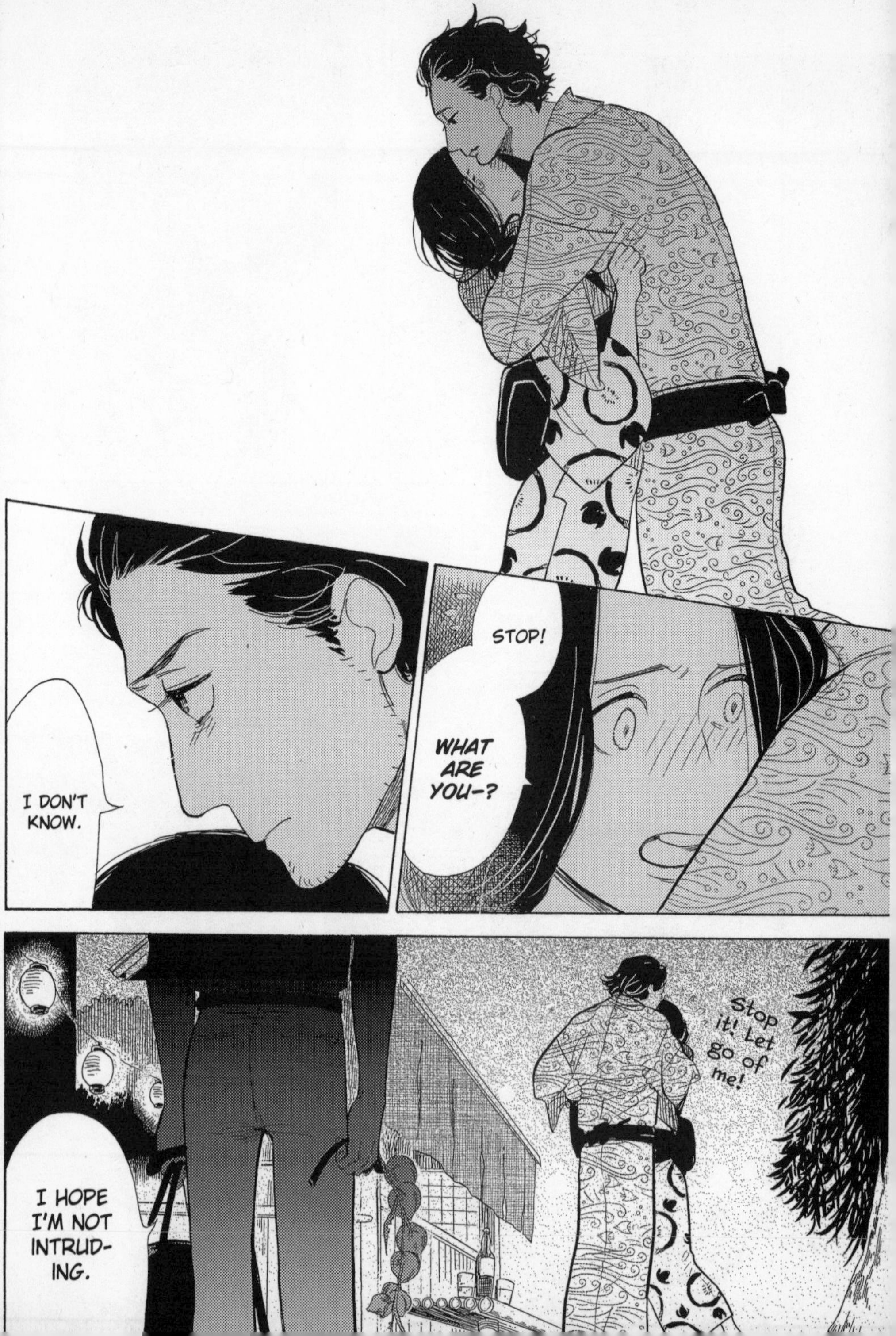
STOP!
WHAT ARE YOU-?
I DON'T KNOW.
Stop it! Let go of me!
I HOPE I'M NOT INTRUD-ING.

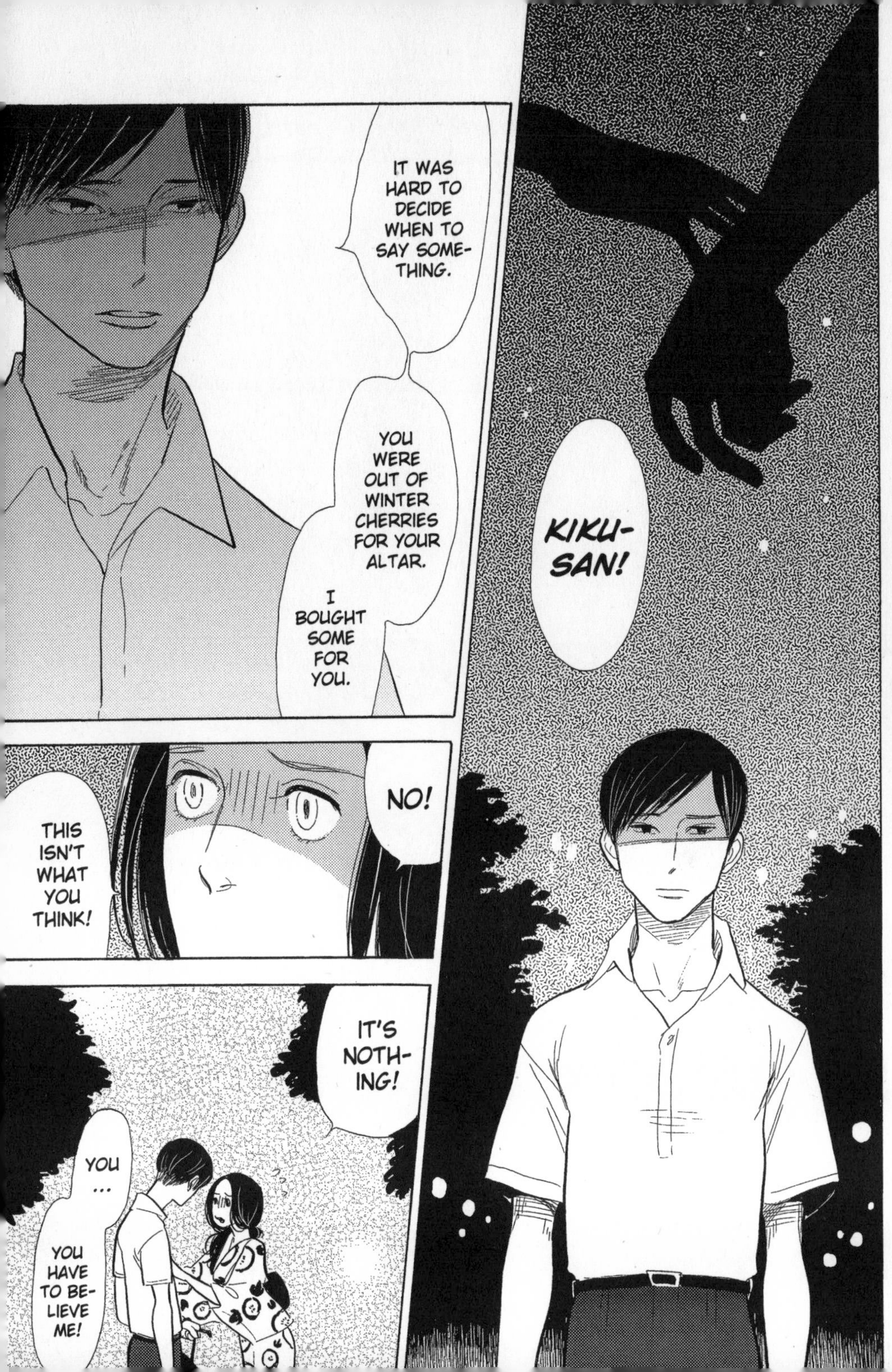
KIKU-SAN!
IT WAS HARD TO DECIDE WHEN TO SAY SOME-THING.
YOU WERE OUT OF WINTER CHERRIES FOR YOUR ALTAR.
I BOUGHT SOME FOR YOU.
NO!
THIS ISN'T WHAT YOU THINK!
IT'S NOTH-ING!
YOU ...
YOU HAVE TO BE-LIEVE ME!

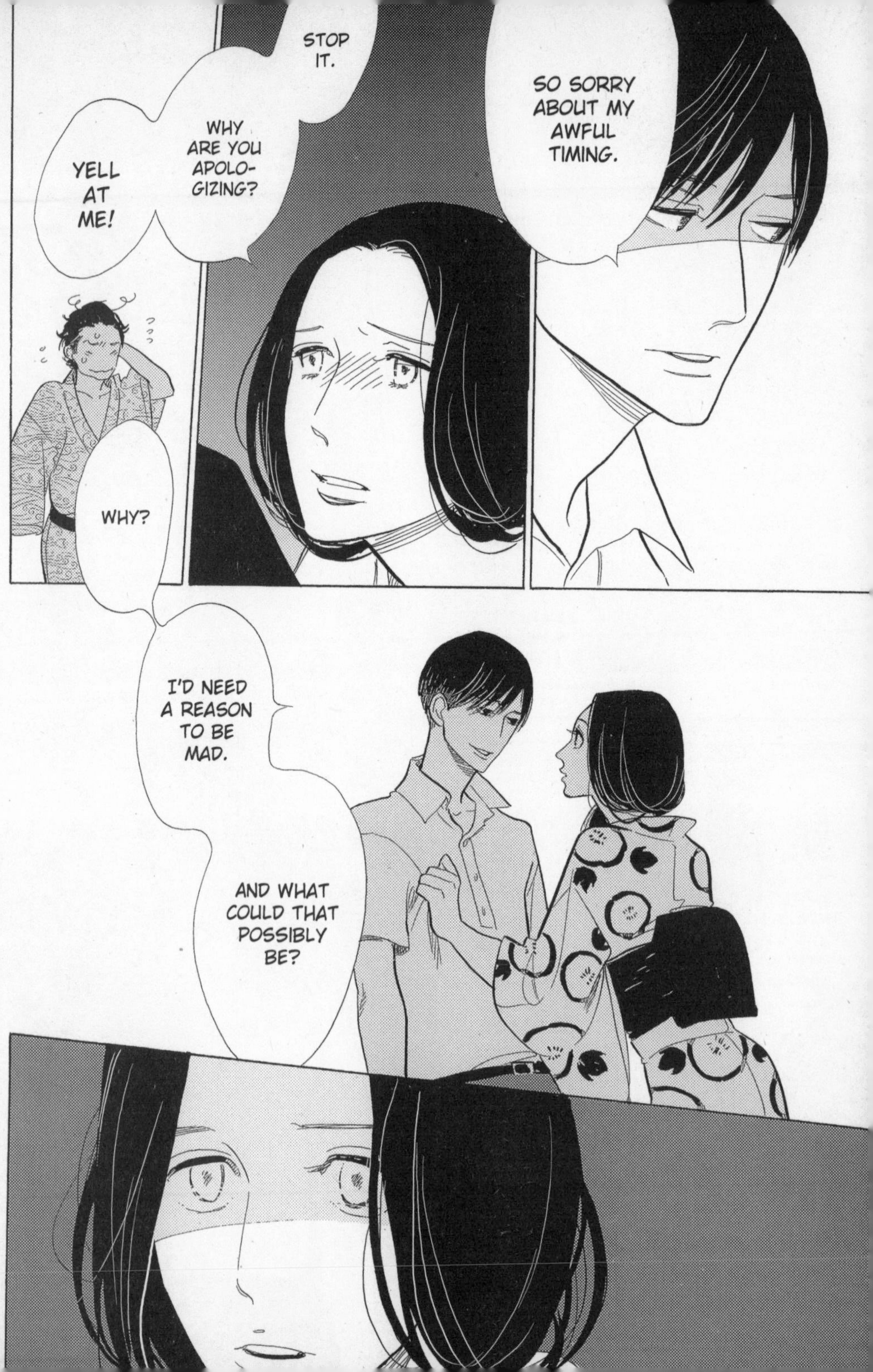
SO SORRY ABOUT MY AWFUL TIMING.
STOP IT.
WHY ARE YOU APOLOGIZING?
YELL AT ME!
WHY?
I'D NEED A REASON TO BE MAD.
AND WHAT COULD THAT POSSIBLY BE?

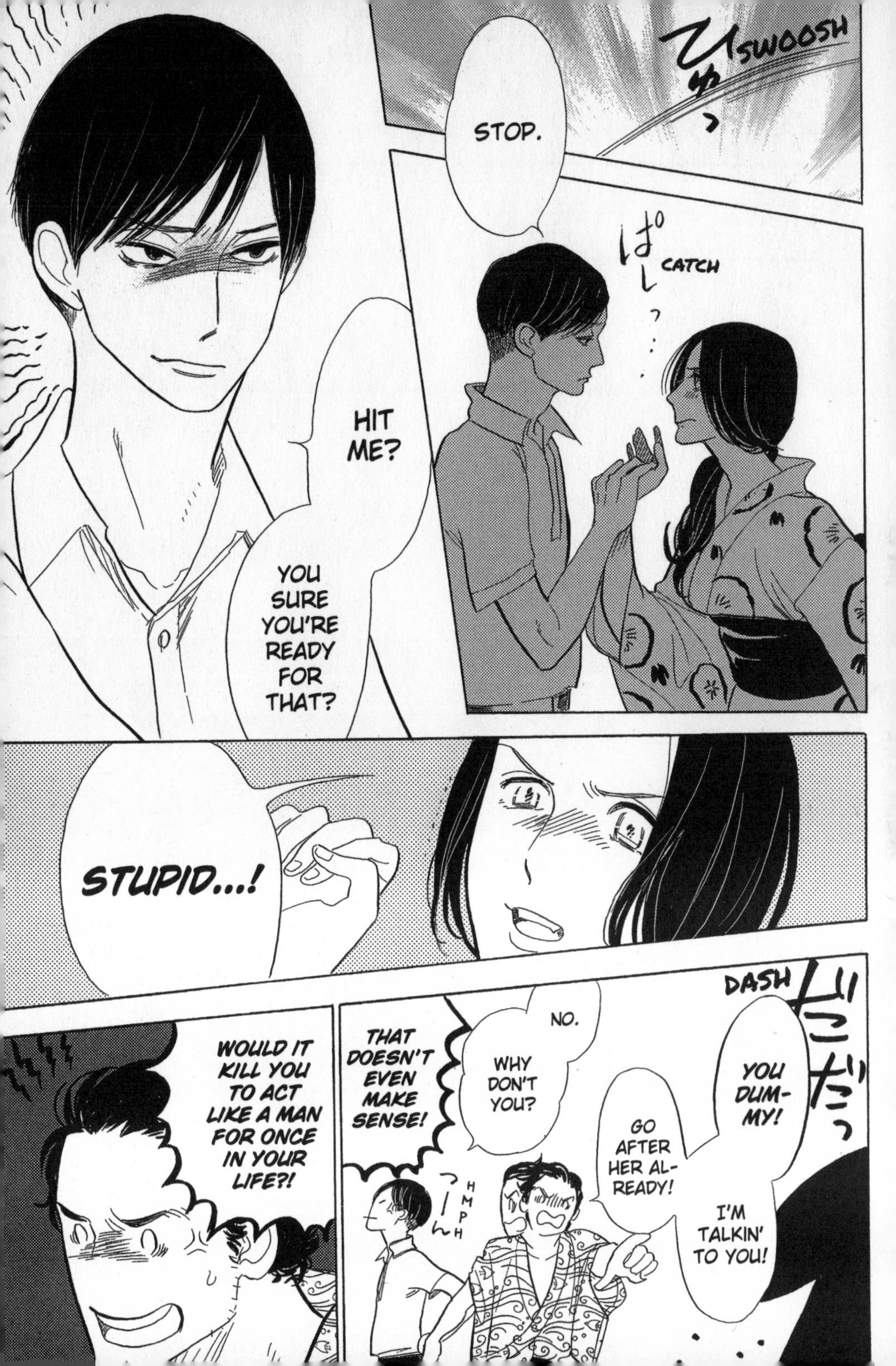

ひゅっ
SWOOSH
STOP.
ぱしっ
CATCH
HIT ME?
YOU SURE YOU'RE READY FOR THAT?
STUPID...!
だだっ
DASH
YOU DUM-MY!
GO AFTER HER AL-READY!
I'M TALKIN' TO YOU!
NO.
WHY DON'T YOU?
THAT DOESN'T EVEN MAKE SENSE!
HMPH
WOULD IT KILL YOU TO ACT LIKE A MAN FOR ONCE IN YOUR LIFE?!

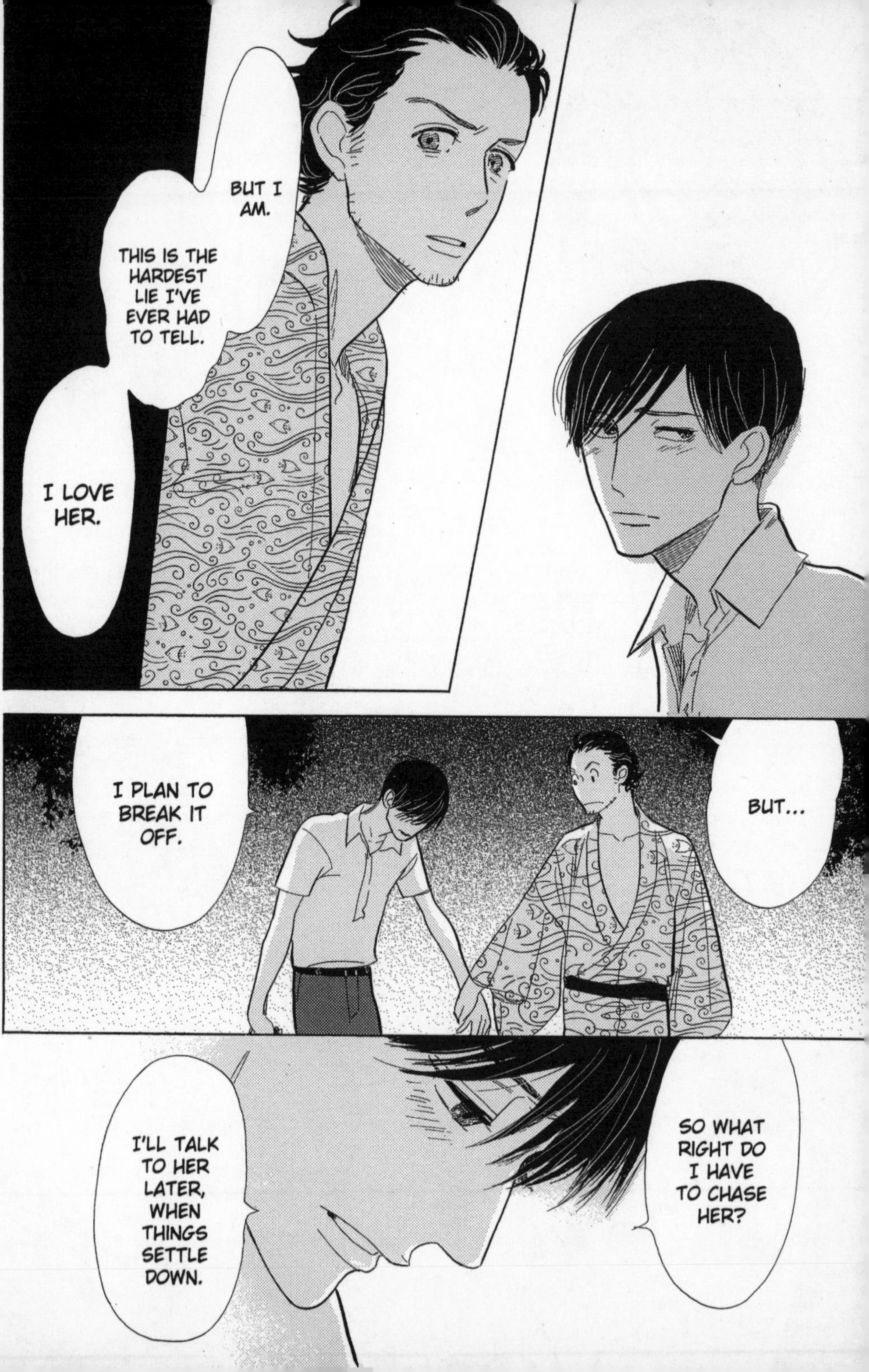
BUT I AM.
THIS IS THE HARDEST LIE I'VE EVER HAD TO TELL.
I LOVE HER.
BUT...
I PLAN TO BREAK IT OFF.
SO WHAT RIGHT DO I HAVE TO CHASE HER?
I'LL TALK TO HER LATER, WHEN THINGS SETTLE DOWN.

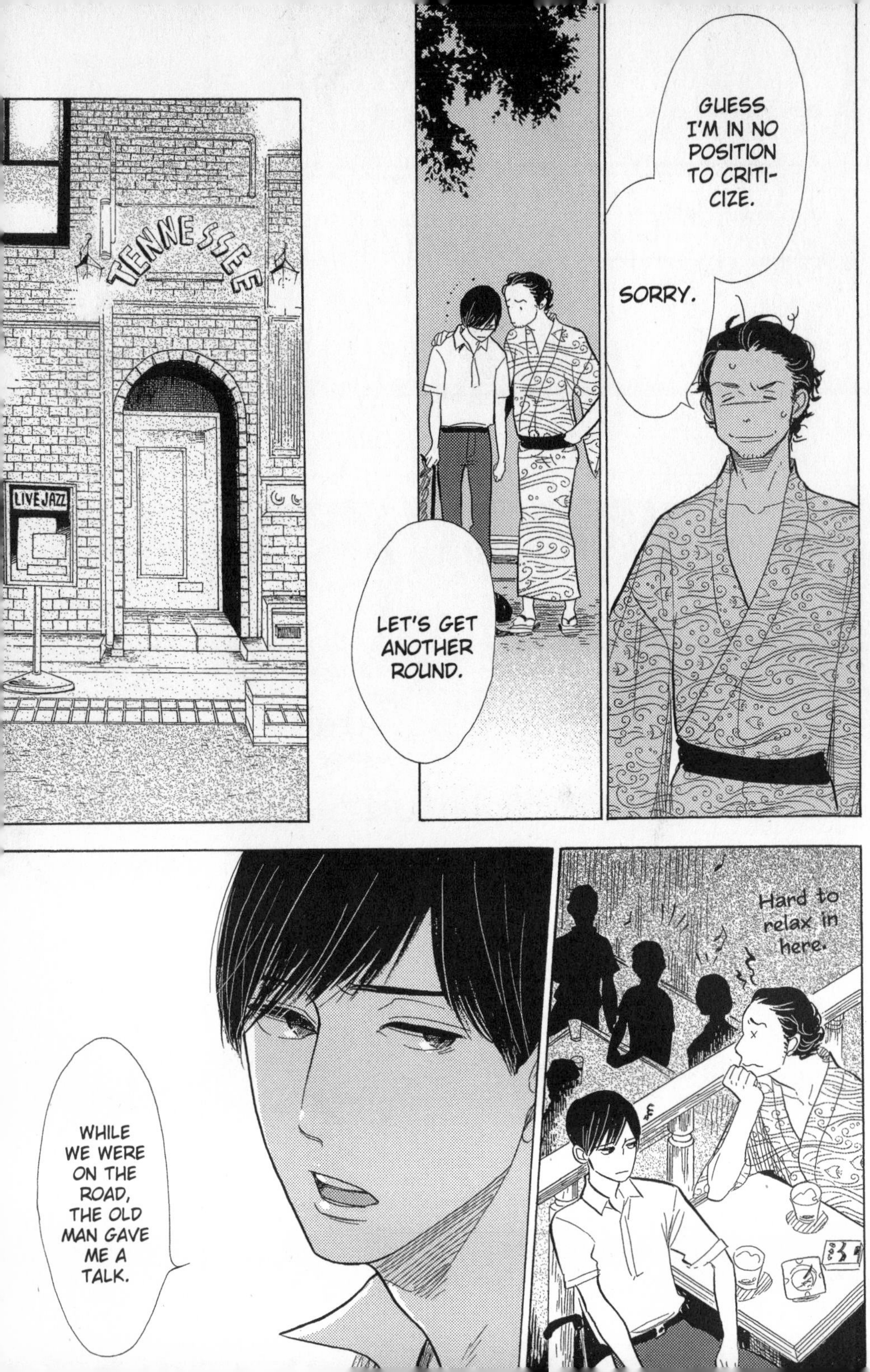
GUESS I'M IN NO POSITION TO CRITI-CIZE.
SORRY.
LET'S GET ANOTHER ROUND.
TENNESSEE
LIVE JAZZ
Hard to relax in here.
WHILE WE WERE ON THE ROAD, THE OLD MAN GAVE ME A TALK.

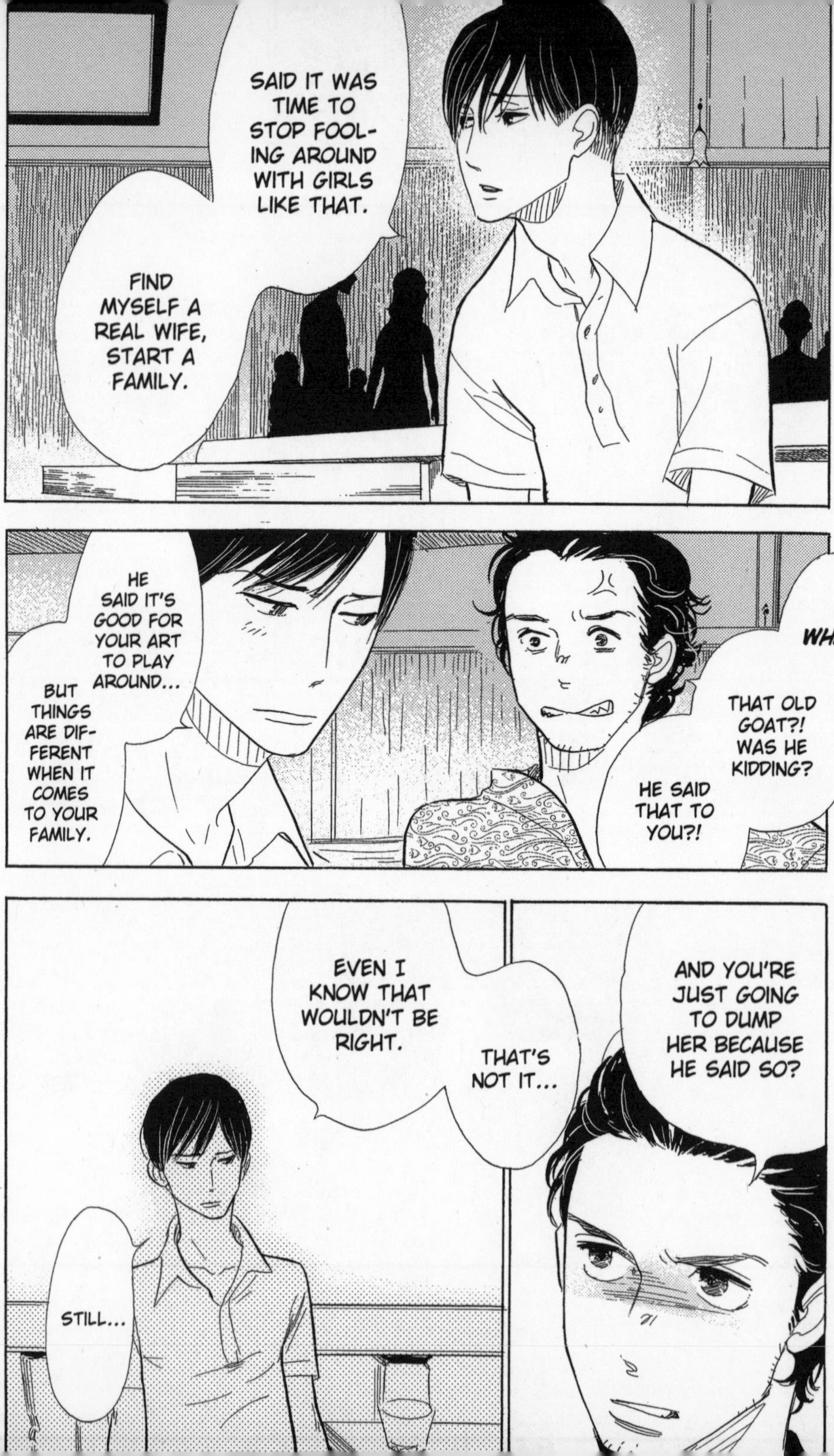
SAID IT WAS TIME TO STOP FOOLING AROUND WITH GIRLS LIKE THAT.
FIND MYSELF A REAL WIFE, START A FAMILY.
WHAT?!
THAT OLD GOAT?! WAS HE KIDDING?
HE SAID THAT TO YOU?!
HE SAID IT'S GOOD FOR YOUR ART TO PLAY AROUND...
BUT THINGS ARE DIFFERENT WHEN IT COMES TO YOUR FAMILY.
AND YOU'RE JUST GOING TO DUMP HER BECAUSE HE SAID SO?
EVEN I KNOW THAT WOULDN'T BE RIGHT.
THAT'S NOT IT...
STILL...

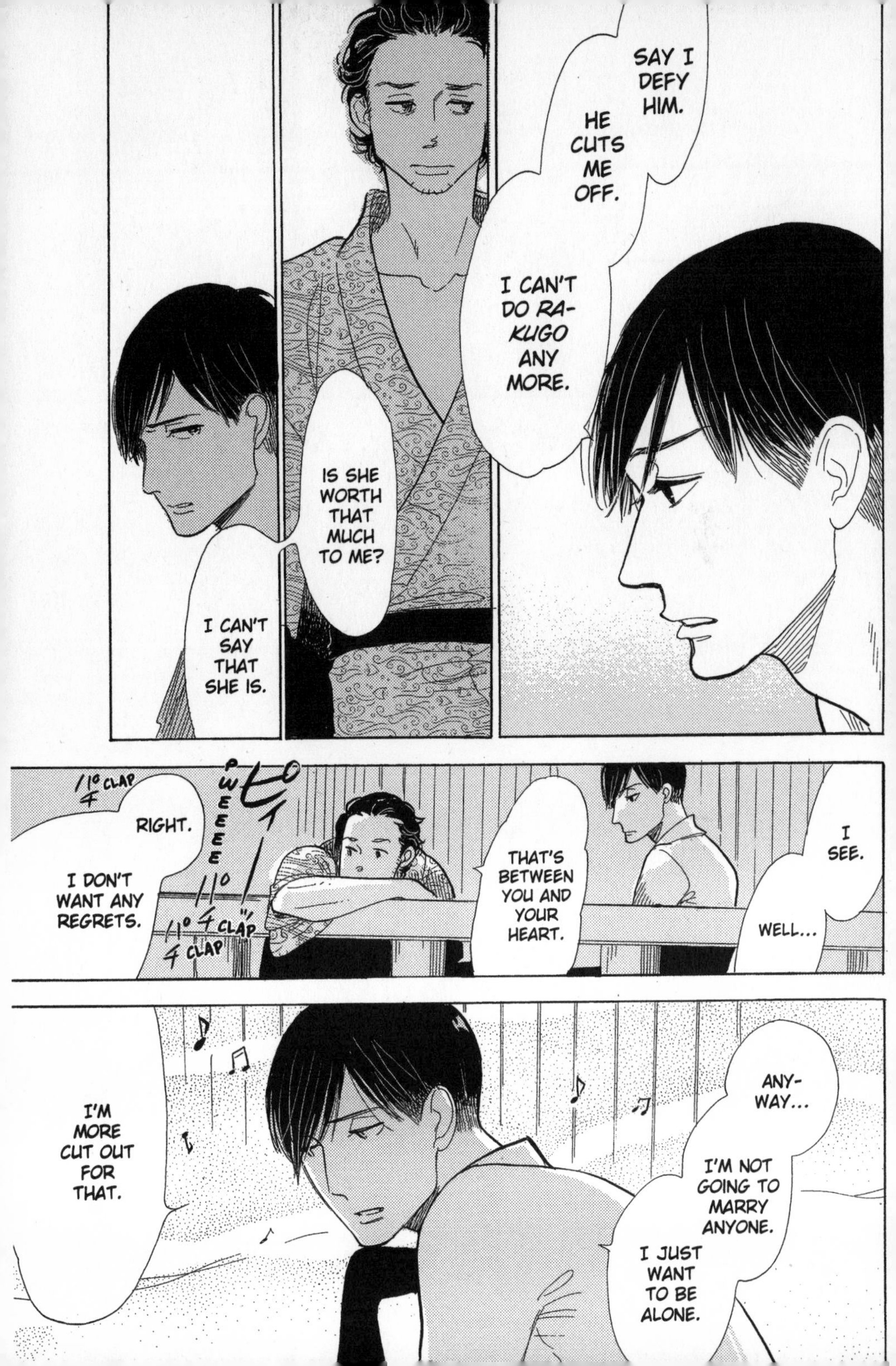
SAY I DEFY HIM.
HE CUTS ME OFF.
I CAN'T DO RA-KUGO ANY MORE.
IS SHE WORTH THAT MUCH TO ME?
I CAN'T SAY THAT SHE IS.
I SEE.
WELL...
THAT'S BETWEEN YOU AND YOUR HEART.
PWEEEEE
CLAP
CLAP
CLAP
RIGHT.
I DON'T WANT ANY REGRETS.
ANY-WAY...
I'M NOT GOING TO MARRY ANYONE.
I JUST WANT TO BE ALONE.
I'M MORE CUT OUT FOR THAT.

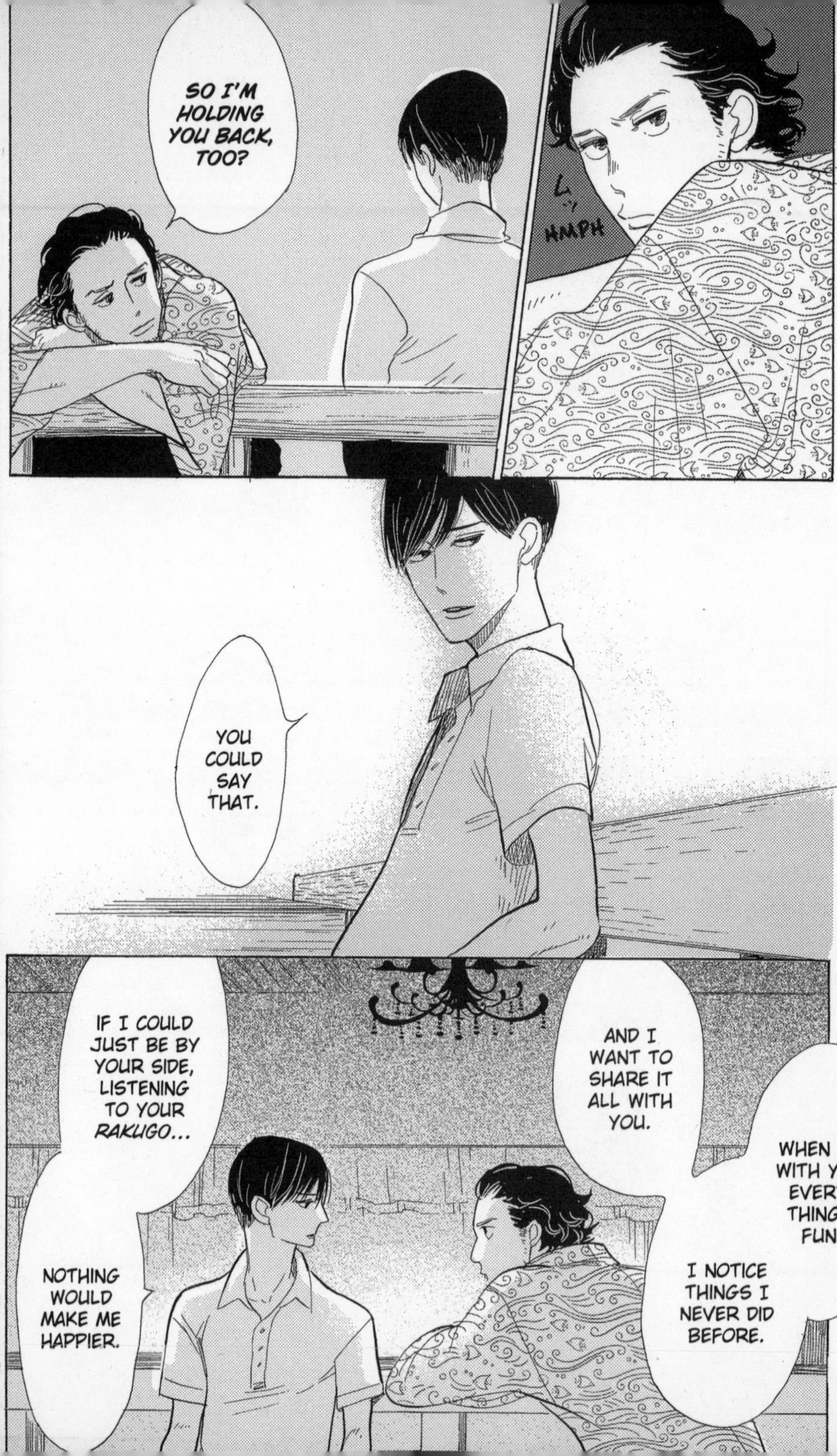

HMPH
SO I'M HOLDING YOU BACK, TOO?
YOU COULD SAY THAT.
WHEN I'M WITH YOU, EVERY-THING'S FUN.
I NOTICE THINGS I NEVER DID BEFORE.
AND I WANT TO SHARE IT ALL WITH YOU.
IF I COULD JUST BE BY YOUR SIDE, LISTENING TO YOUR *RAKUGO*...
NOTHING WOULD MAKE ME HAPPIER.

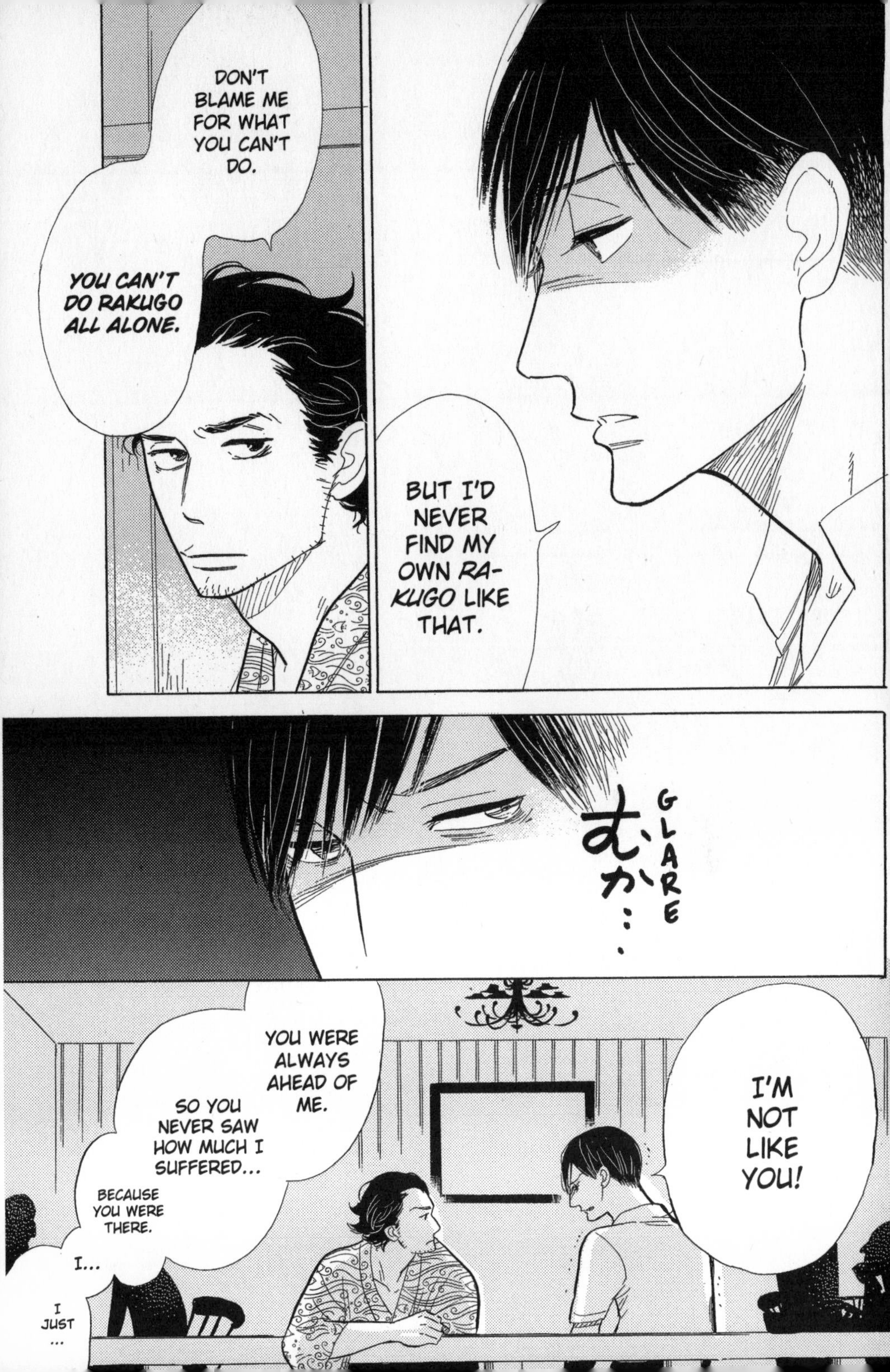
BUT I'D NEVER FIND MY OWN *RAKUGO* LIKE THAT.
DON'T BLAME ME FOR WHAT YOU CAN'T DO.
YOU CAN'T DO RAKUGO ALL ALONE.
GLARE
むか…
I'M NOT LIKE YOU!
YOU WERE ALWAYS AHEAD OF ME.
SO YOU NEVER SAW HOW MUCH I SUFFERED...
BECAUSE YOU WERE THERE.
I...
I JUST ...

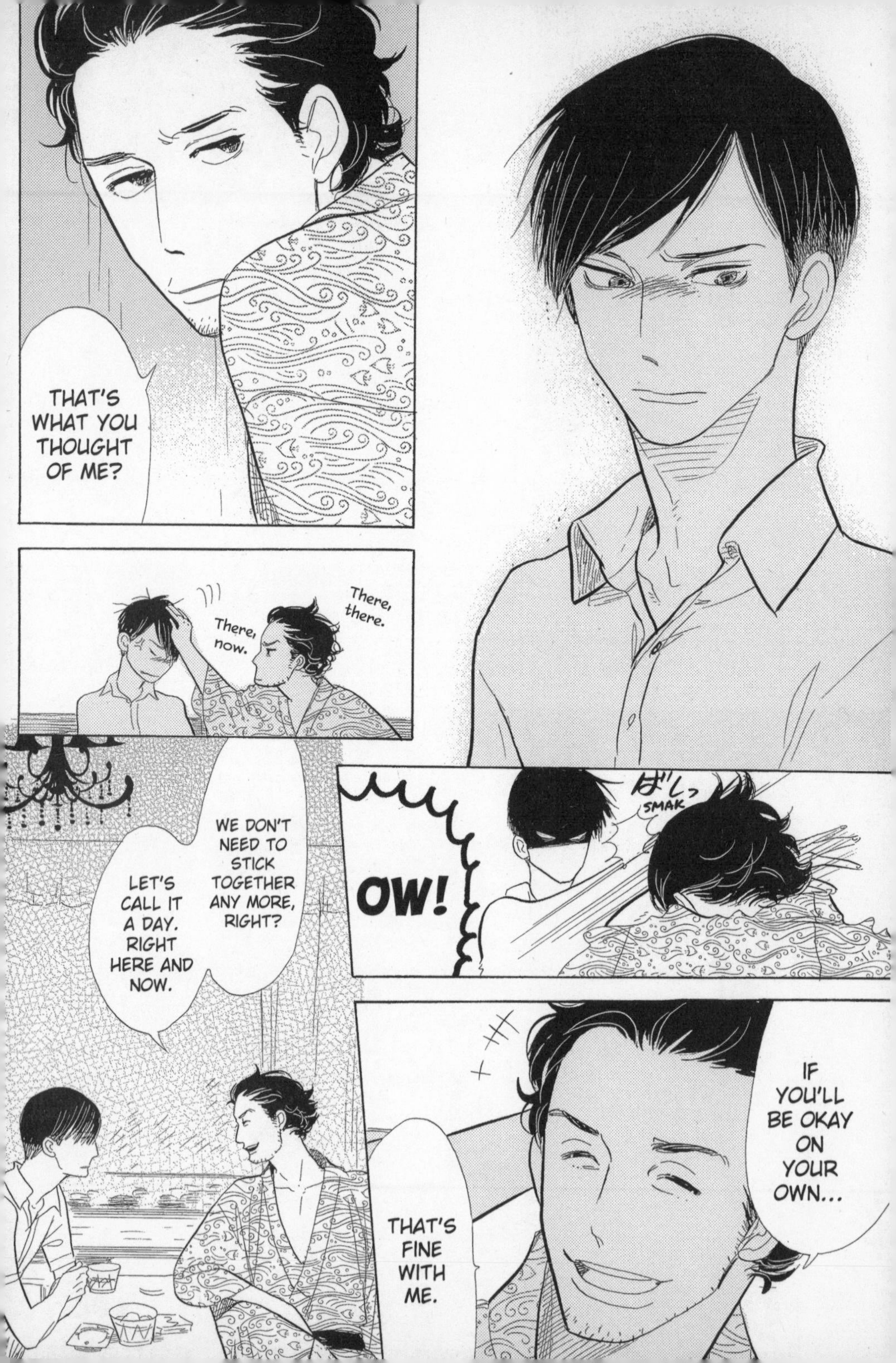
THAT'S WHAT YOU THOUGHT OF ME?
There, there.
There, now.
ばしっ
SMAK
OW!
IF YOU'LL BE OKAY ON YOUR OWN...
THAT'S FINE WITH ME.
WE DON'T NEED TO STICK TOGETHER ANY MORE, RIGHT?
LET'S CALL IT A DAY. RIGHT HERE AND NOW.

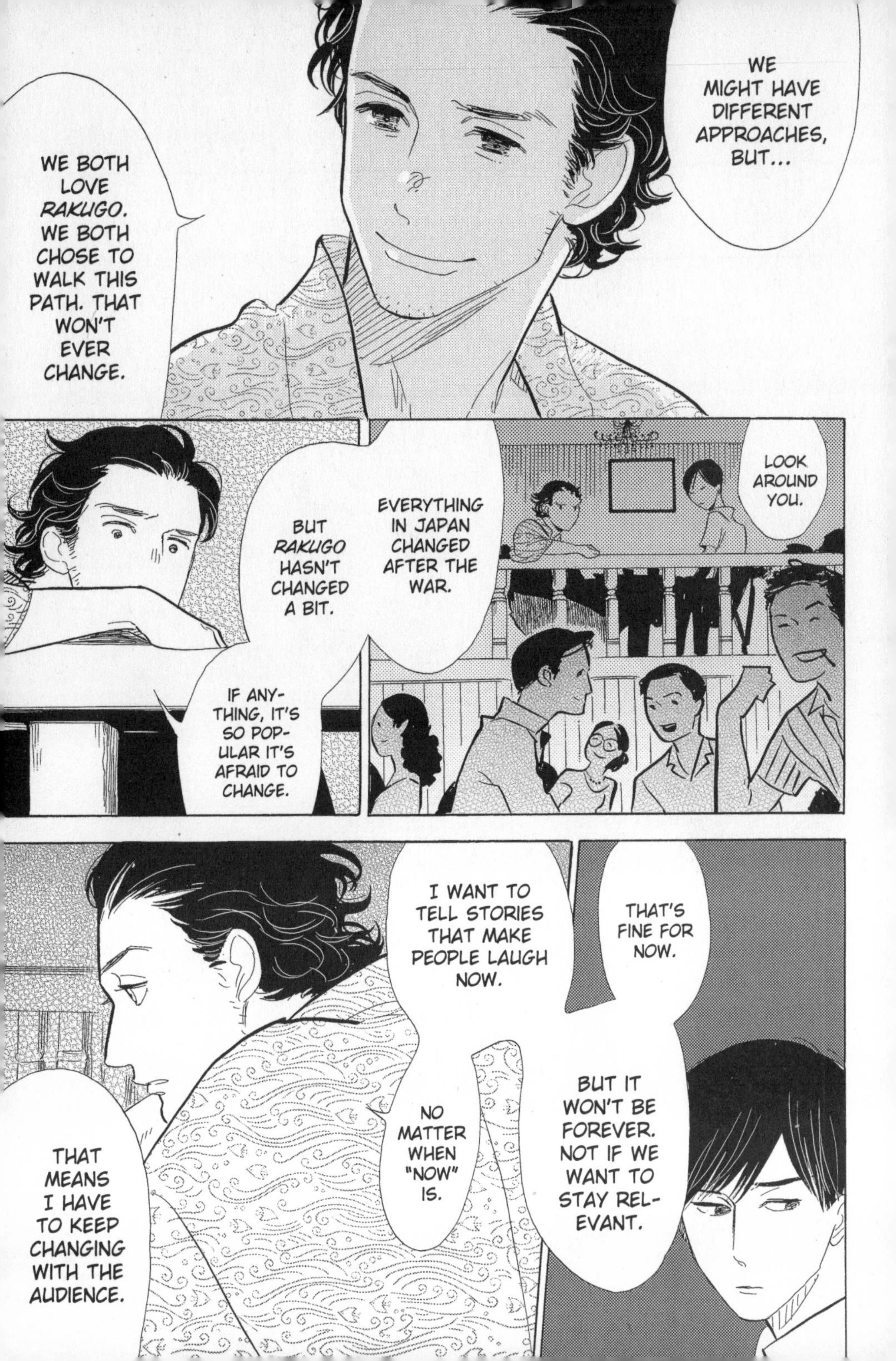
WE MIGHT HAVE DIFFERENT APPROACHES, BUT...
WE BOTH LOVE RAKUGO. WE BOTH CHOSE TO WALK THIS PATH. THAT WON'T EVER CHANGE.
LOOK AROUND YOU.
EVERYTHING IN JAPAN CHANGED AFTER THE WAR.
BUT RAKUGO HASN'T CHANGED A BIT.
IF ANY-THING, IT'S SO POP-ULAR IT'S AFRAID TO CHANGE.
THAT'S FINE FOR NOW.
BUT IT WON'T BE FOREVER. NOT IF WE WANT TO STAY REL-EVANT.
I WANT TO TELL STORIES THAT MAKE PEOPLE LAUGH NOW.
NO MATTER WHEN "NOW" IS.
THAT MEANS I HAVE TO KEEP CHANGING WITH THE AUDIENCE.

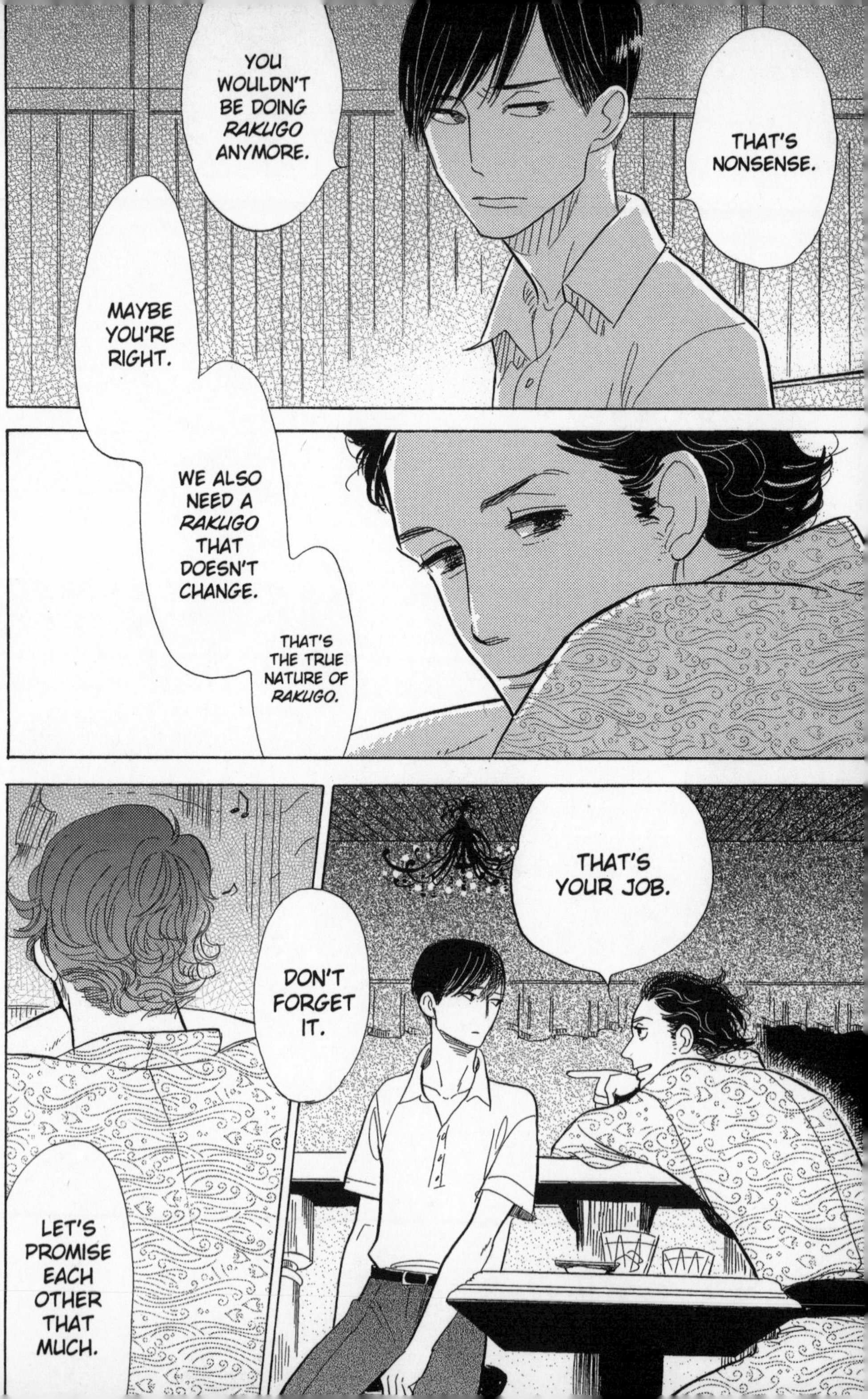
THAT'S NONSENSE.
YOU WOULDN'T BE DOING *RAKUGO* ANYMORE.
MAYBE YOU'RE RIGHT.
WE ALSO NEED A *RAKUGO* THAT DOESN'T CHANGE.
THAT'S THE TRUE NATURE OF *RAKUGO*.
THAT'S YOUR JOB.
DON'T FORGET IT.
LET'S PROMISE EACH OTHER THAT MUCH.

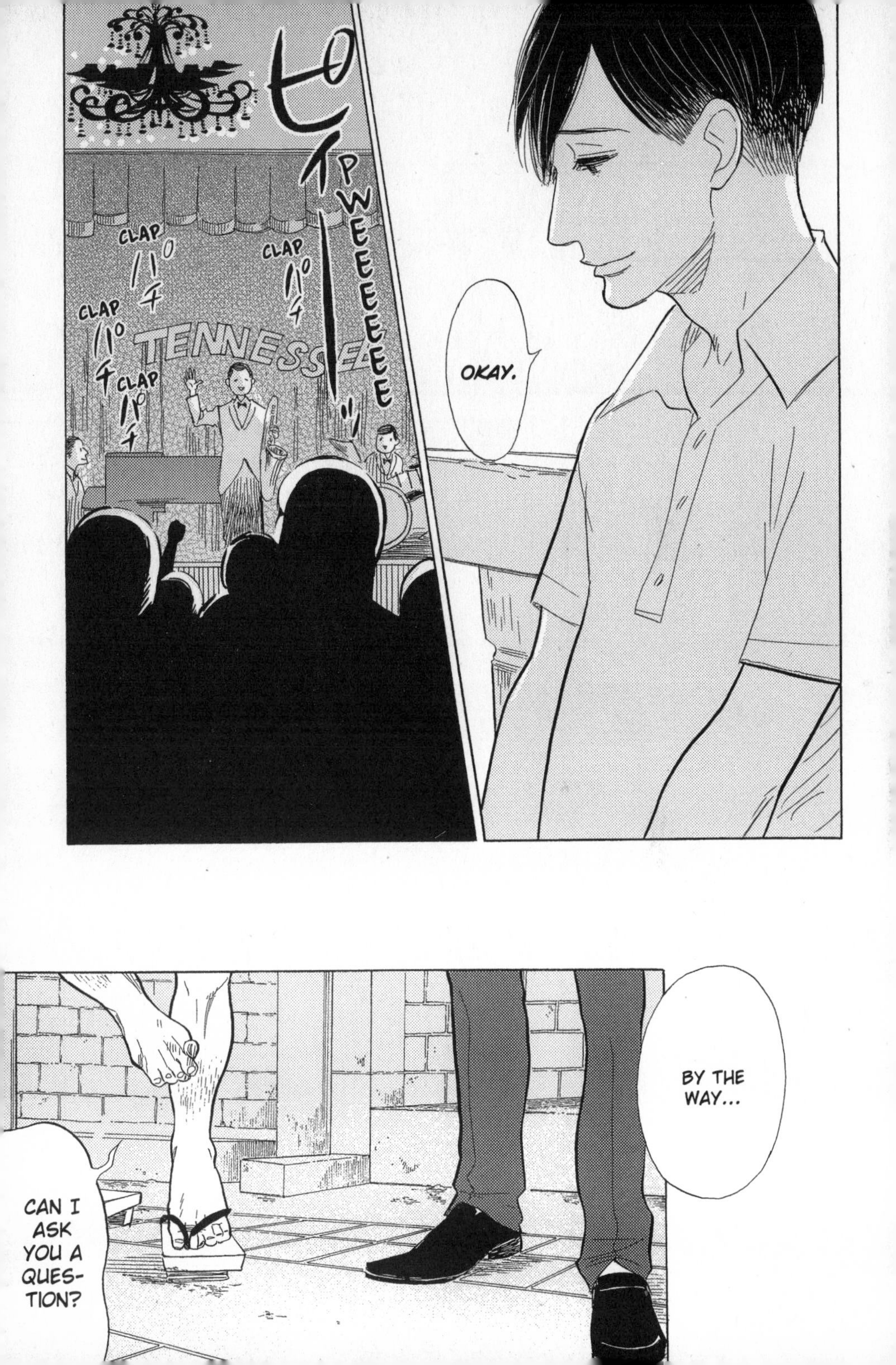
OKAY.
ピイーッ
PWEEEEEEEEE
CLAP
パチ
CLAP
パチ
CLAP
パチ
CLAP
パチ
BY THE WAY...
CAN I ASK YOU A QUES-TION?

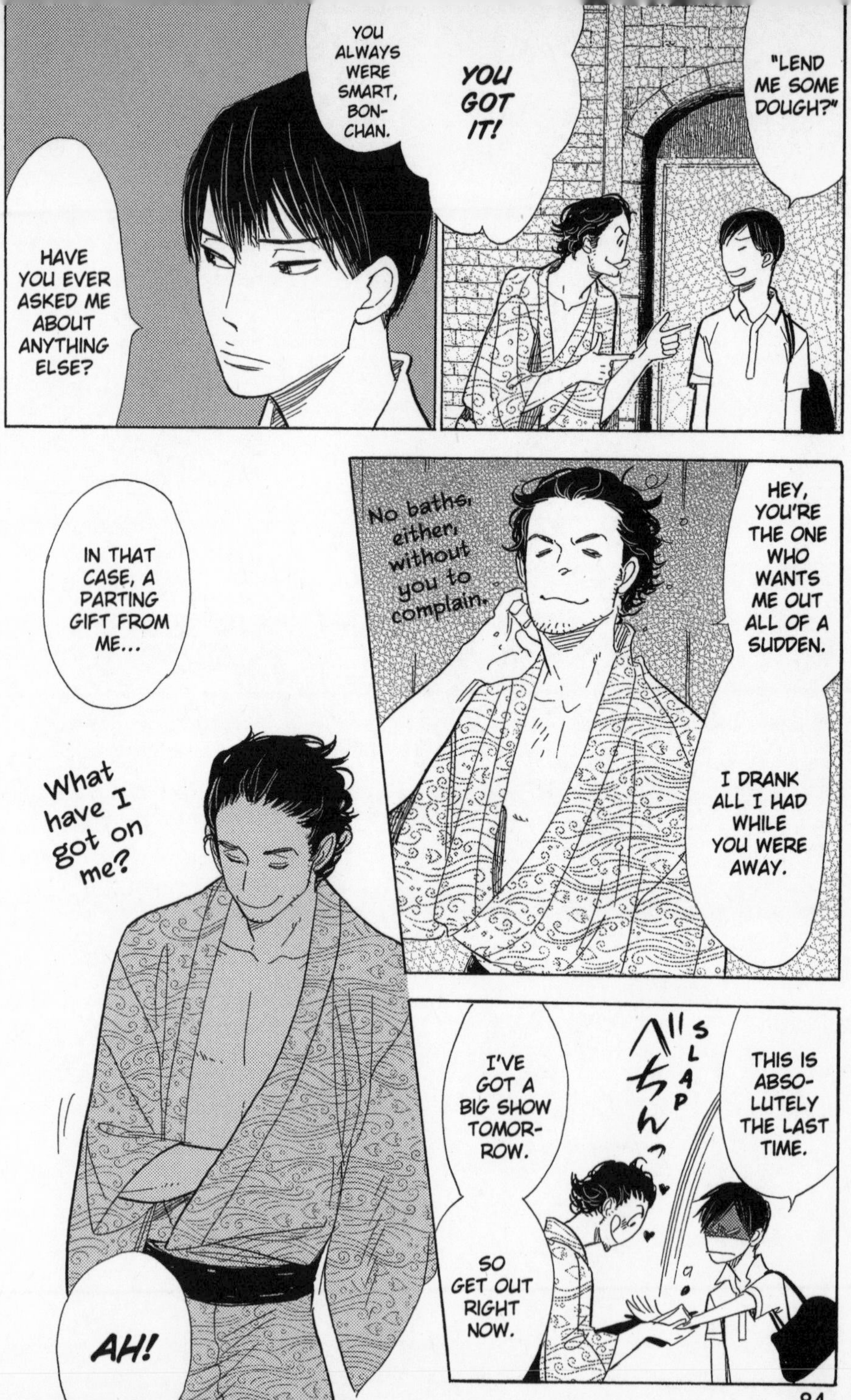
"LEND ME SOME DOUGH?"
YOU GOT IT!
YOU ALWAYS WERE SMART, BON-CHAN.
HAVE YOU EVER ASKED ME ABOUT ANYTHING ELSE?
HEY, YOU'RE THE ONE WHO WANTS ME OUT ALL OF A SUDDEN.
No baths, either, without you to complain.
I DRANK ALL I HAD WHILE YOU WERE AWAY.
THIS IS ABSOLUTELY THE LAST TIME.
SLAP
I'VE GOT A BIG SHOW TOMORROW.
SO GET OUT RIGHT NOW.
IN THAT CASE, A PARTING GIFT FROM ME...
What have I got on me?
AH!

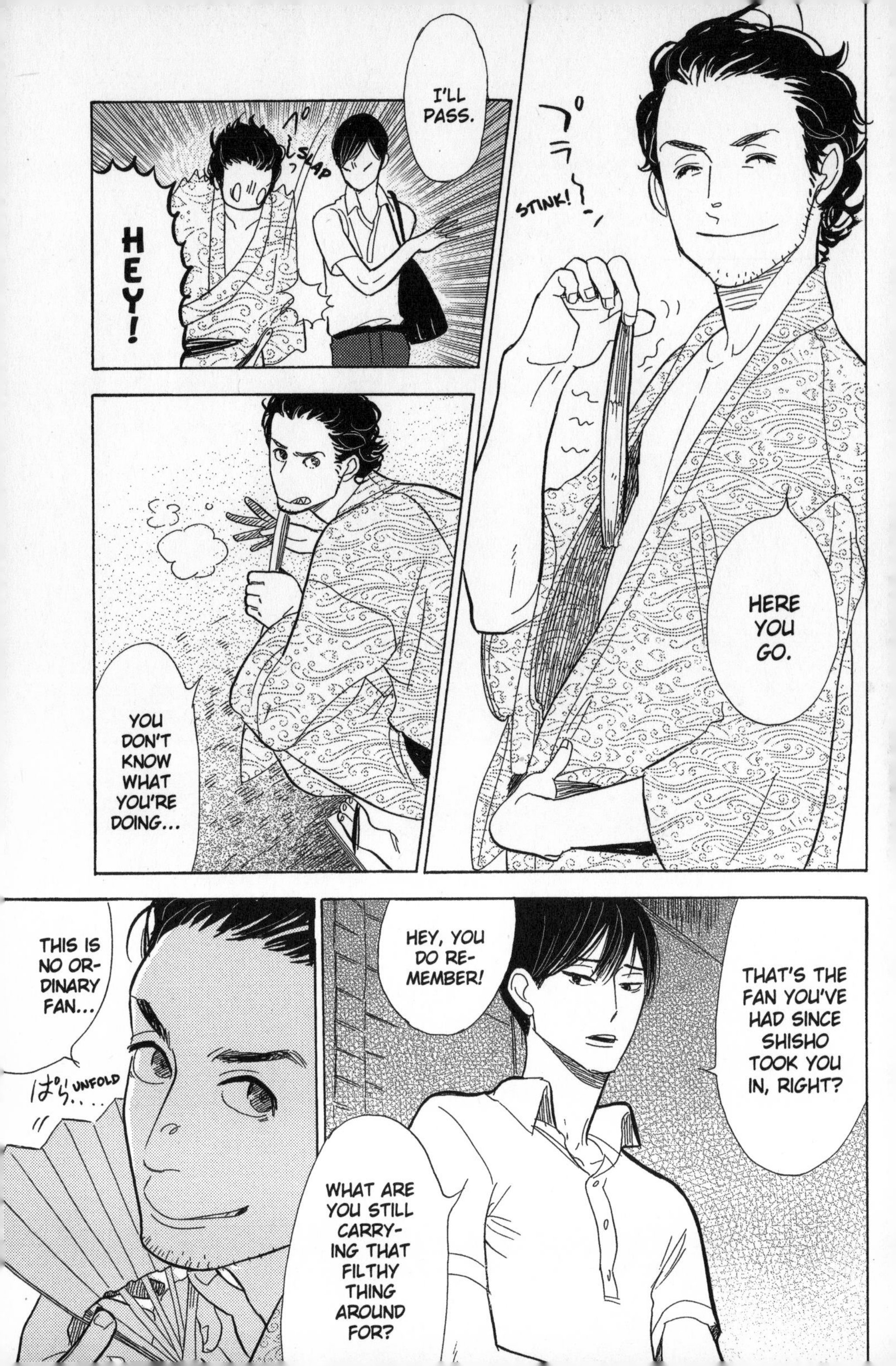
STINK!
HERE YOU GO.
I'LL PASS.
SLAP
HEY!
YOU DON'T KNOW WHAT YOU'RE DOING...
THAT'S THE FAN YOU'VE HAD SINCE SHISHO TOOK YOU IN, RIGHT?
HEY, YOU DO RE-MEMBER!
WHAT ARE YOU STILL CARRY-ING THAT FILTHY THING AROUND FOR?
THIS IS NO OR-DINARY FAN...
ぱら UNFOLD

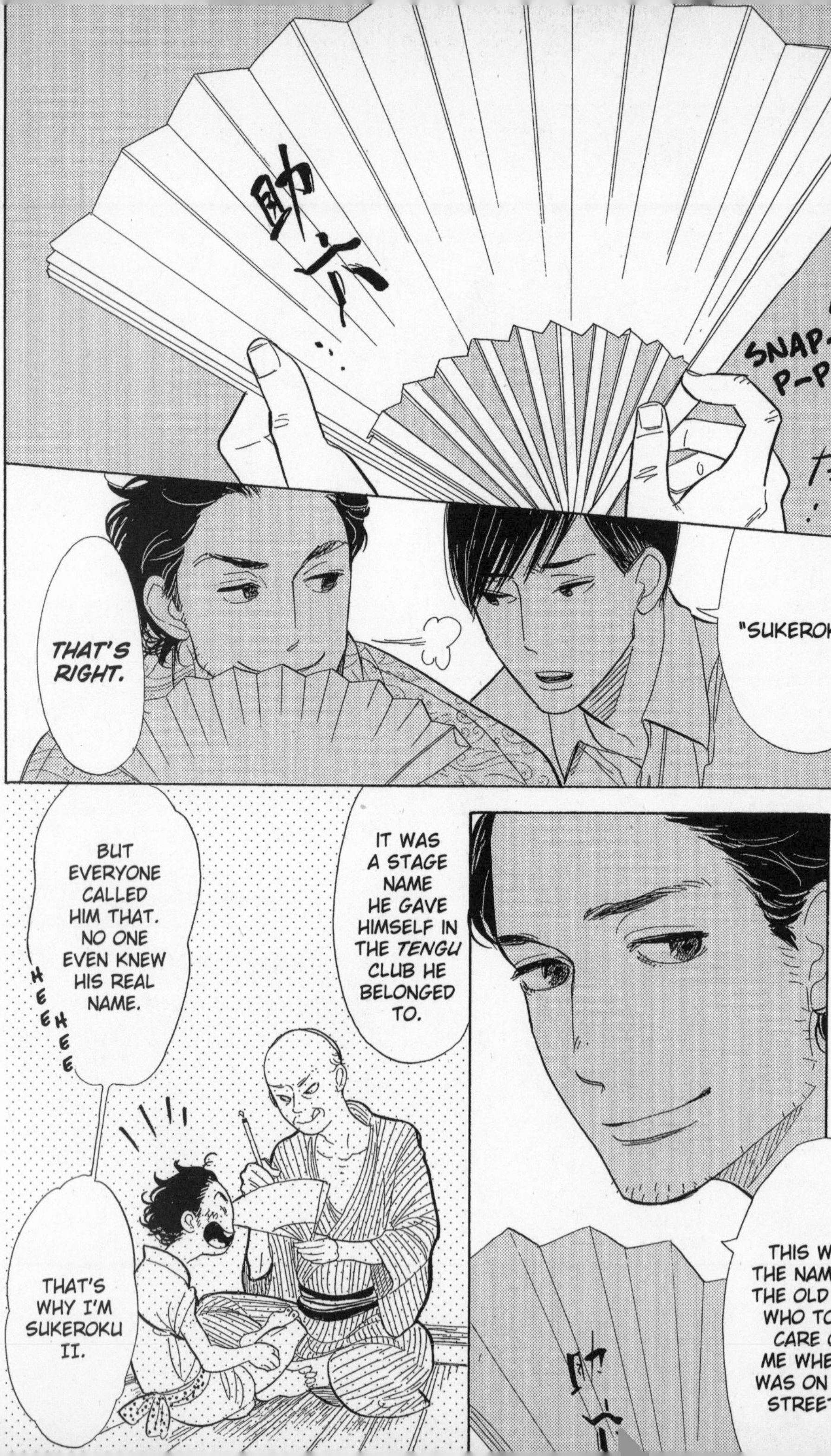
助六
ぱ
SNAP-P-P
たた
"SUKEROKU"?
THAT'S RIGHT.
THIS WAS THE NAME OF THE OLD MAN WHO TOOK CARE OF ME WHEN I WAS ON THE STREETS.
IT WAS A STAGE NAME HE GAVE HIMSELF IN THE *TENGU* CLUB HE BELONGED TO.
BUT EVERYONE CALLED HIM THAT. NO ONE EVEN KNEW HIS REAL NAME.
HEE HEE HEE
THAT'S WHY I'M SUKEROKU II.

Note: A *tengu* club was a group of amateurs who performed *rakugo* for each other.

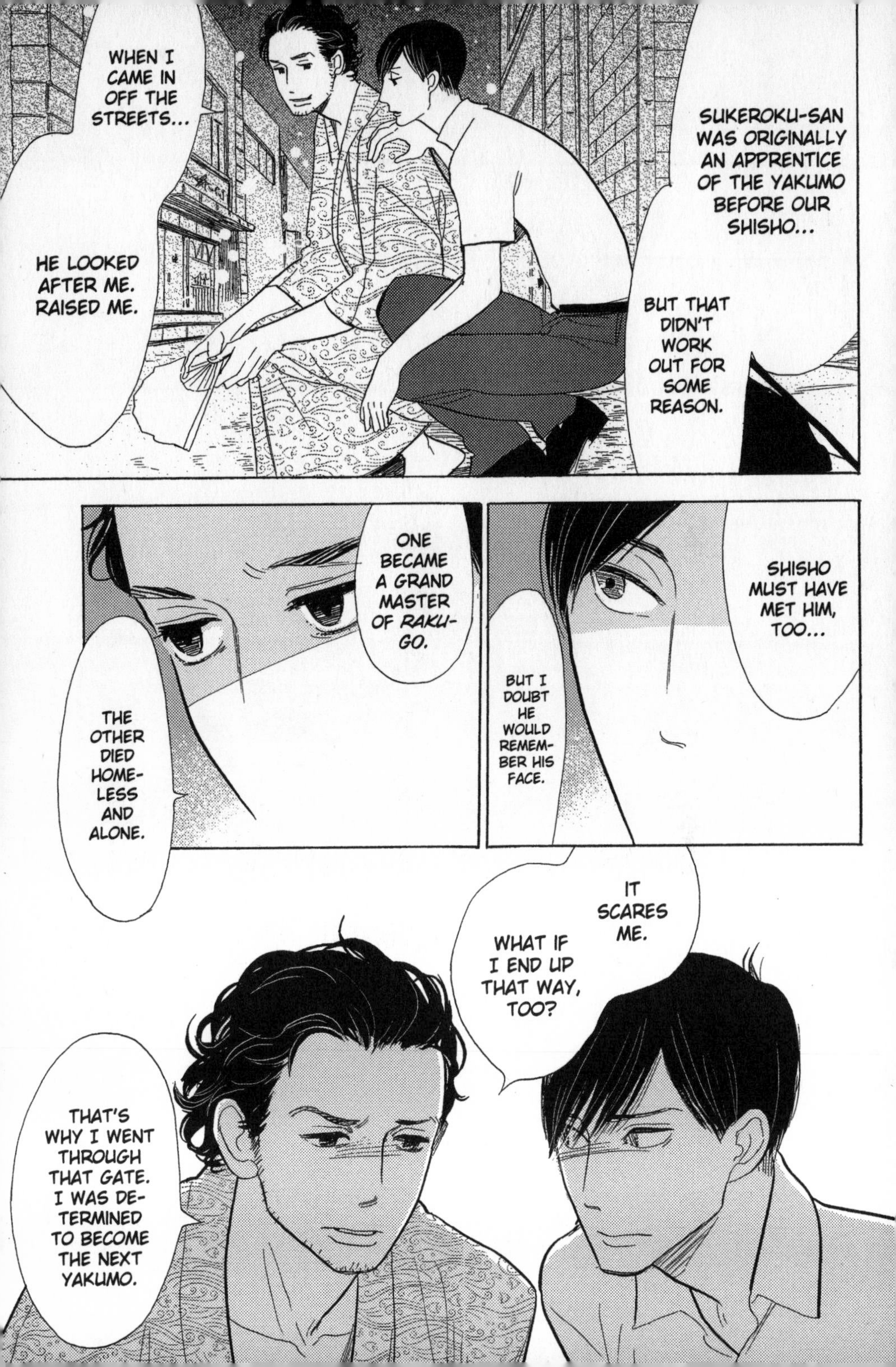
SUKEROKU-SAN WAS ORIGINALLY AN APPRENTICE OF THE YAKUMO BEFORE OUR SHISHO...
BUT THAT DIDN'T WORK OUT FOR SOME REASON.
WHEN I CAME IN OFF THE STREETS...
HE LOOKED AFTER ME. RAISED ME.
SHISHO MUST HAVE MET HIM, TOO...
BUT I DOUBT HE WOULD REMEMBER HIS FACE.
ONE BECAME A GRAND MASTER OF *RAKUGO*.
THE OTHER DIED HOMELESS AND ALONE.
IT SCARES ME.
WHAT IF I END UP THAT WAY, TOO?
THAT'S WHY I WENT THROUGH THAT GATE. I WAS DETERMINED TO BECOME THE NEXT YAKUMO.

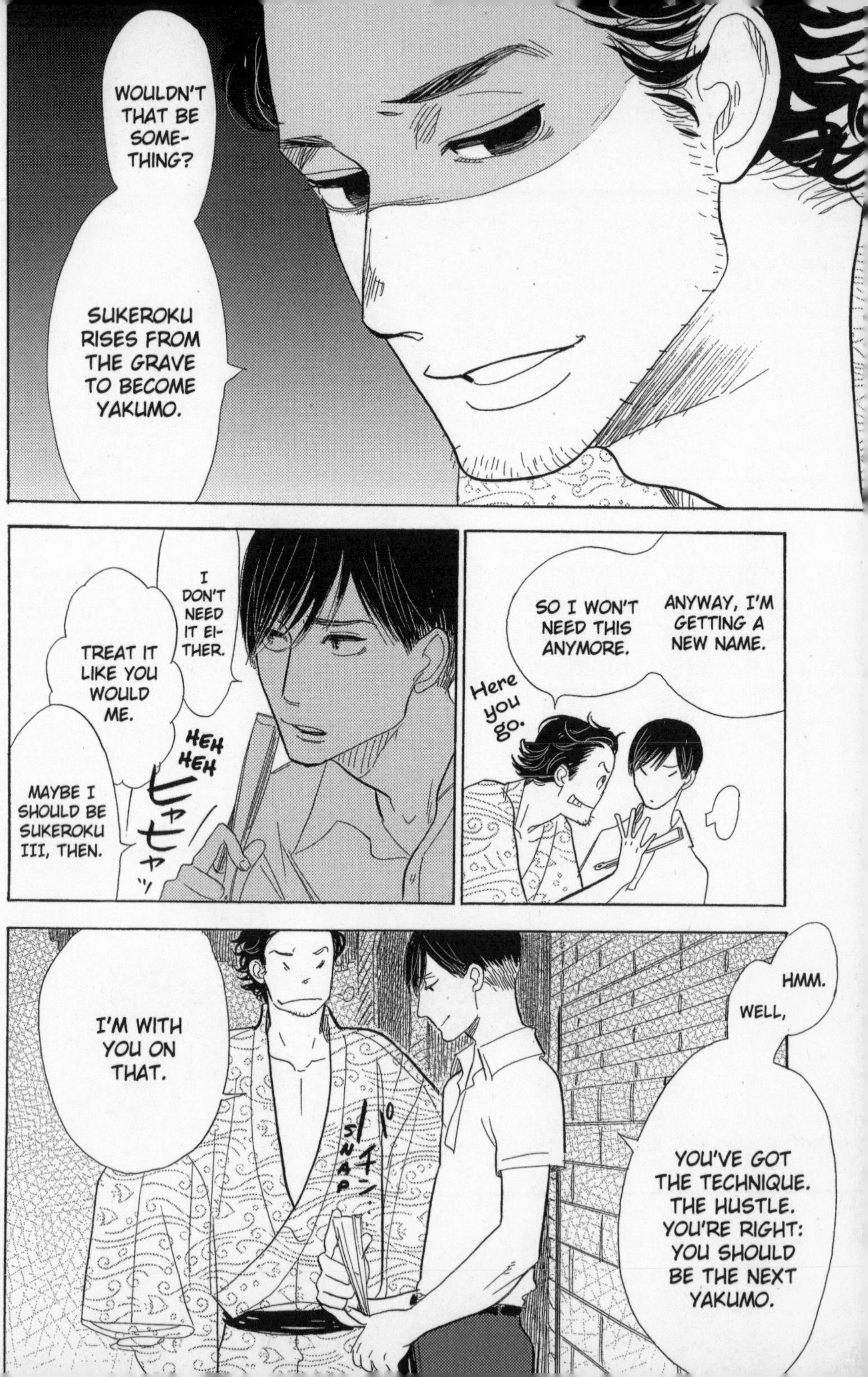
WOULDN'T THAT BE SOME-THING?
SUKEROKU RISES FROM THE GRAVE TO BECOME YAKUMO.
ANYWAY, I'M GETTING A NEW NAME.
SO I WON'T NEED THIS ANYMORE.
Here you go.
I DON'T NEED IT EI-THER.
TREAT IT LIKE YOU WOULD ME.
HEH HEH
MAYBE I SHOULD BE SUKEROKU III, THEN.
HMM.
WELL,
YOU'VE GOT THE TECHNIQUE. THE HUSTLE. YOU'RE RIGHT: YOU SHOULD BE THE NEXT YAKUMO.
I'M WITH YOU ON THAT.
SNAP

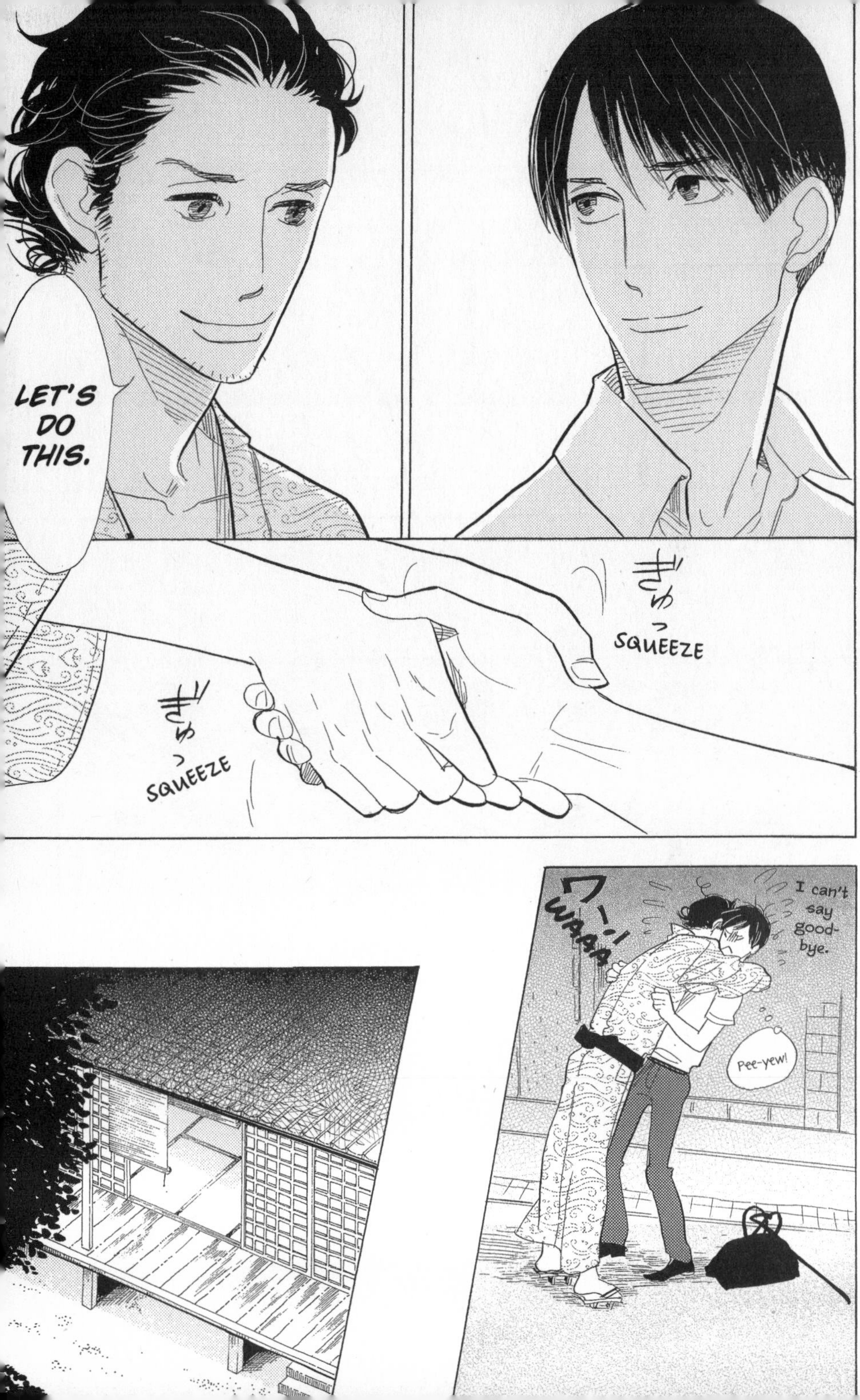
LET'S DO THIS.
ぎゅっ
SQUEEZE
ぎゅっ
SQUEEZE
WAAA
I can't say good-bye.
Pee-yew!

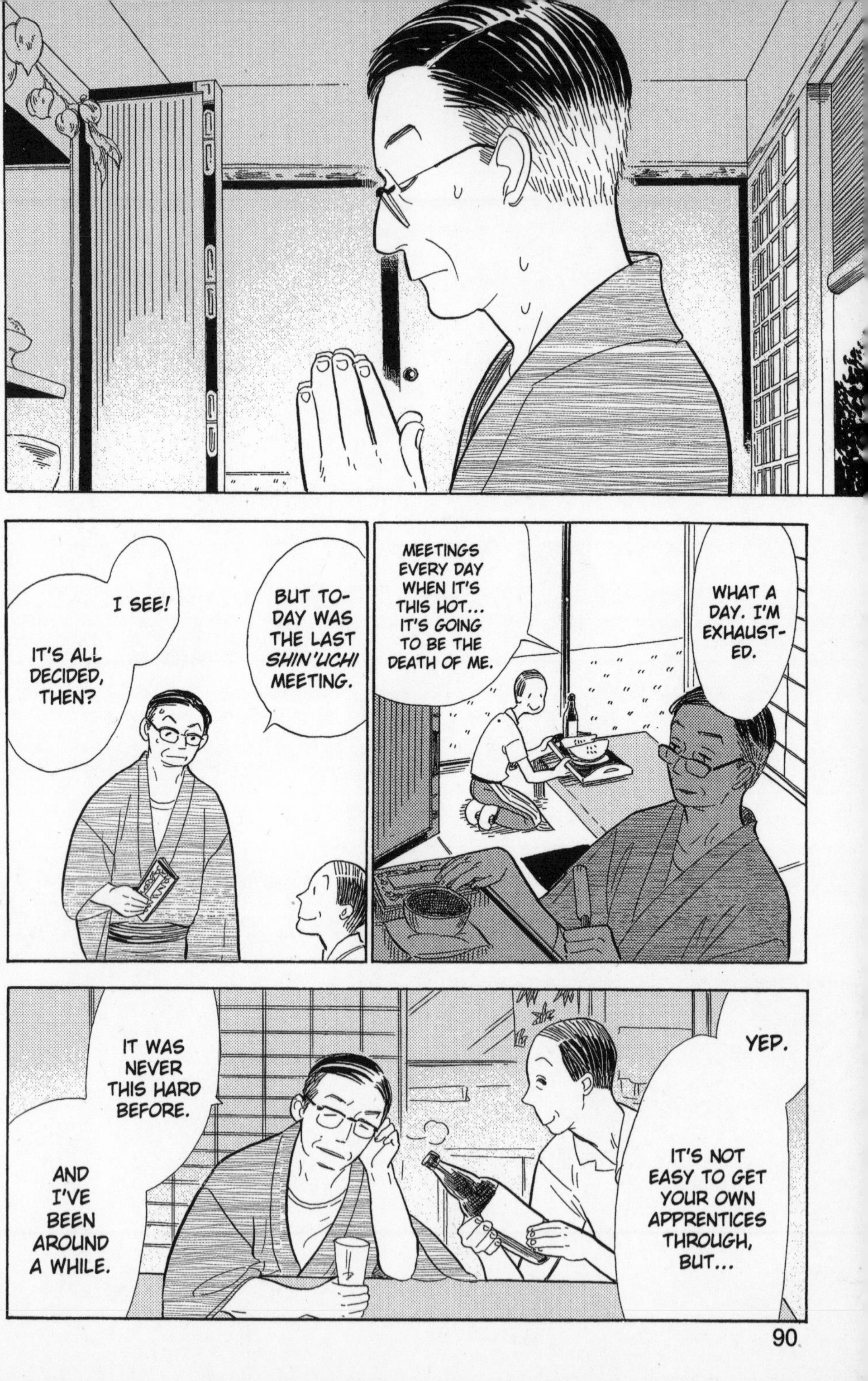
WHAT A DAY. I'M EXHAUSTED.
MEETINGS EVERY DAY WHEN IT'S THIS HOT... IT'S GOING TO BE THE DEATH OF ME.
BUT TODAY WAS THE LAST *SHIN'UCHI* MEETING.
I SEE!
IT'S ALL DECIDED, THEN?
YEP.
IT'S NOT EASY TO GET YOUR OWN APPRENTICES THROUGH, BUT...
IT WAS NEVER THIS HARD BEFORE.
AND I'VE BEEN AROUND A WHILE.

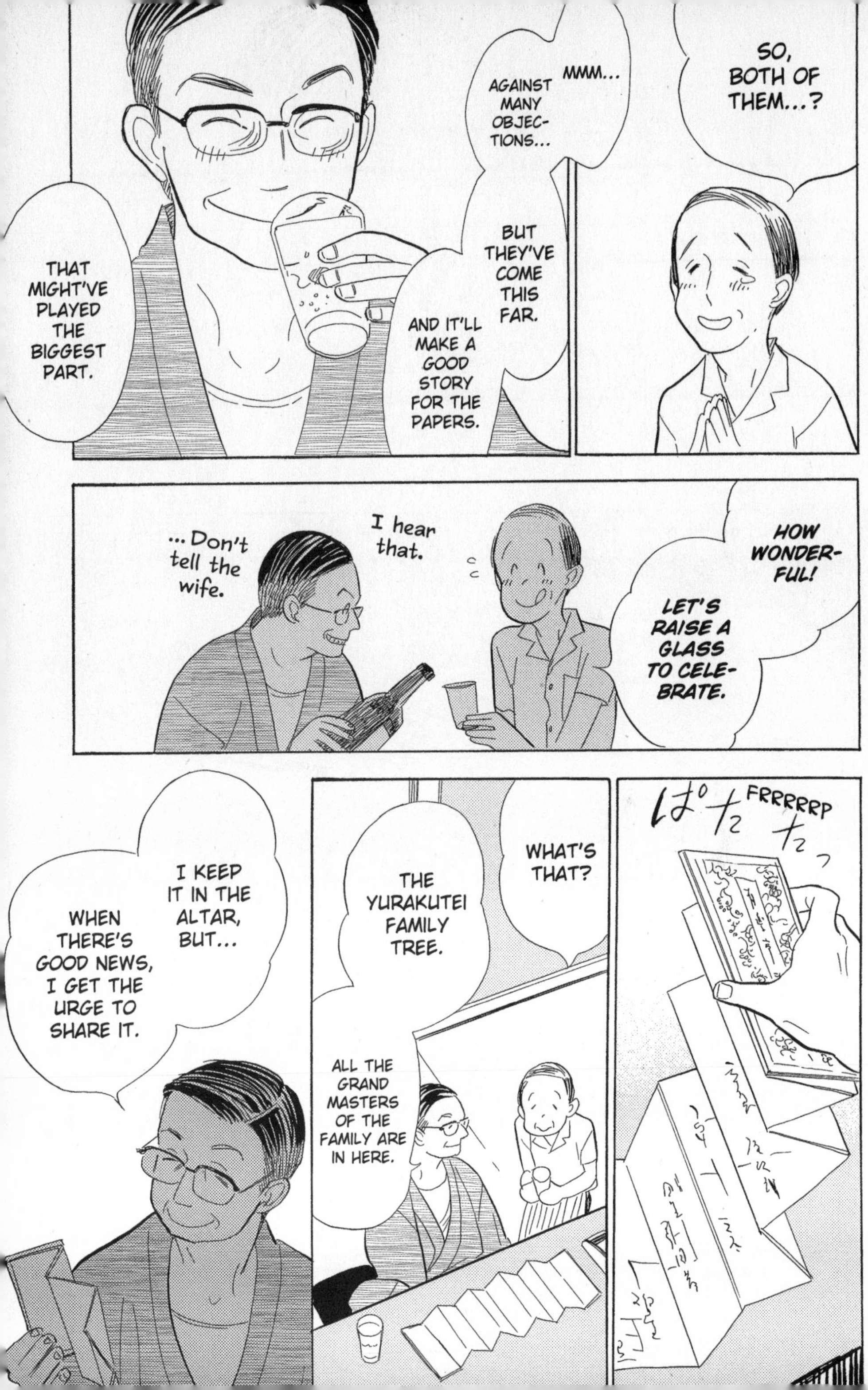
SO, BOTH OF THEM...?
MMM...
AGAINST MANY OBJECTIONS...
BUT THEY'VE COME THIS FAR.
AND IT'LL MAKE A GOOD STORY FOR THE PAPERS.
THAT MIGHT'VE PLAYED THE BIGGEST PART.
HOW WONDERFUL!
LET'S RAISE A GLASS TO CELEBRATE.
I hear that.
...Don't tell the wife.
ぱた
FRRRRRP
たた
WHAT'S THAT?
THE YURAKUTEI FAMILY TREE.
ALL THE GRAND MASTERS OF THE FAMILY ARE IN HERE.
I KEEP IT IN THE ALTAR, BUT...
WHEN THERE'S GOOD NEWS, I GET THE URGE TO SHARE IT.

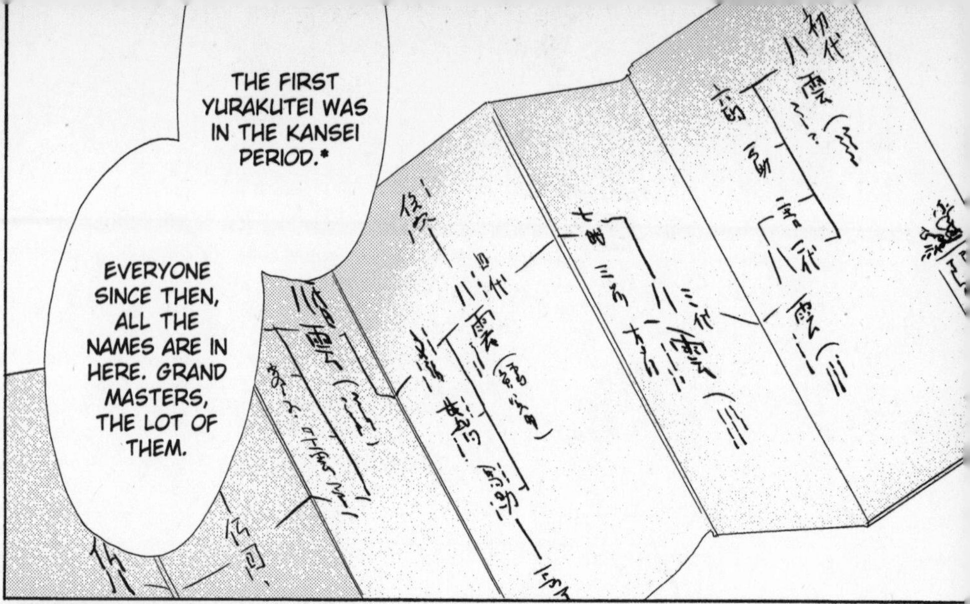
THE FIRST YURAKUTEI WAS IN THE KANSEI PERIOD.*
EVERYONE SINCE THEN, ALL THE NAMES ARE IN HERE. GRAND MASTERS, THE LOT OF THEM.

*1789–1801 CE

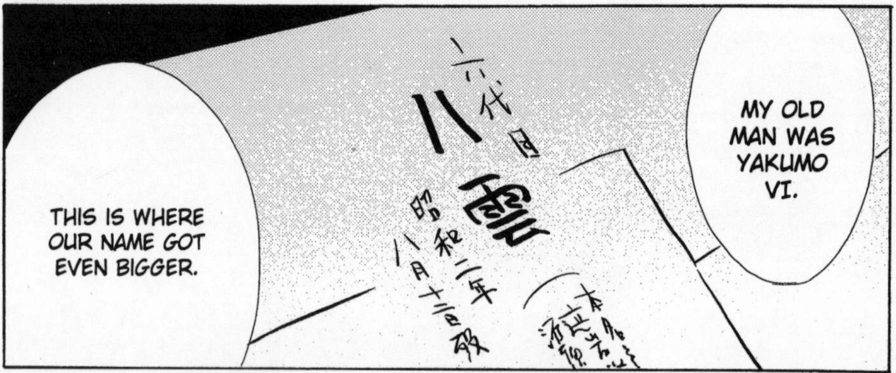
MY OLD MAN WAS YAKUMO VI.
六代目
八雲
昭和二年
THIS IS WHERE OUR NAME GOT EVEN BIGGER.

*D. August 12, 1927.

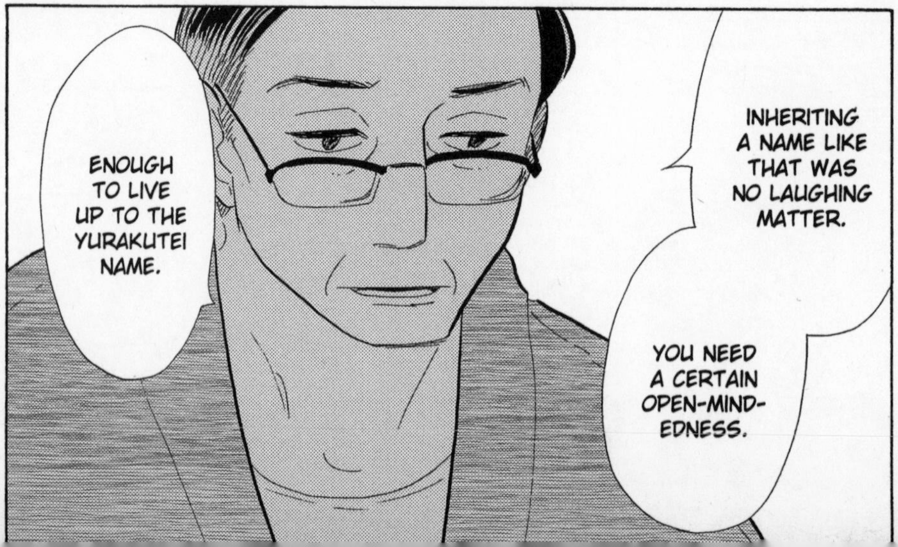
INHERITING A NAME LIKE THAT WAS NO LAUGHING MATTER.
YOU NEED A CERTAIN OPEN-MIND-EDNESS.
ENOUGH TO LIVE UP TO THE YURAKUTEI NAME.

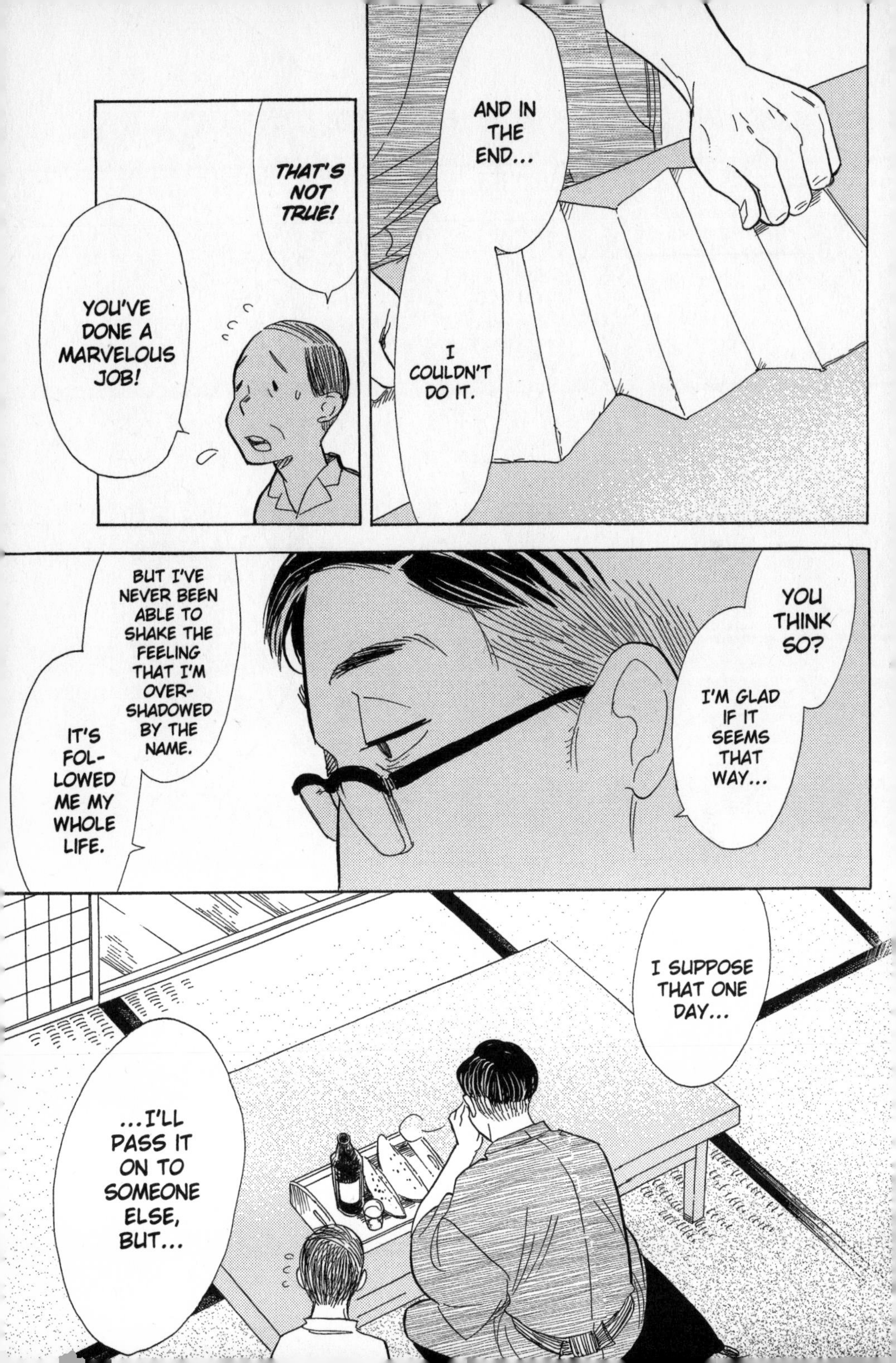
AND IN THE END...
I COULDN'T DO IT.
THAT'S NOT TRUE!
YOU'VE DONE A MARVELOUS JOB!
YOU THINK SO?
I'M GLAD IF IT SEEMS THAT WAY...
BUT I'VE NEVER BEEN ABLE TO SHAKE THE FEELING THAT I'M OVER-SHADOWED BY THE NAME.
IT'S FOL-LOWED ME MY WHOLE LIFE.
I SUPPOSE THAT ONE DAY...
...I'LL PASS IT ON TO SOMEONE ELSE, BUT...

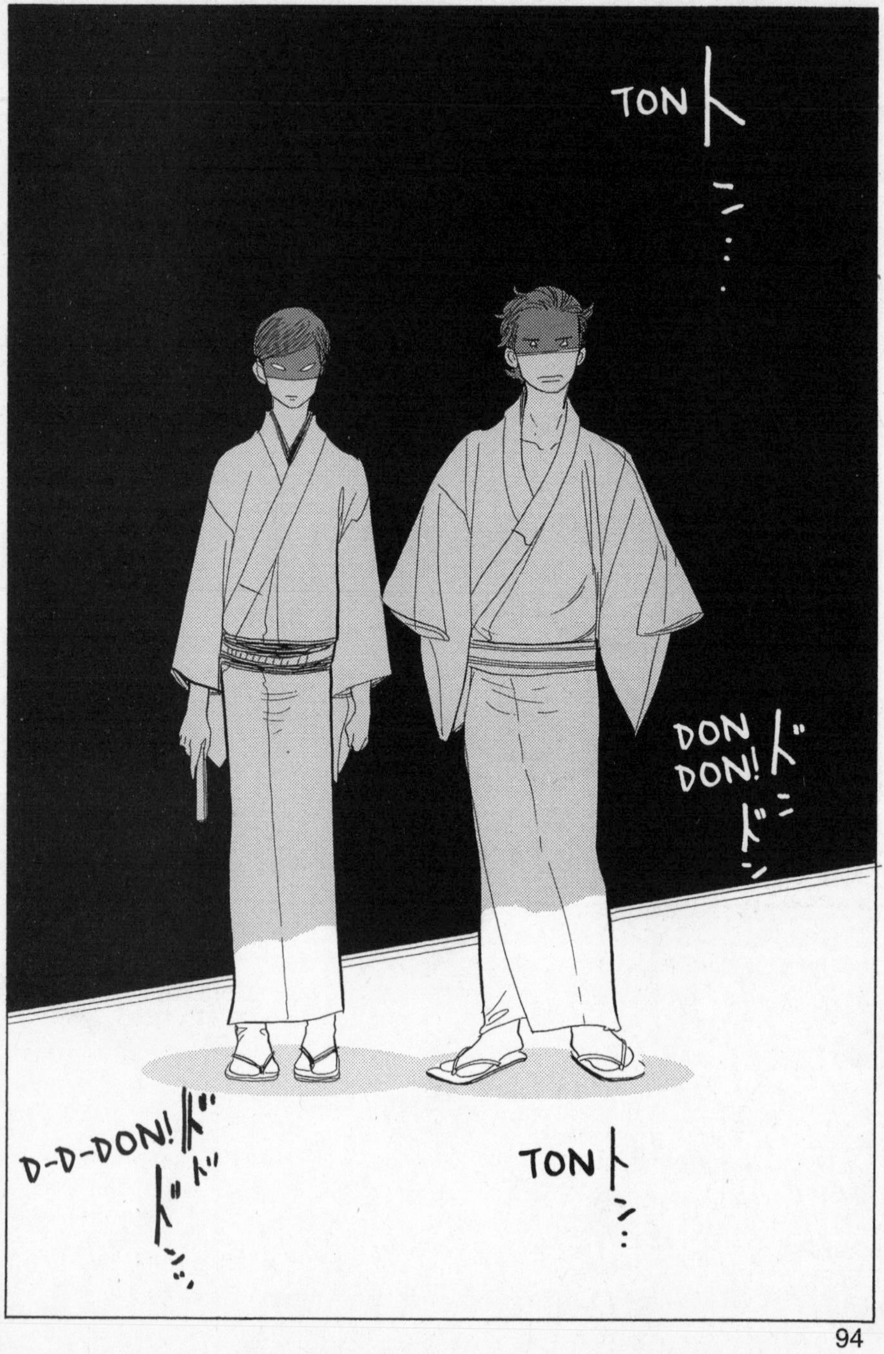
TON トン…
DON DON! ドンドン
TON トン…
D-D-DON! ドドドン…

DESCENDING
STORIES

SHOWA
GENROKU
RAKUGO
SHINJU

HARUKO KUMOTA

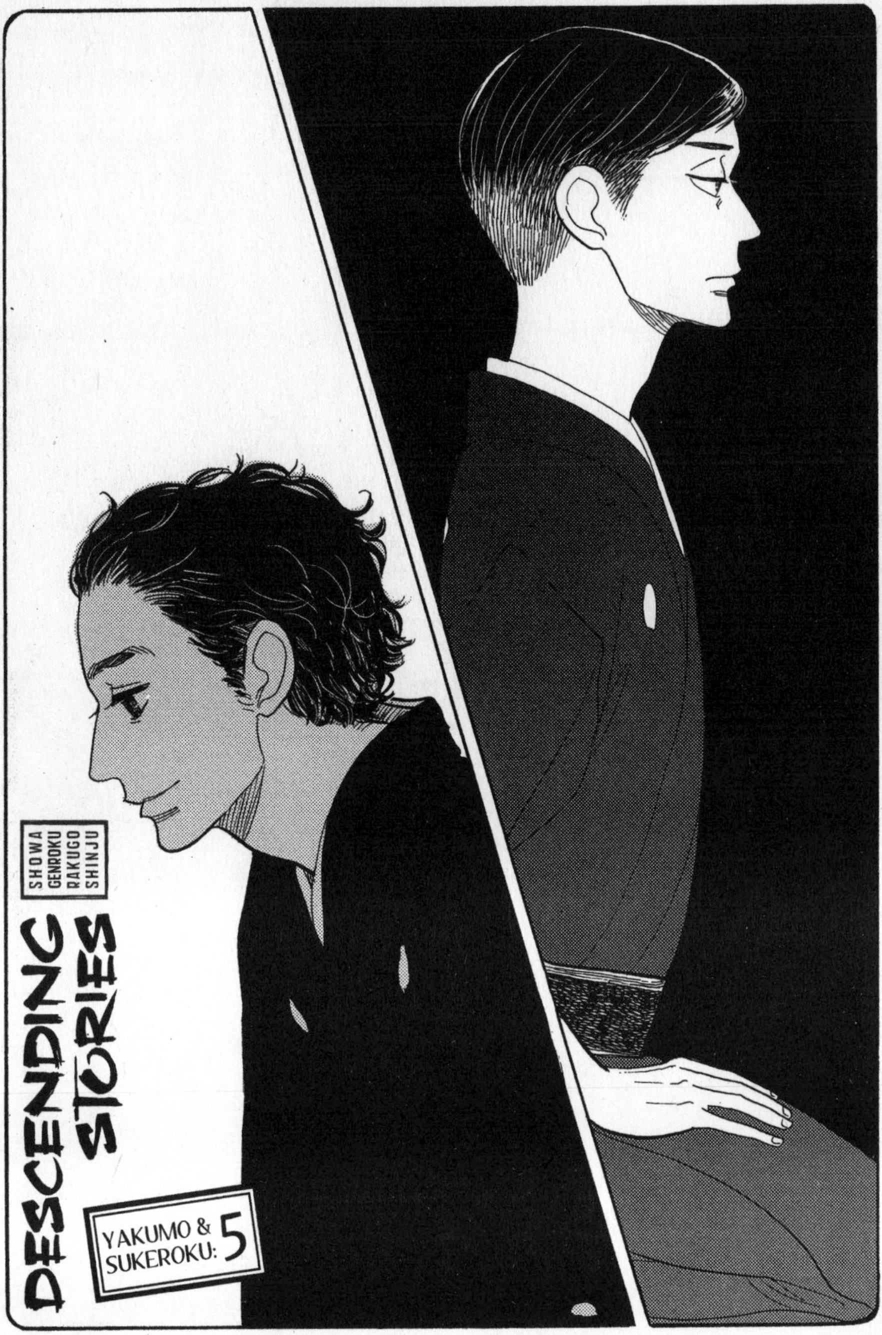
DESCENDING STORIES
SHOWA GENROKU RAKUGO SHINJU
YAKUMO & SUKEROKU: 5

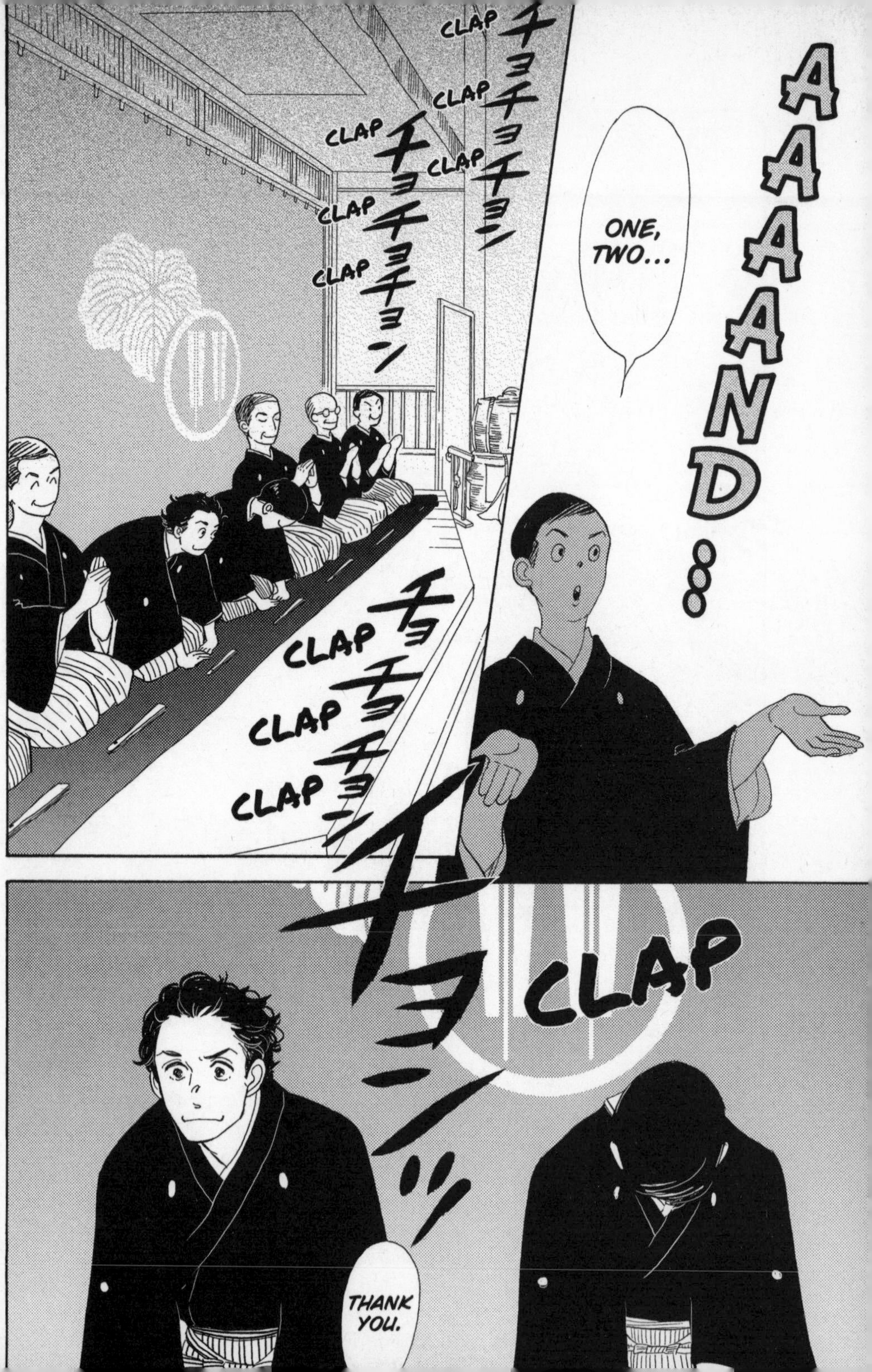
ONE, TWO...
AAAAAND...
CLAP
CLAP
CLAP
チョチョチョン
CLAP
CLAP
CLAP
チョチョチョン
CLAP
CLAP
CLAP
チョチョチョン
CLAP
THANK YOU.

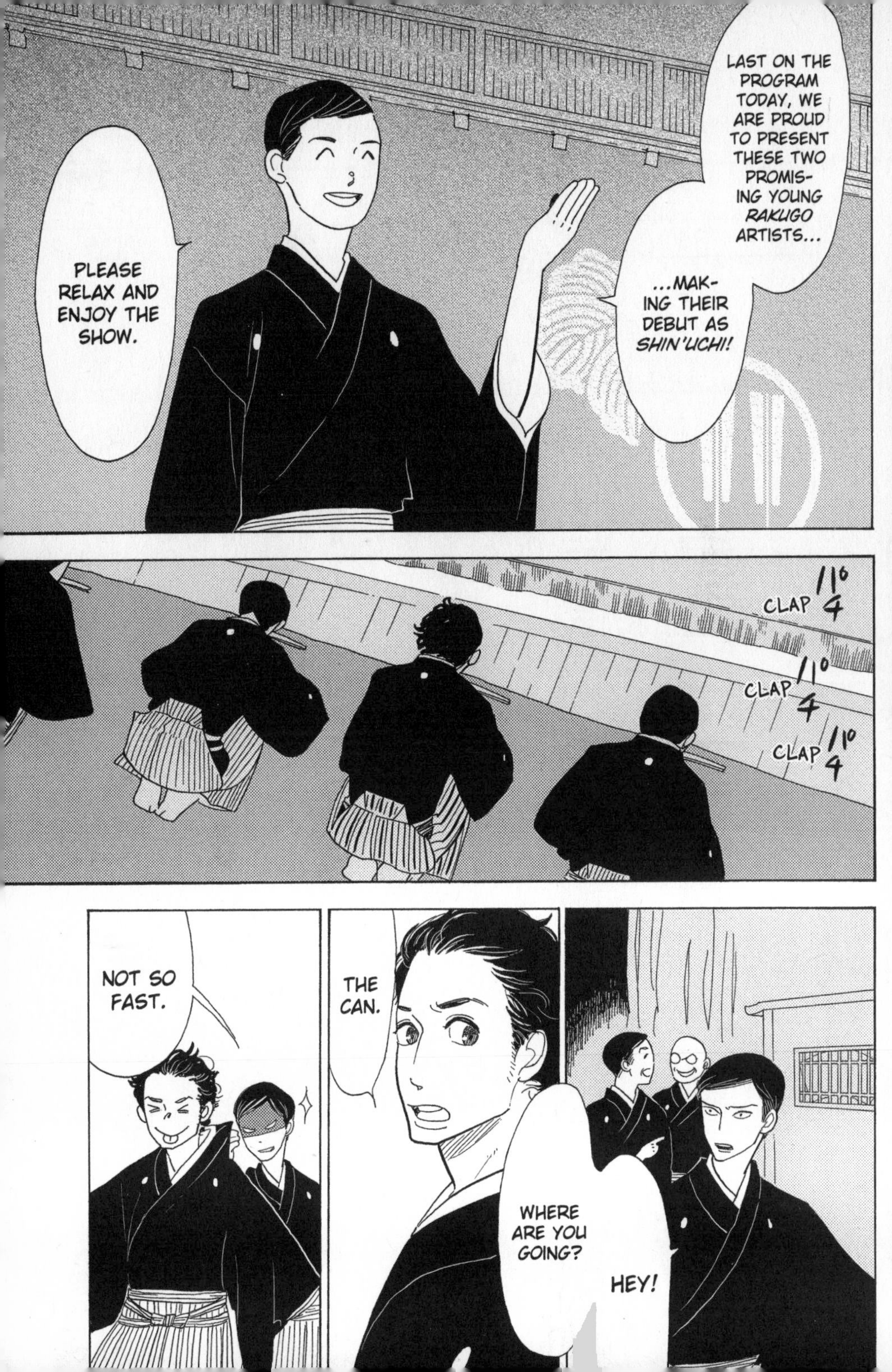
LAST ON THE PROGRAM TODAY, WE ARE PROUD TO PRESENT THESE TWO PROMISING YOUNG *RAKUGO* ARTISTS...
...MAKING THEIR DEBUT AS *SHIN'UCHI*!
PLEASE RELAX AND ENJOY THE SHOW.
CLAP
CLAP
CLAP
HEY!
WHERE ARE YOU GOING?
THE CAN.
NOT SO FAST.

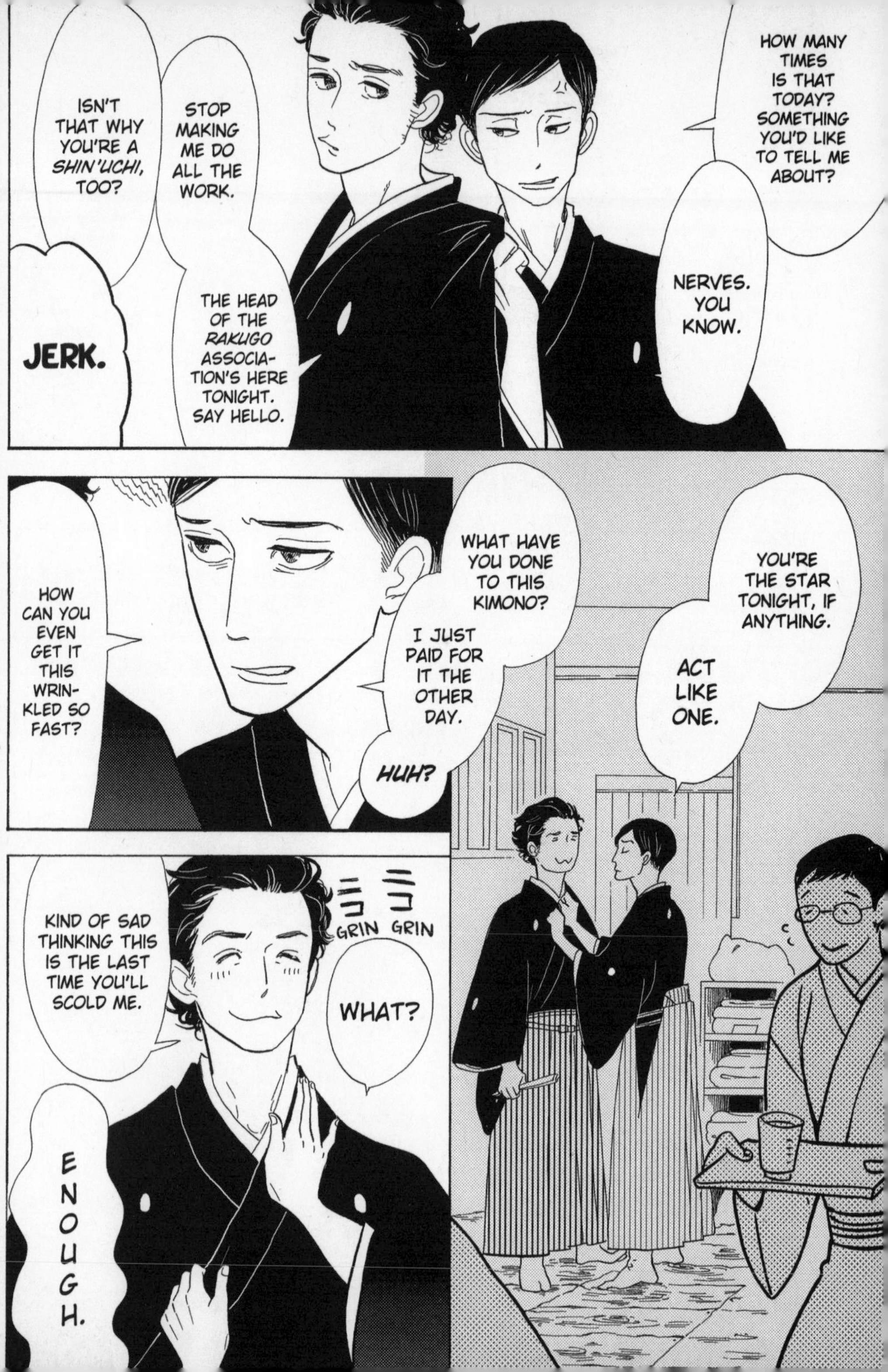
HOW MANY TIMES IS THAT TODAY? SOMETHING YOU'D LIKE TO TELL ME ABOUT?
NERVES. YOU KNOW.
STOP MAKING ME DO ALL THE WORK.
THE HEAD OF THE *RAKUGO* ASSOCIA-TION'S HERE TONIGHT. SAY HELLO.
ISN'T THAT WHY YOU'RE A *SHIN'UCHI*, TOO?
JERK.
YOU'RE THE STAR TONIGHT, IF ANYTHING.
ACT LIKE ONE.
WHAT HAVE YOU DONE TO THIS KIMONO?
I JUST PAID FOR IT THE OTHER DAY.
HOW CAN YOU EVEN GET IT THIS WRIN-KLED SO FAST?
HUH?
GRIN GRIN
KIND OF SAD THINKING THIS IS THE LAST TIME YOU'LL SCOLD ME.
WHAT?
ENOUGH.

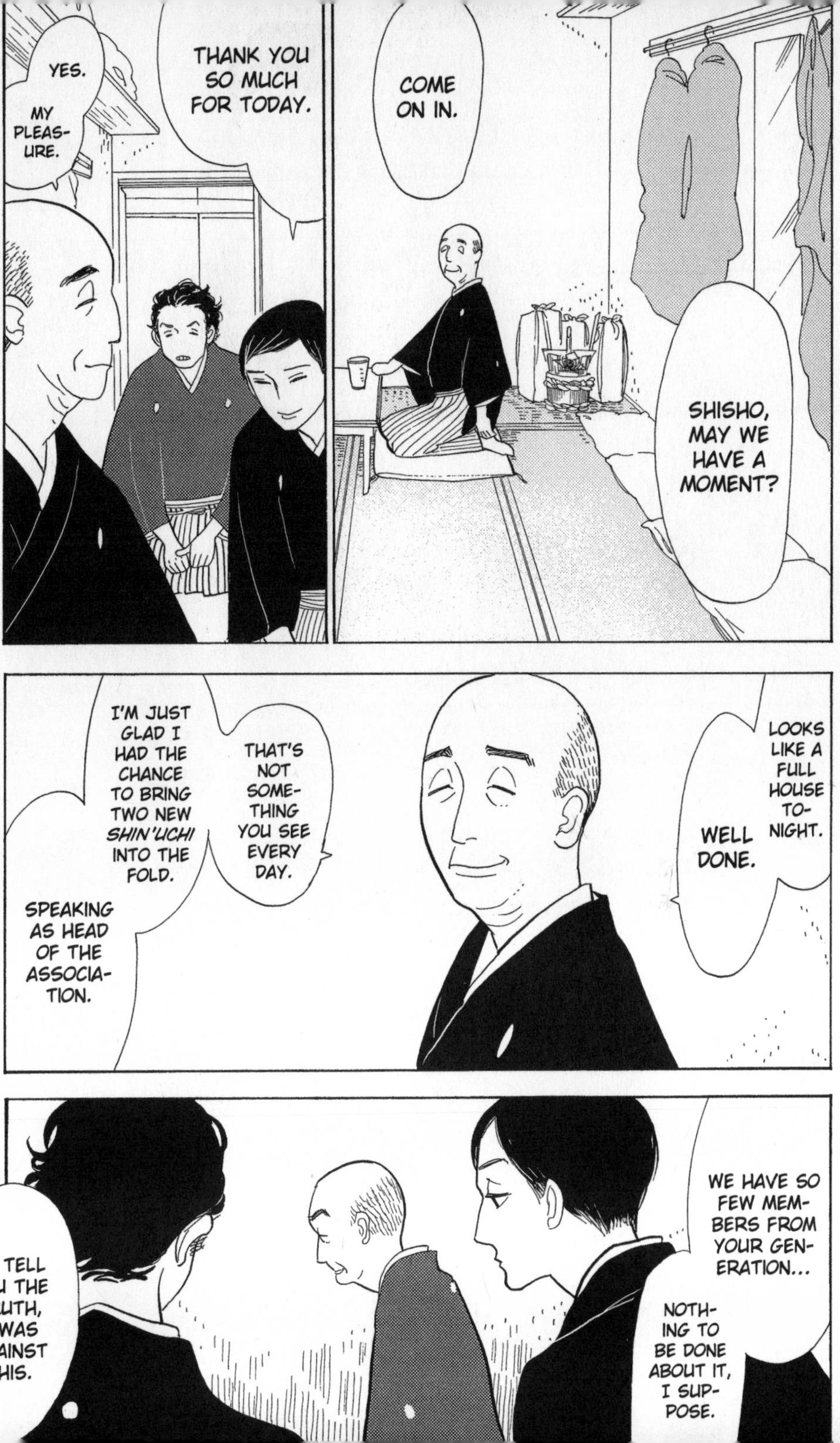
SHISHO, MAY WE HAVE A MOMENT?
COME ON IN.
THANK YOU SO MUCH FOR TODAY.
YES. MY PLEASURE.
LOOKS LIKE A FULL HOUSE TONIGHT.
WELL DONE.
THAT'S NOT SOMETHING YOU SEE EVERY DAY.
I'M JUST GLAD I HAD THE CHANCE TO BRING TWO NEW *SHIN'UCHI* INTO THE FOLD.
SPEAKING AS HEAD OF THE ASSOCIATION.
WE HAVE SO FEW MEMBERS FROM YOUR GENERATION...
NOTHING TO BE DONE ABOUT IT, I SUPPOSE.
TO TELL YOU THE TRUTH, I WAS AGAINST THIS.

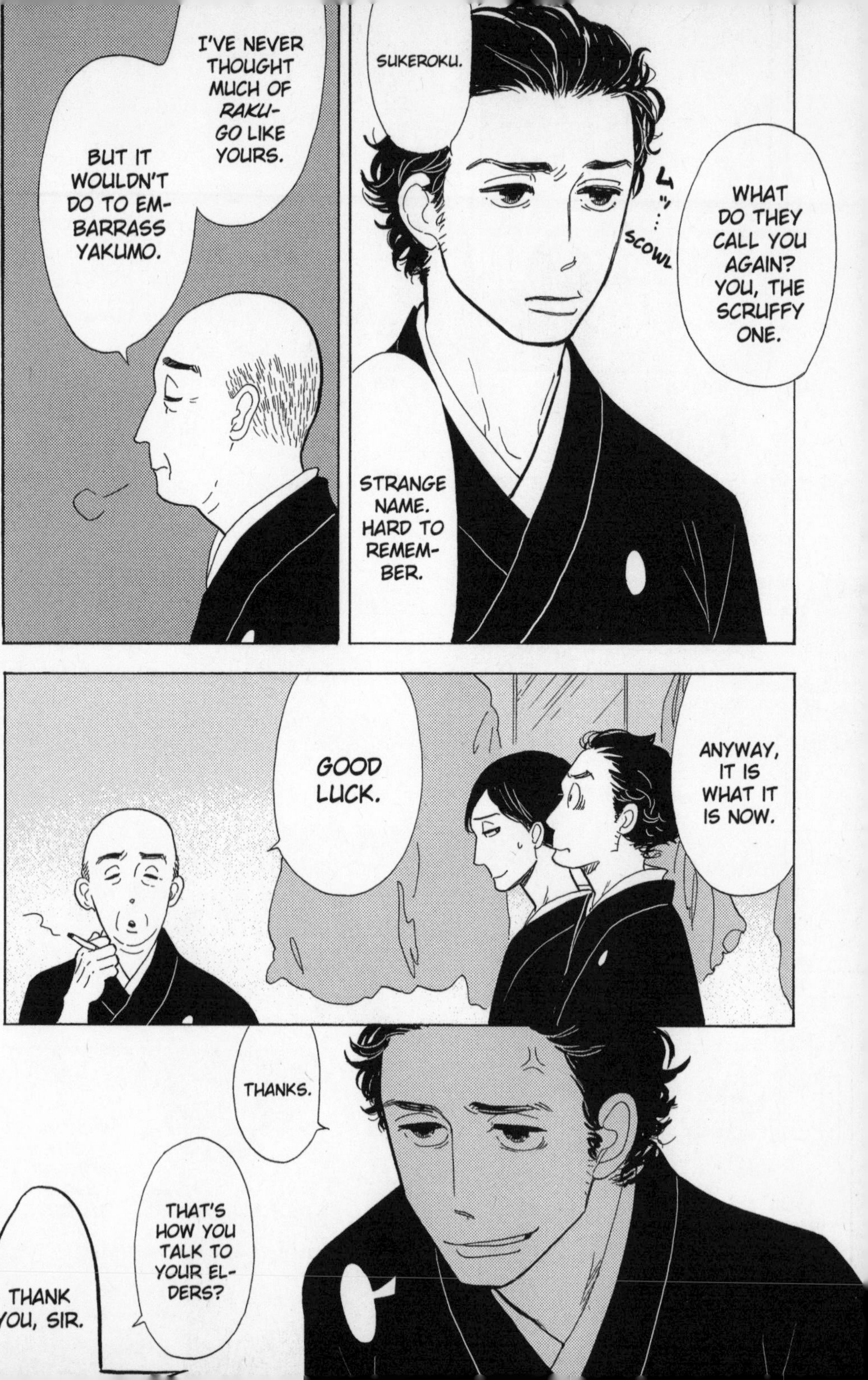
WHAT DO THEY CALL YOU AGAIN? YOU, THE SCRUFFY ONE.
SCOWL
SUKEROKU.
STRANGE NAME. HARD TO REMEMBER.
I'VE NEVER THOUGHT MUCH OF *RAKU-GO* LIKE YOURS.
BUT IT WOULDN'T DO TO EMBARRASS YAKUMO.
ANYWAY, IT IS WHAT IT IS NOW.
GOOD LUCK.
THANKS.
THAT'S HOW YOU TALK TO YOUR ELDERS?
THANK YOU, SIR.

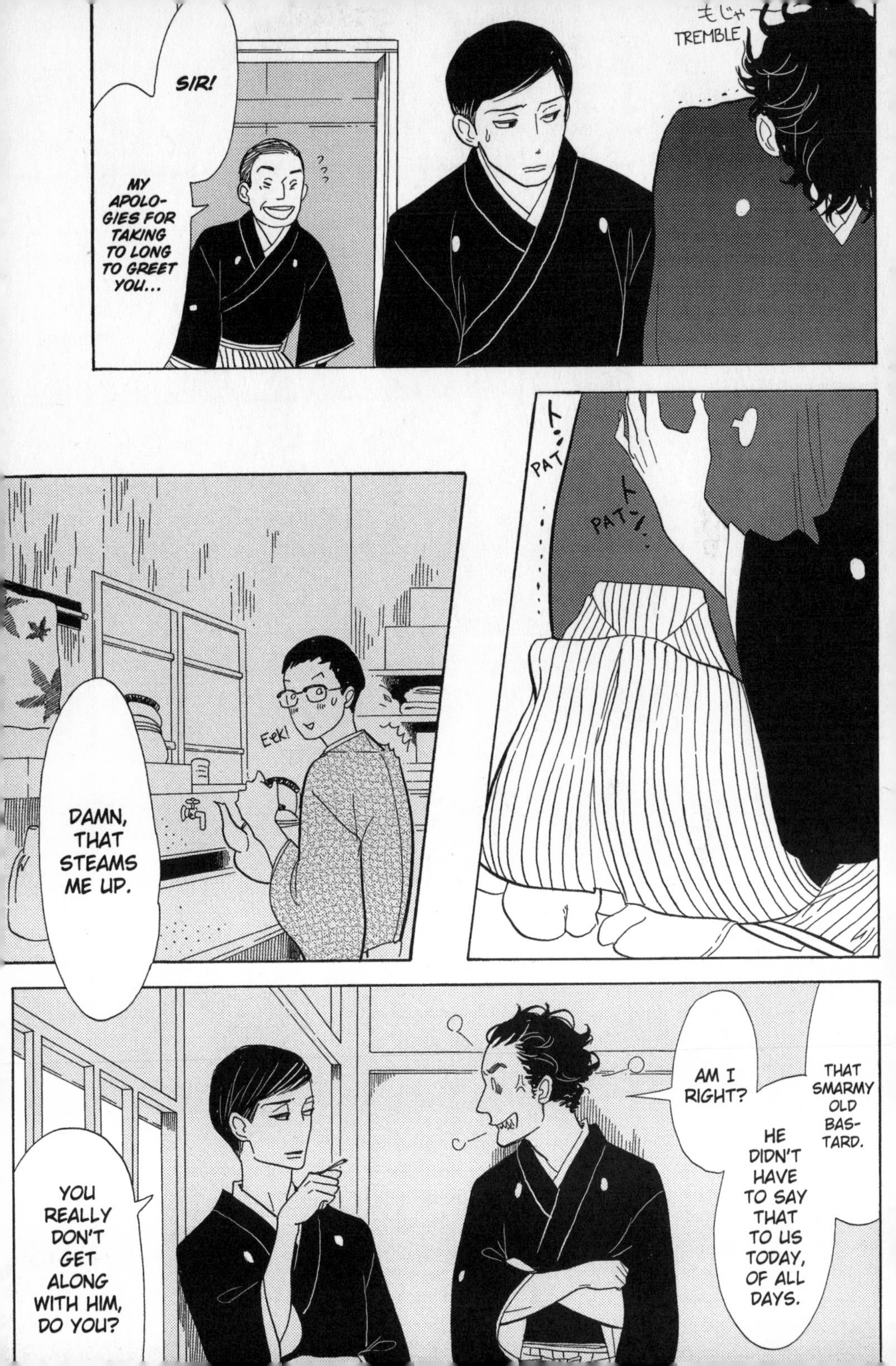
もじゃ
TREMBLE
SIR!
MY APOLOGIES FOR TAKING TO LONG TO GREET YOU...
PAT
PAT
Eek!
DAMN, THAT STEAMS ME UP.
THAT SMARMY OLD BASTARD.
HE DIDN'T HAVE TO SAY THAT TO US TODAY, OF ALL DAYS.
AM I RIGHT?
YOU REALLY DON'T GET ALONG WITH HIM, DO YOU?

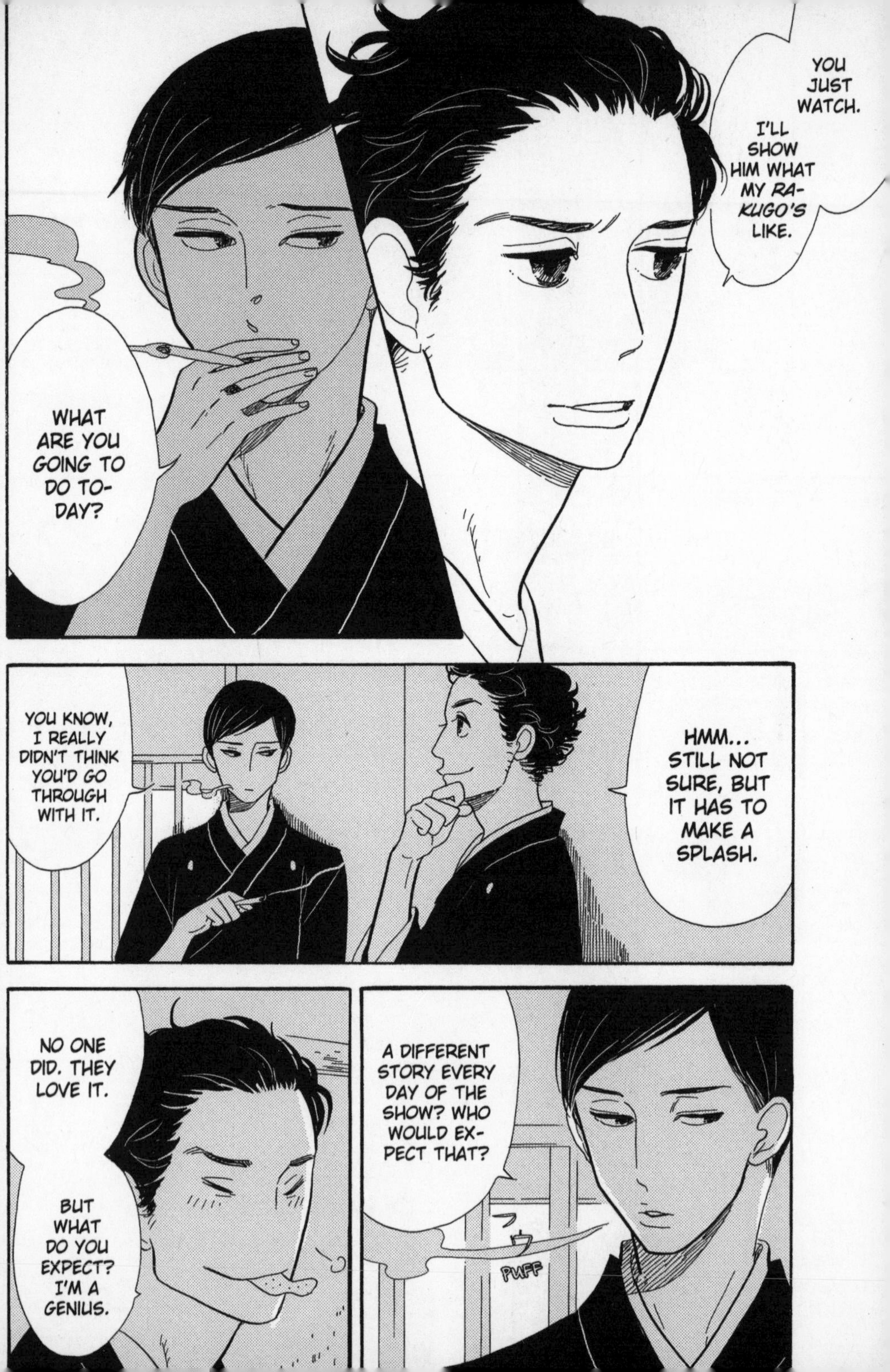
YOU JUST WATCH.
I'LL SHOW HIM WHAT MY *RA-KUGO'S* LIKE.
WHAT ARE YOU GOING TO DO TO-DAY?
HMM... STILL NOT SURE, BUT IT HAS TO MAKE A SPLASH.
YOU KNOW, I REALLY DIDN'T THINK YOU'D GO THROUGH WITH IT.
A DIFFERENT STORY EVERY DAY OF THE SHOW? WHO WOULD EX-PECT THAT?
PUFF
NO ONE DID. THEY LOVE IT.
BUT WHAT DO YOU EXPECT? I'M A GENIUS.

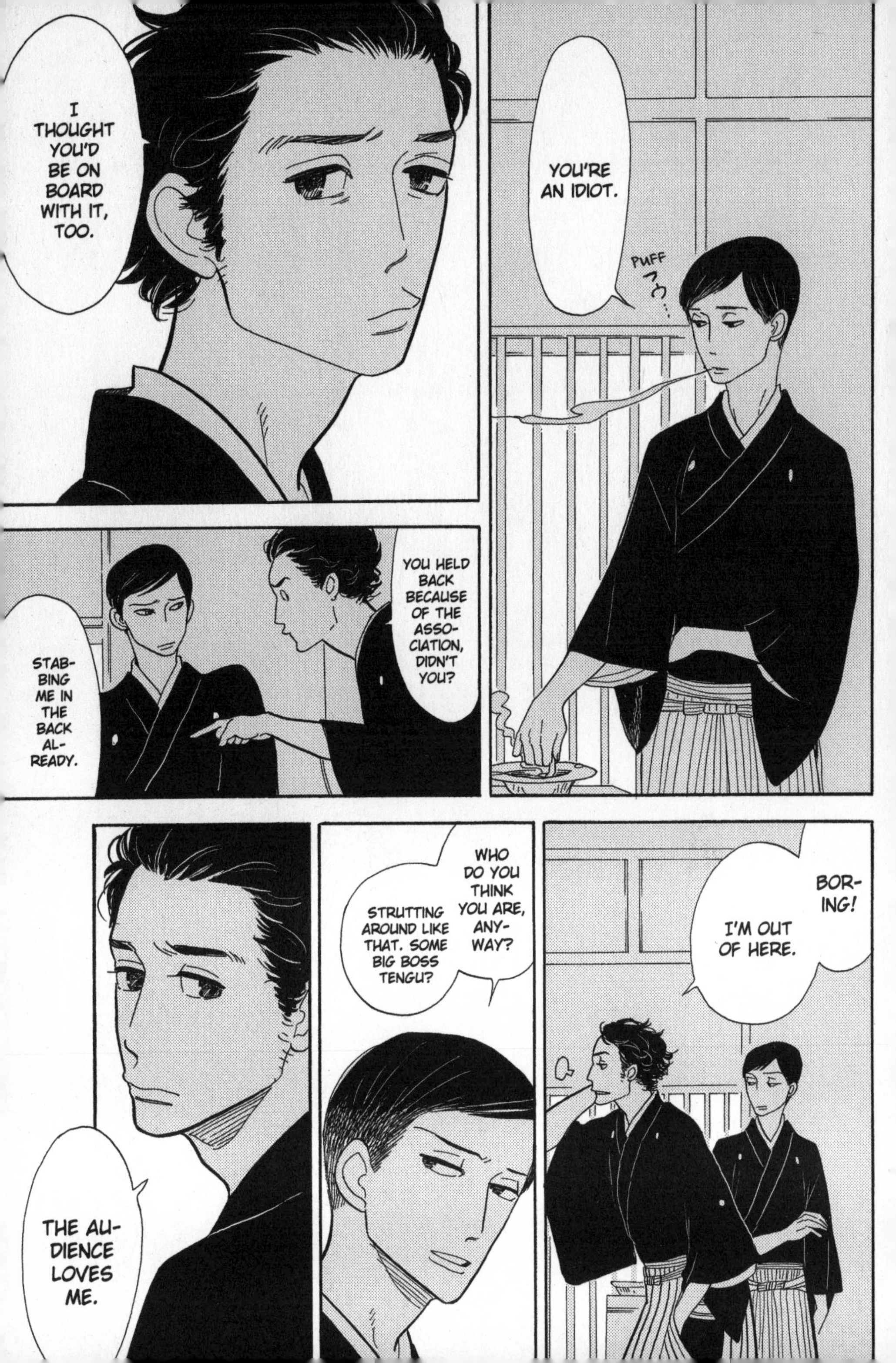
YOU'RE AN IDIOT.
PUFF
I THOUGHT YOU'D BE ON BOARD WITH IT, TOO.
YOU HELD BACK BECAUSE OF THE ASSO-CIATION, DIDN'T YOU?
STAB-BING ME IN THE BACK AL-READY.
BOR-ING!
I'M OUT OF HERE.
WHO DO YOU THINK YOU ARE, ANY-WAY?
STRUTTING AROUND LIKE THAT. SOME BIG BOSS TENGU?
THE AU-DIENCE LOVES ME.

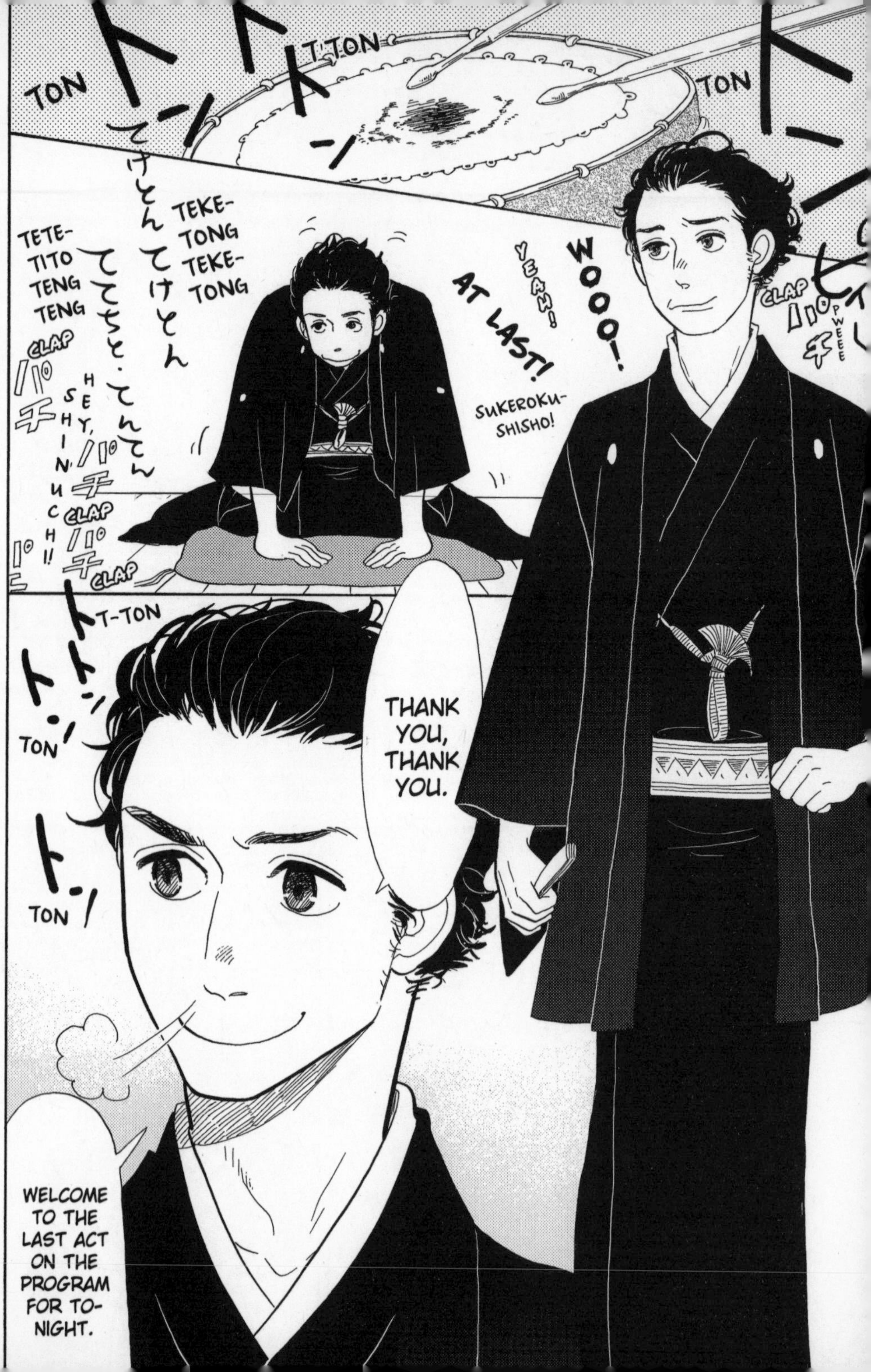
TON
T'TON
TON
CLAP
PWEEE
WOOO!
YEAH!
AT LAST!
SUKEROKU-SHISHO!
てけとんてけとん
TEKE-TONG TEKE-TONG
てててちと・てんてん
TETE-TITO TENG TENG
CLAP
HEY, SHINUCHI!
CLAP
CLAP
THANK YOU, THANK YOU.
T-TON
TON
TON
WELCOME TO THE LAST ACT ON THE PROGRAM FOR TO-NIGHT.

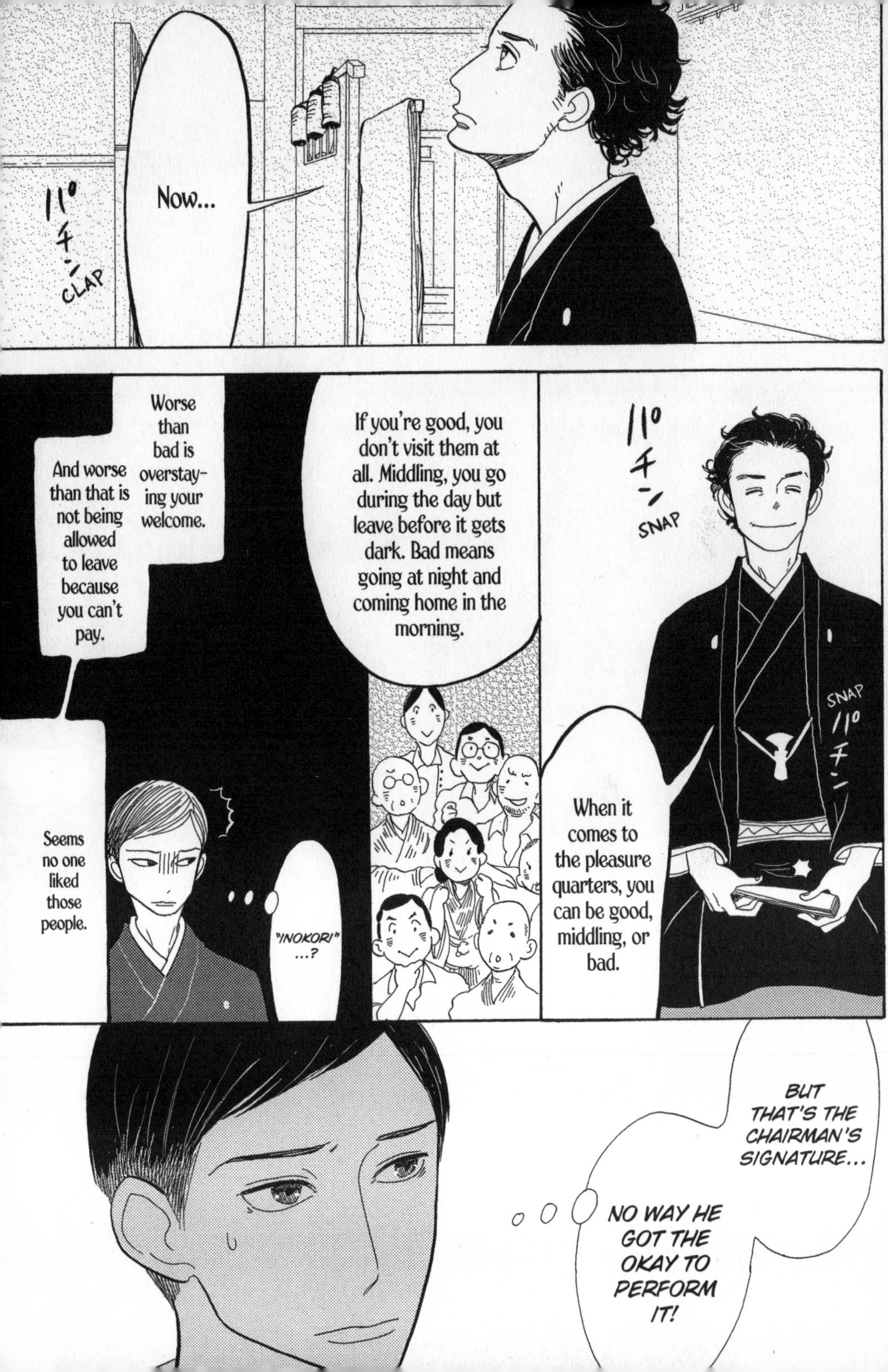
Now...
パチン
CLAP
パチン
SNAP
SNAP
パチン
When it comes to the pleasure quarters, you can be good, middling, or bad.
If you're good, you don't visit them at all. Middling, you go during the day but leave before it gets dark. Bad means going at night and coming home in the morning.
Worse than bad is overstaying your welcome.
And worse than that is not being allowed to leave because you can't pay.
Seems no one liked those people.
"INOKORI" ...?
BUT THAT'S THE CHAIRMAN'S SIGNATURE...
NO WAY HE GOT THE OKAY TO PERFORM IT!

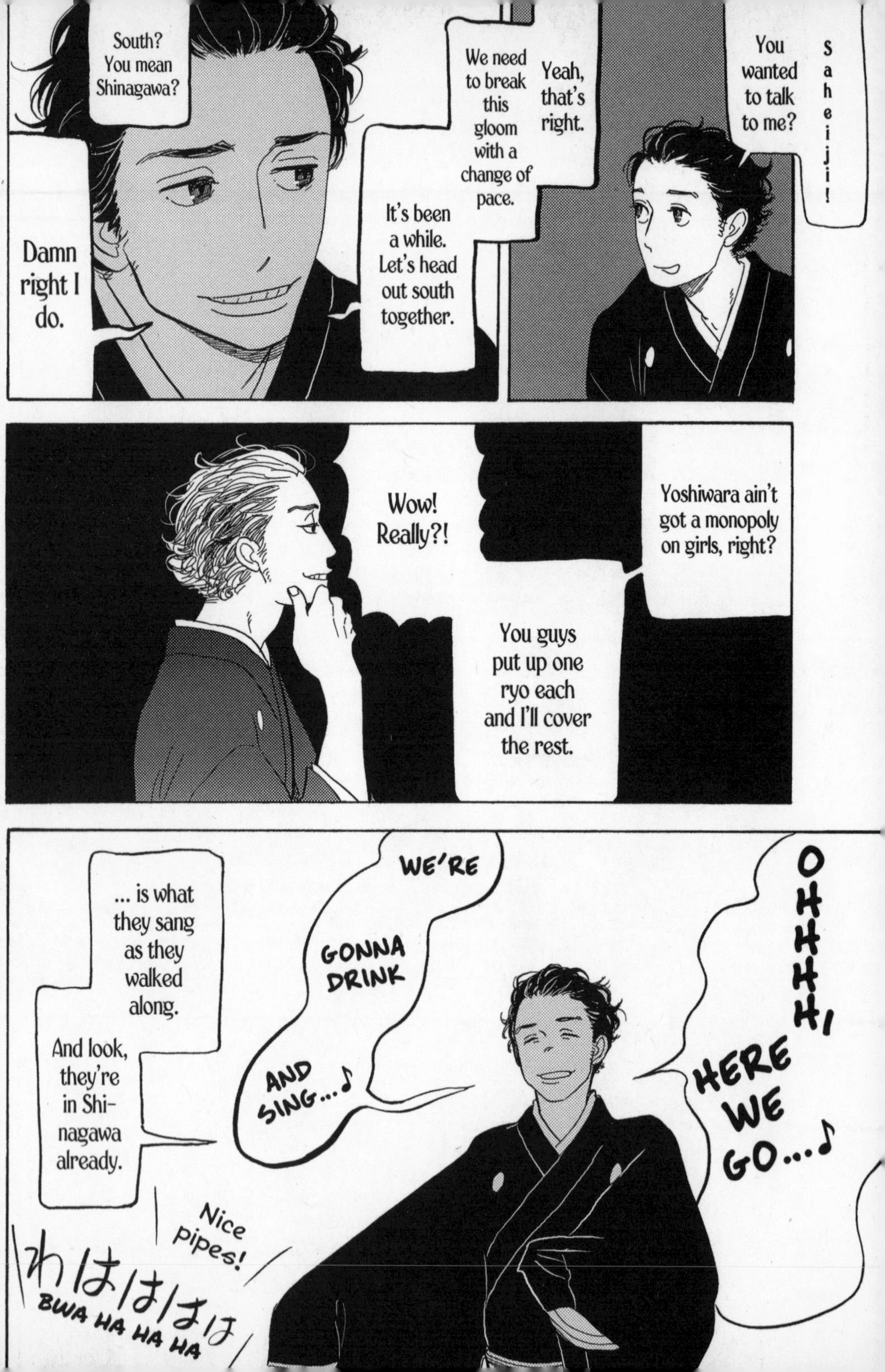

You wanted to talk to me? Saheiji!
Yeah, that's right.
We need to break this gloom with a change of pace.
It's been a while. Let's head out south together.
South? You mean Shinagawa?
Damn right I do.
Yoshiwara ain't got a monopoly on girls, right?
You guys put up one ryo each and I'll cover the rest.
Wow! Really?!
OHHHH, HERE WE GO...♪
WE'RE GONNA DRINK AND SING...♪
... is what they sang as they walked along.
And look, they're in Shinagawa already.
Nice pipes!
わはははは
BWA HA HA HA

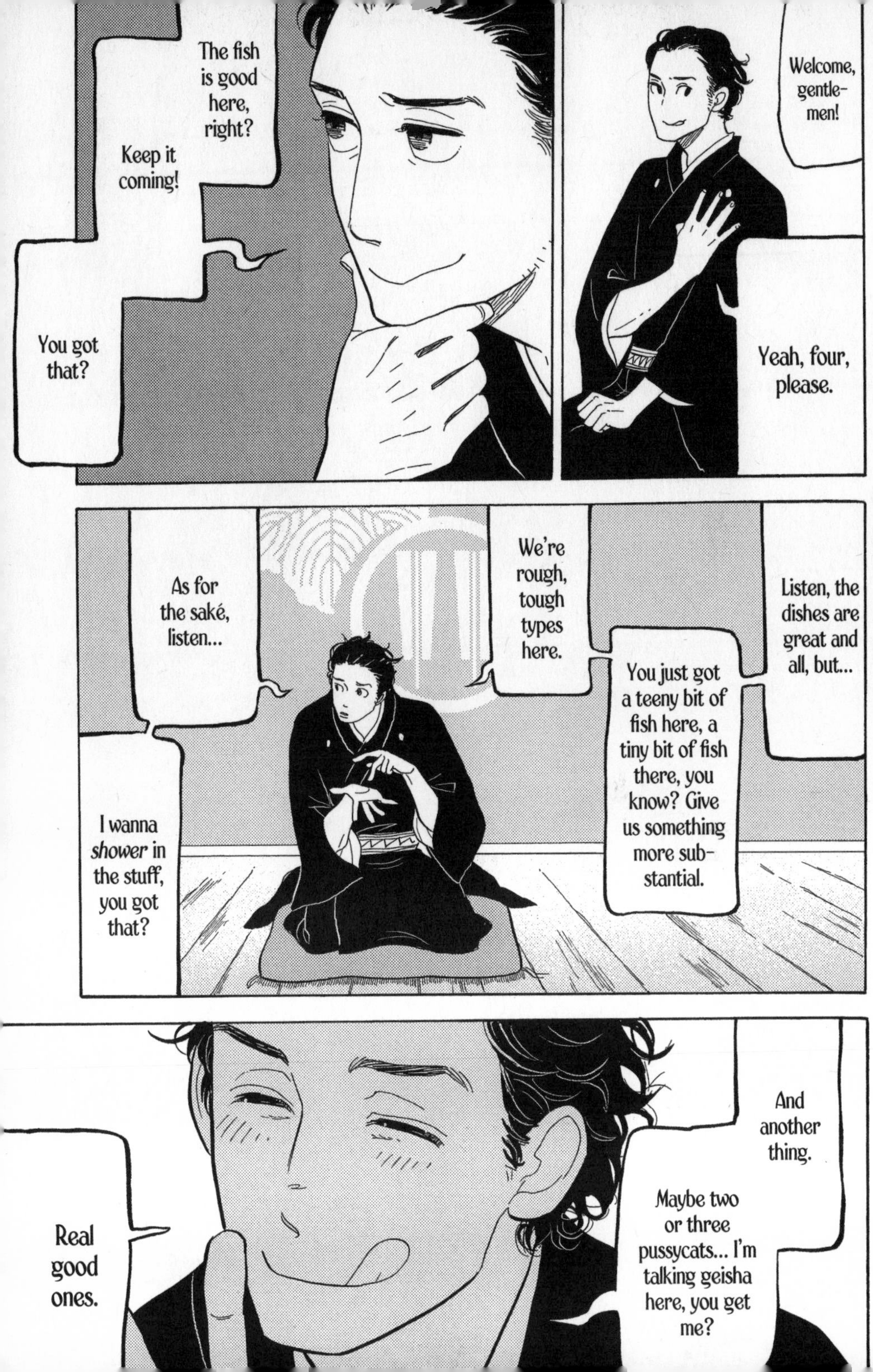
Welcome, gentle-men!
Yeah, four, please.
The fish is good here, right?
Keep it coming!
You got that?
Listen, the dishes are great and all, but...
You just got a teeny bit of fish here, a tiny bit of fish there, you know? Give us something more sub-stantial.
We're rough, tough types here.
As for the saké, listen...
I wanna *shower* in the stuff, you got that?
And another thing.
Maybe two or three pussycats... I'm talking geisha here, you get me?
Real good ones.

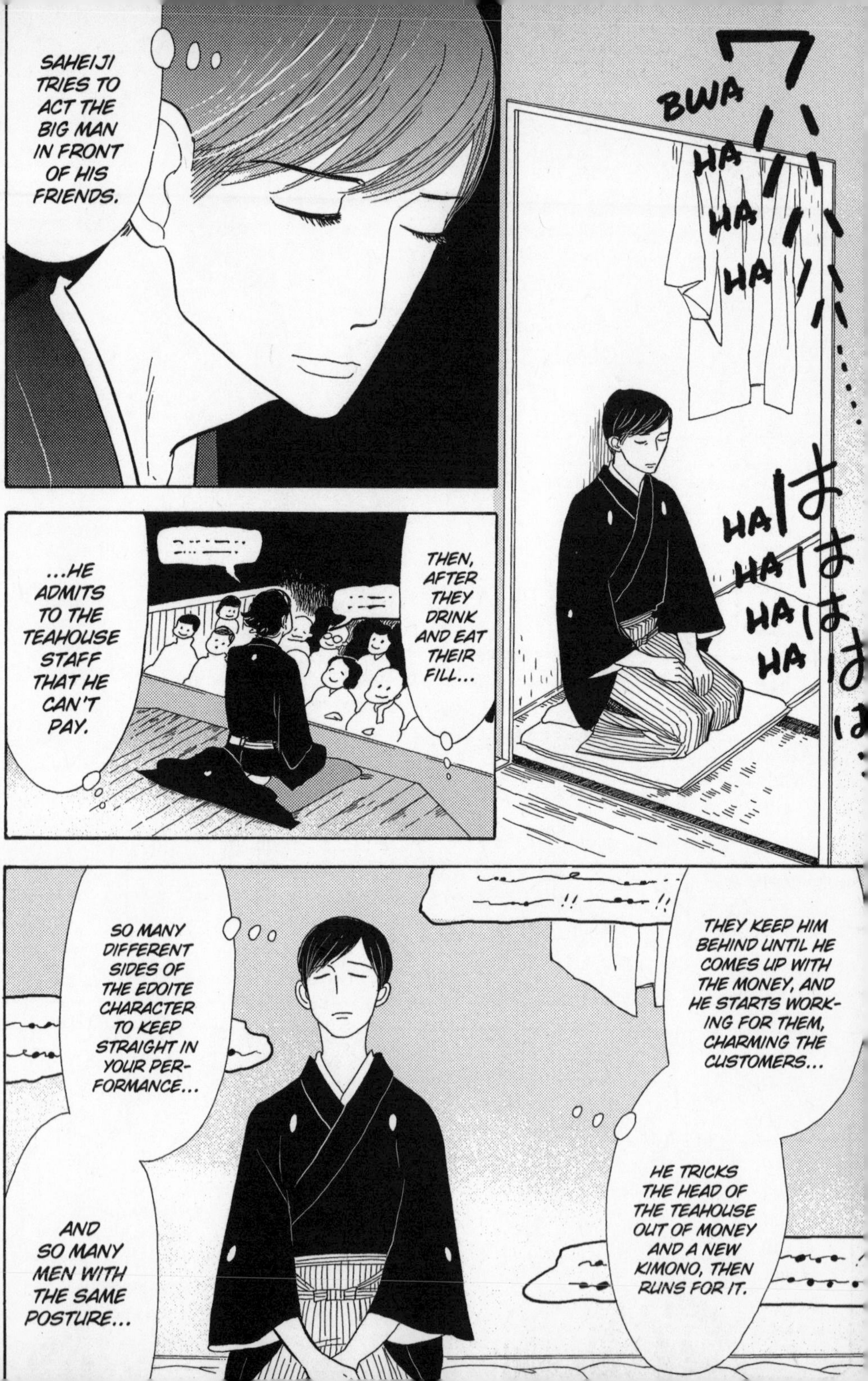
BWA HA HA HA HA
HA HA HA HA
SAHEIJI TRIES TO ACT THE BIG MAN IN FRONT OF HIS FRIENDS.
THEN, AFTER THEY DRINK AND EAT THEIR FILL...
...HE ADMITS TO THE TEAHOUSE STAFF THAT HE CAN'T PAY.
THEY KEEP HIM BEHIND UNTIL HE COMES UP WITH THE MONEY, AND HE STARTS WORKING FOR THEM, CHARMING THE CUSTOMERS...
HE TRICKS THE HEAD OF THE TEAHOUSE OUT OF MONEY AND A NEW KIMONO, THEN RUNS FOR IT.
SO MANY DIFFERENT SIDES OF THE EDOITE CHARACTER TO KEEP STRAIGHT IN YOUR PERFORMANCE...
AND SO MANY MEN WITH THE SAME POSTURE...

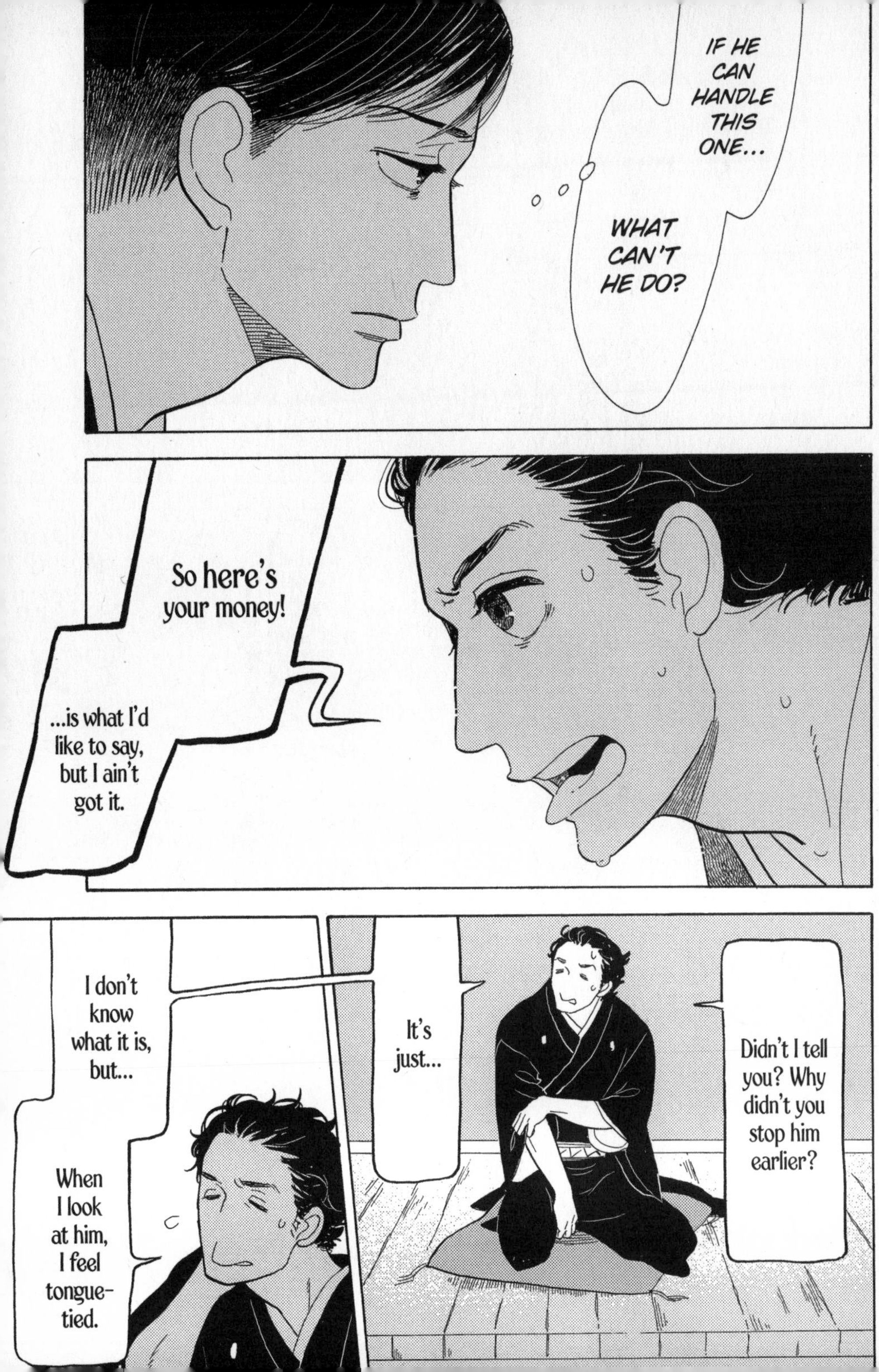
IF HE CAN HANDLE THIS ONE...
WHAT CAN'T HE DO?
So here's your money!
...is what I'd like to say, but I ain't got it.
Didn't I tell you? Why didn't you stop him earlier?
It's just...
I don't know what it is, but...
When I look at him, I feel tongue-tied.

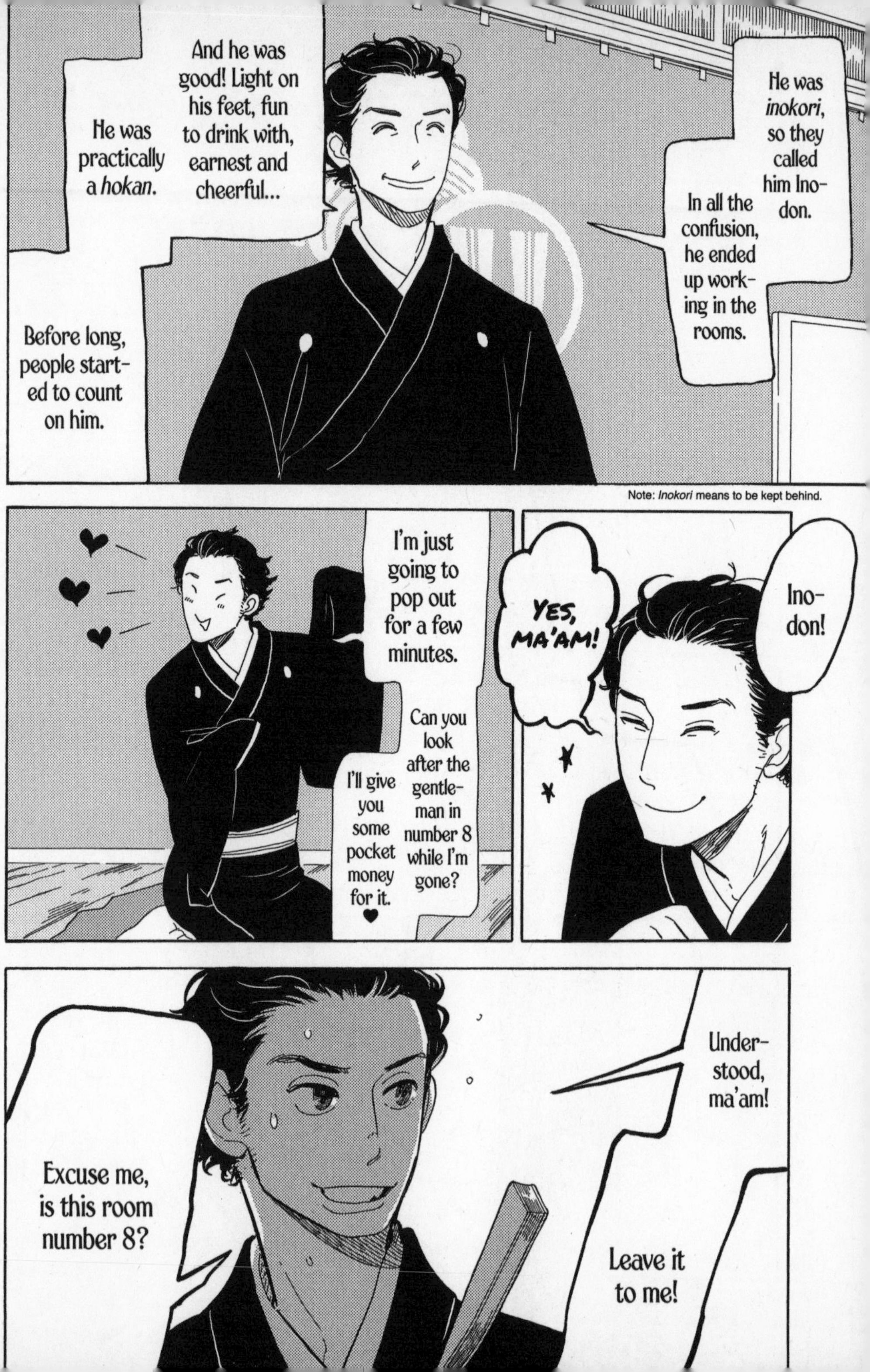
He was *inokori*, so they called him Ino-don.
In all the confusion, he ended up working in the rooms.
And he was good! Light on his feet, fun to drink with, earnest and cheerful...
He was practically a *hokan*.
Before long, people started to count on him.
Ino-don!
YES, MA'AM!
I'm just going to pop out for a few minutes.
Can you look after the gentleman in number 8 while I'm gone?
I'll give you some pocket money for it. ♥
Understood, ma'am!
Leave it to me!
Excuse me, is this room number 8?

Note: *Inokori* means to be kept behind.

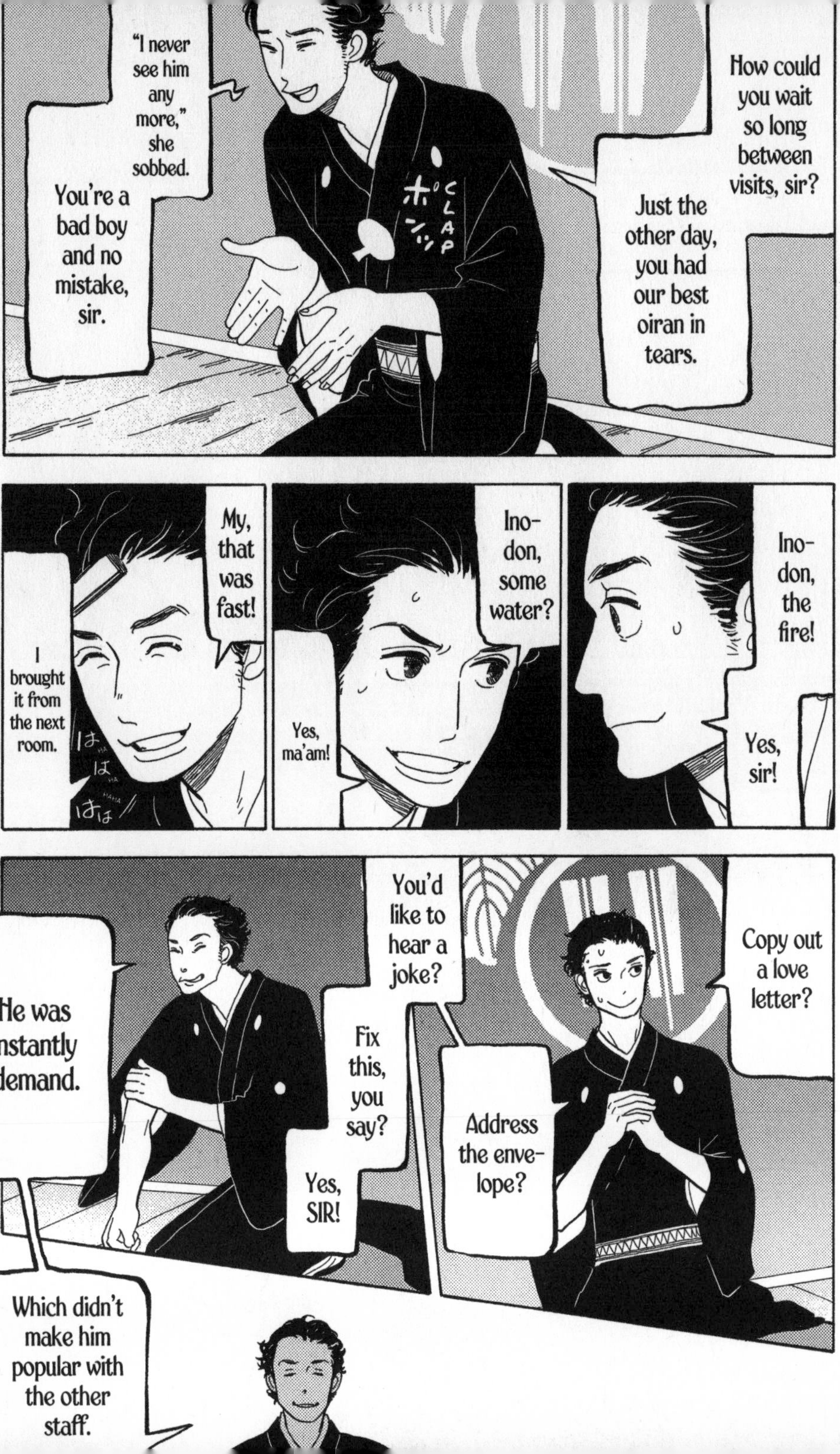
How could you wait so long between visits, sir?
Just the other day, you had our best oiran in tears.
"I never see him any more," she sobbed.
You're a bad boy and no mistake, sir.
CLAP
Ino-don, the fire!
Yes, sir!
Ino-don, some water?
Yes, ma'am!
My, that was fast!
I brought it from the next room.
HA HA HAHA
Copy out a love letter?
Address the envelope?
You'd like to hear a joke?
Fix this, you say?
Yes, SIR!
...He was constantly in demand.
Which didn't make him popular with the other staff.

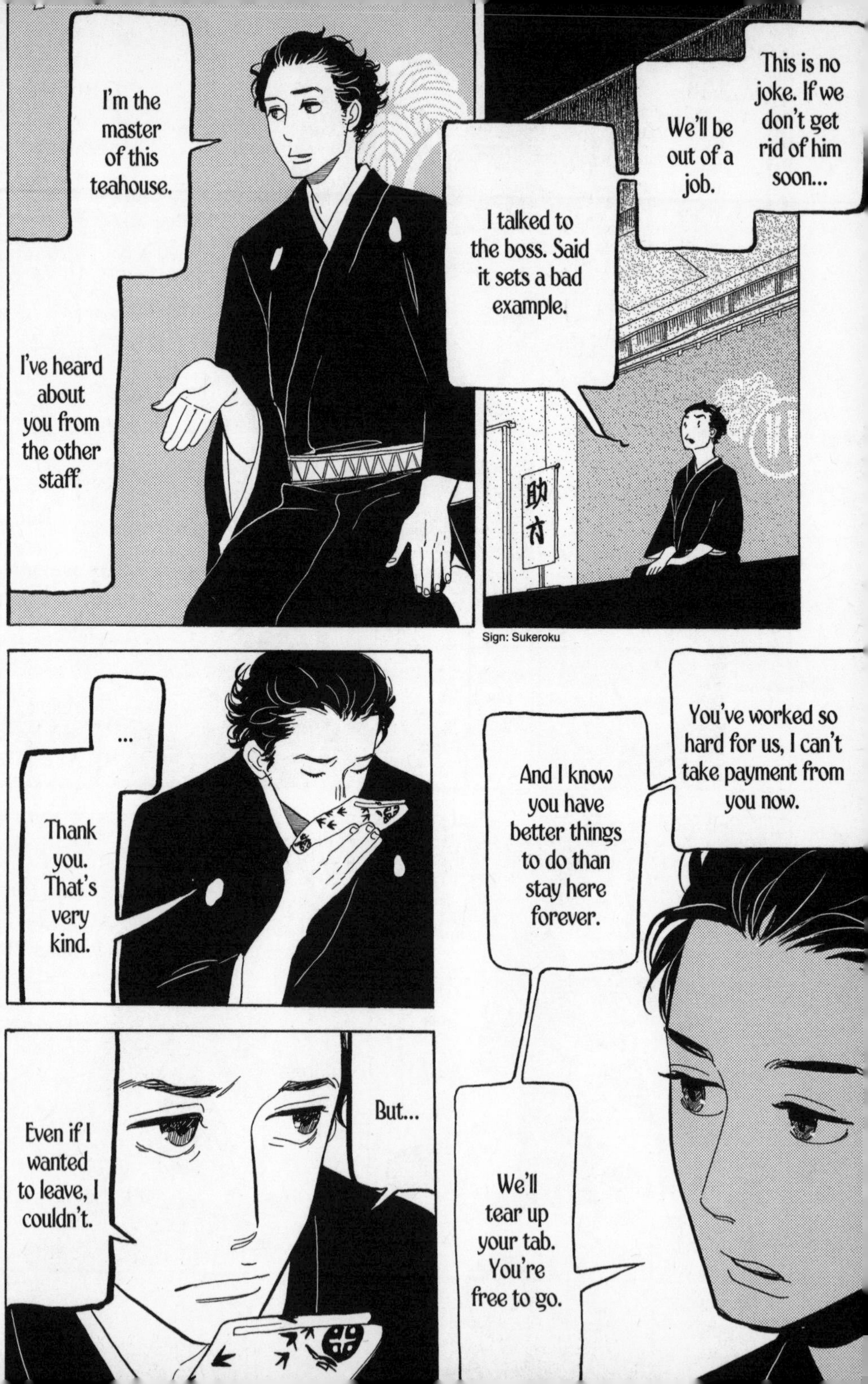
This is no joke. If we don't get rid of him soon...
We'll be out of a job.
I talked to the boss. Said it sets a bad example.
助六
I'm the master of this teahouse.
I've heard about you from the other staff.
You've worked so hard for us, I can't take payment from you now.
And I know you have better things to do than stay here forever.
We'll tear up your tab. You're free to go.
...
Thank you. That's very kind.
But...
Even if I wanted to leave, I couldn't.
Sign: Sukeroku

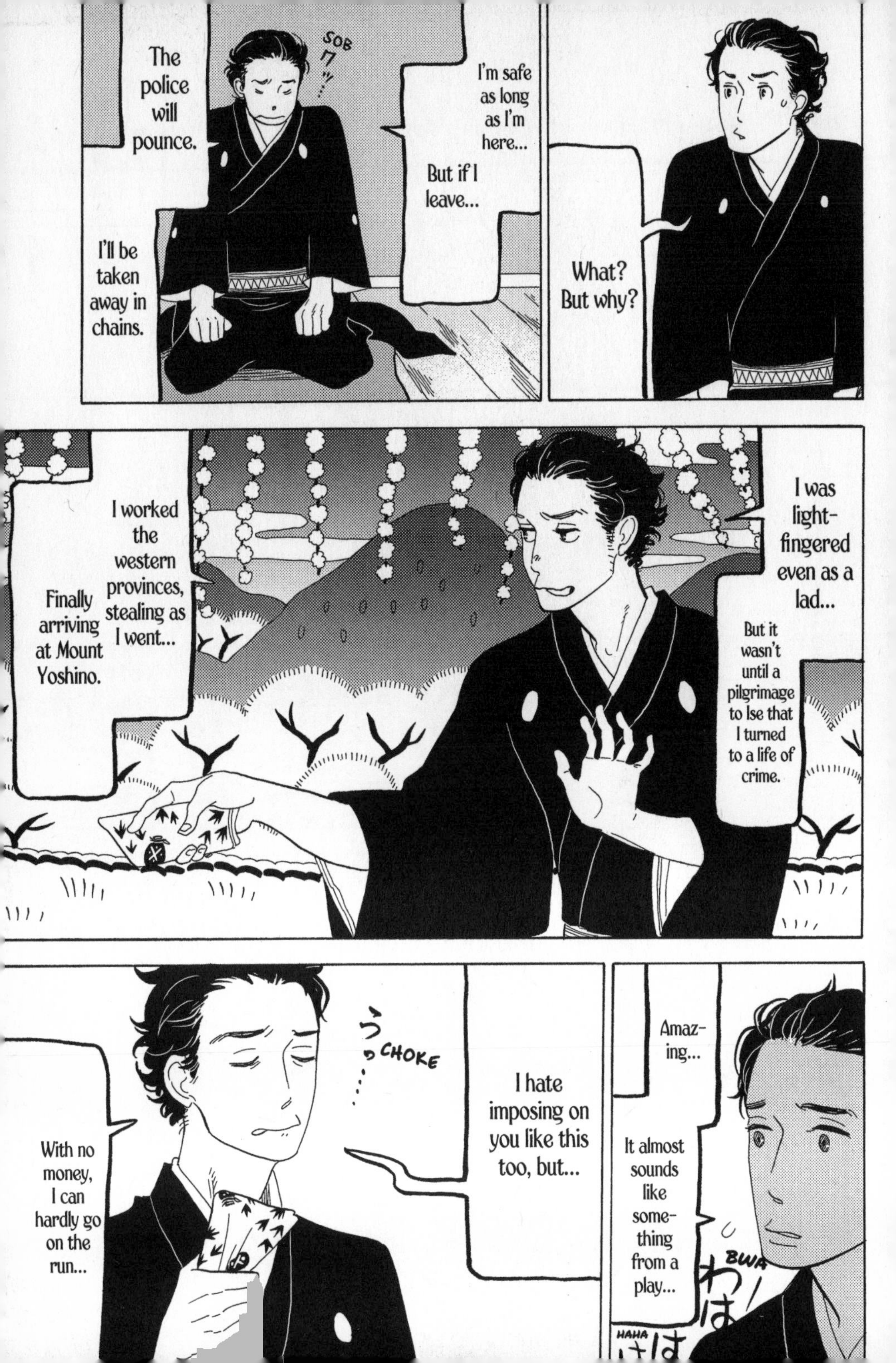
What? But why?
I'm safe as long as I'm here...
SOB
But if I leave...
The police will pounce.
I'll be taken away in chains.
I was light-fingered even as a lad...
But it wasn't until a pilgrimage to Ise that I turned to a life of crime.
I worked the western provinces, stealing as I went...
Finally arriving at Mount Yoshino.
Amaz-ing...
It almost sounds like some-thing from a play...
BWA
HAHA
I hate imposing on you like this too, but...
CHOKE
With no money, I can hardly go on the run...

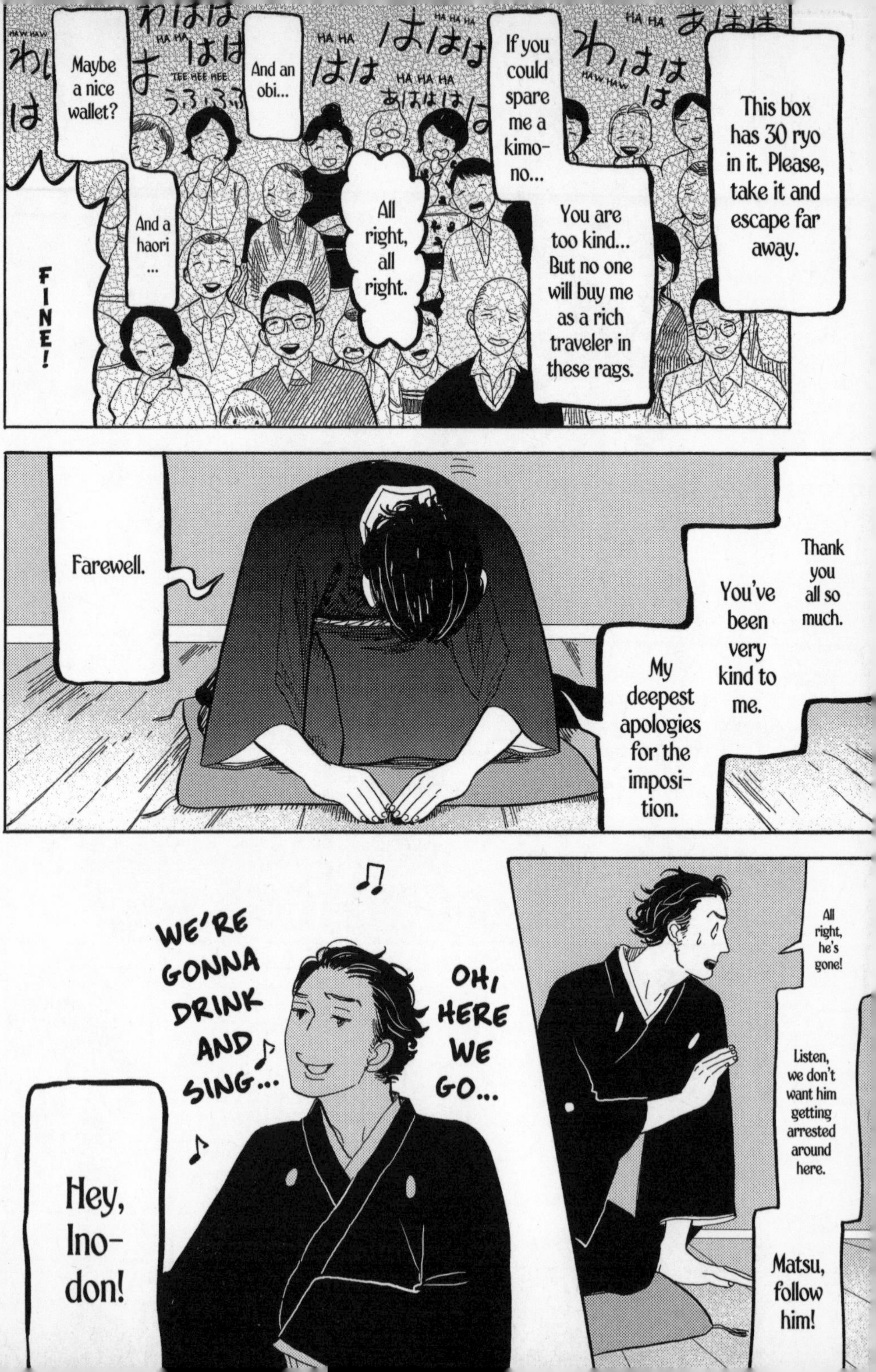

This box has 30 ryo in it. Please, take it and escape far away.
You are too kind... But no one will buy me as a rich traveler in these rags.
If you could spare me a kimono...
All right, all right.
And an obi...
And a haori ...
Maybe a nice wallet?
FINE!
HA HA あはは
HAW HAW わははは
HA HA HA あはははは
HA HA ははは
TEE HEE HEE うふふふ
HA HA ははは
HAW HAW わはは
Thank you all so much.
You've been very kind to me.
My deepest apologies for the imposition.
Farewell.
All right, he's gone!
Listen, we don't want him getting arrested around here.
Matsu, follow him!
OH, HERE WE GO...
WE'RE GONNA DRINK AND SING...
Hey, Ino-don!

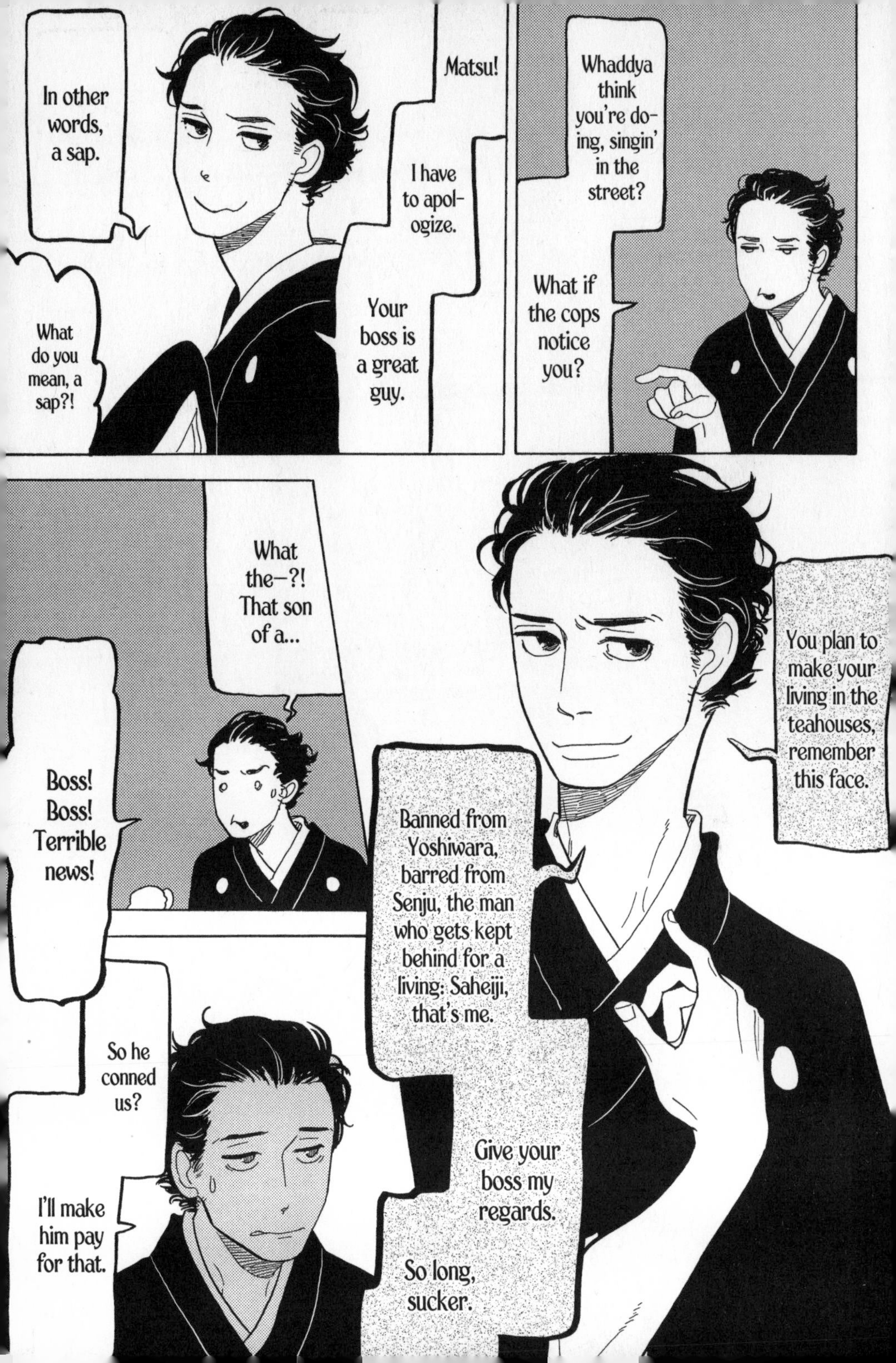
Whaddya think you're doing, singin' in the street?
What if the cops notice you?
Matsu!
I have to apologize.
Your boss is a great guy.
In other words, a sap.
What do you mean, a sap?!
You plan to make your living in the teahouses, remember this face.
Banned from Yoshiwara, barred from Senju, the man who gets kept behind for a living: Saheiji, that's me.
Give your boss my regards.
So long, sucker.
What the—?! That son of a...
Boss! Boss! Terrible news!
So he conned us?
I'll make him pay for that.

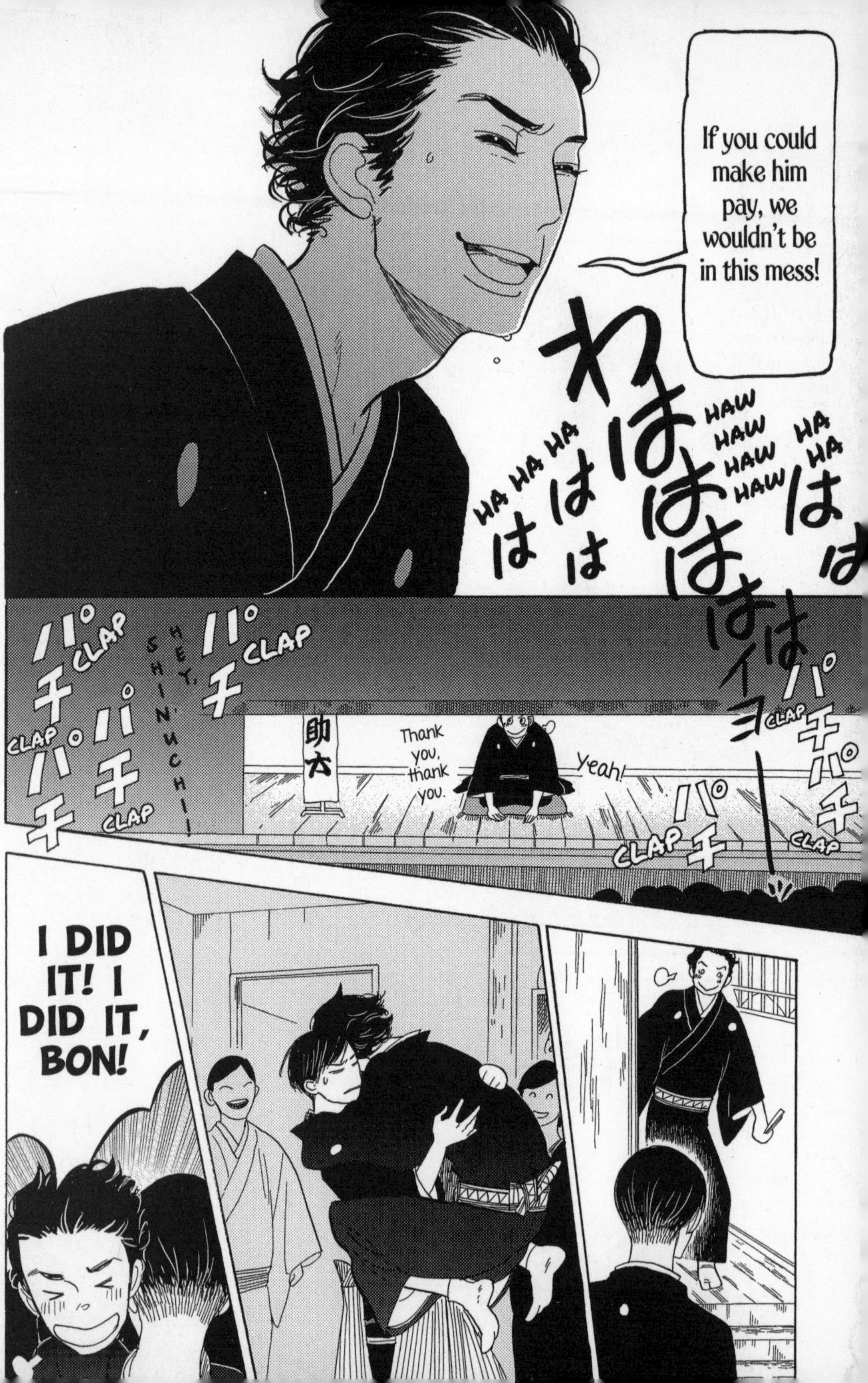
If you could make him pay, we wouldn't be in this mess!
HAW HAW HAW HAW
HA HA
HA HA HA
CLAP
Yeah!
Thank you, thank you.
HEY, SHIN'UCHI!
I DID IT! I DID IT, BON!

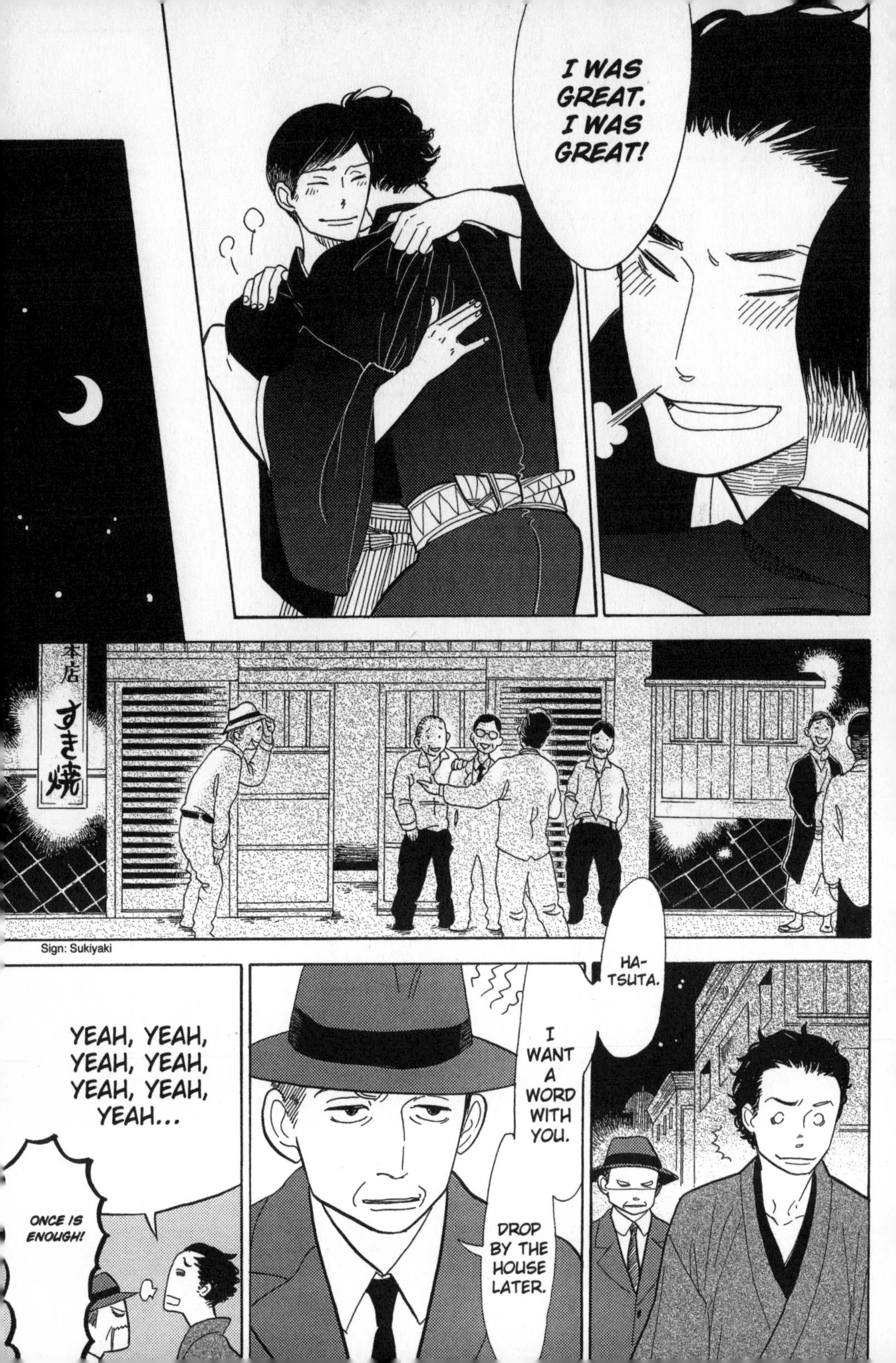
I WAS GREAT. I WAS GREAT!
本店
すき焼
HA-TSUTA.
I WANT A WORD WITH YOU.
DROP BY THE HOUSE LATER.
YEAH, YEAH, YEAH, YEAH, YEAH, YEAH, YEAH...
ONCE IS ENOUGH!

Sign: Sukiyaki

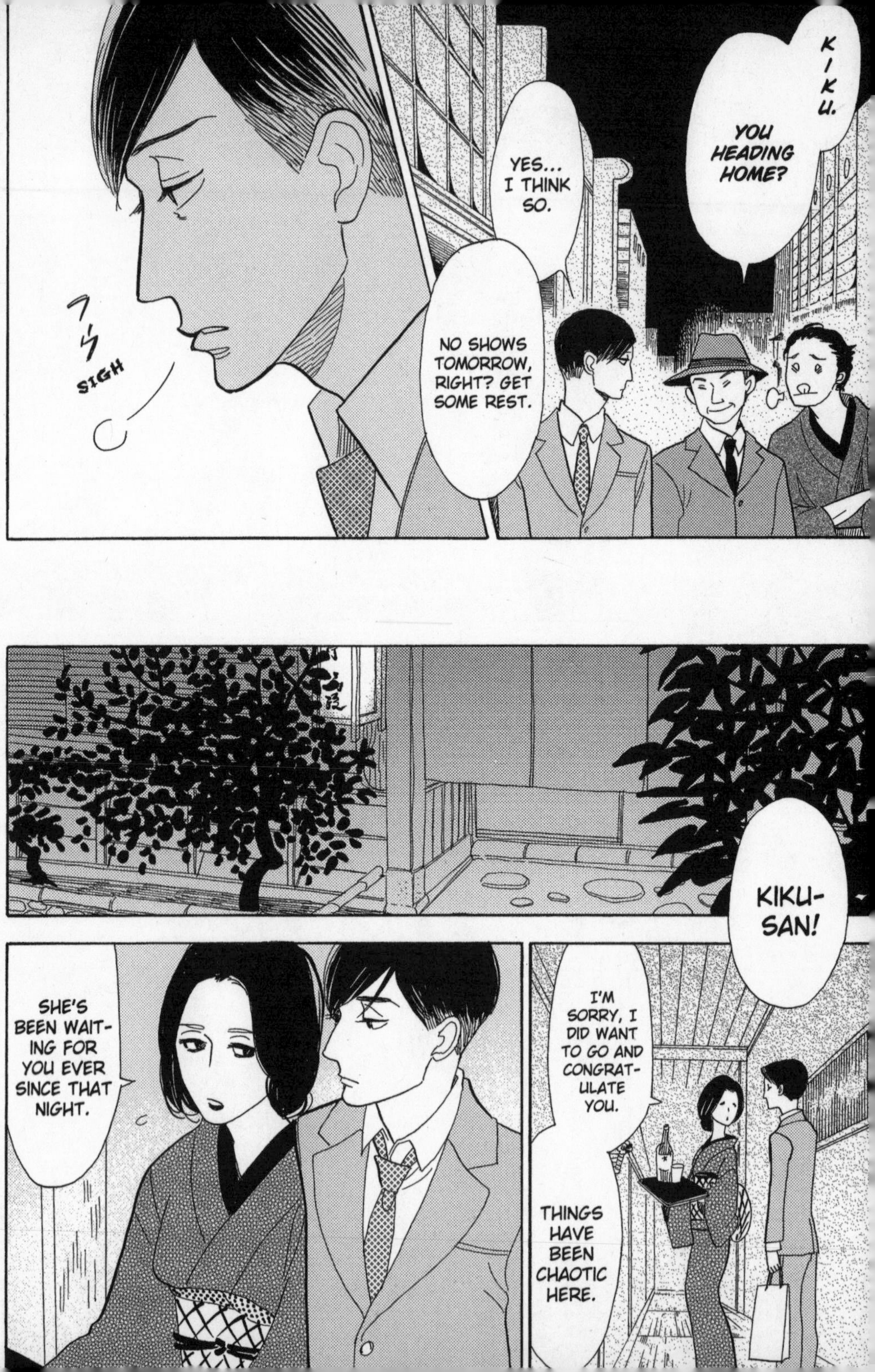

KIKU.
YOU HEADING HOME?
YES... I THINK SO.
NO SHOWS TOMORROW, RIGHT? GET SOME REST.
SIGH
KIKU-SAN!
I'M SORRY, I DID WANT TO GO AND CONGRAT-ULATE YOU.
THINGS HAVE BEEN CHAOTIC HERE.
SHE'S BEEN WAIT-ING FOR YOU EVER SINCE THAT NIGHT.

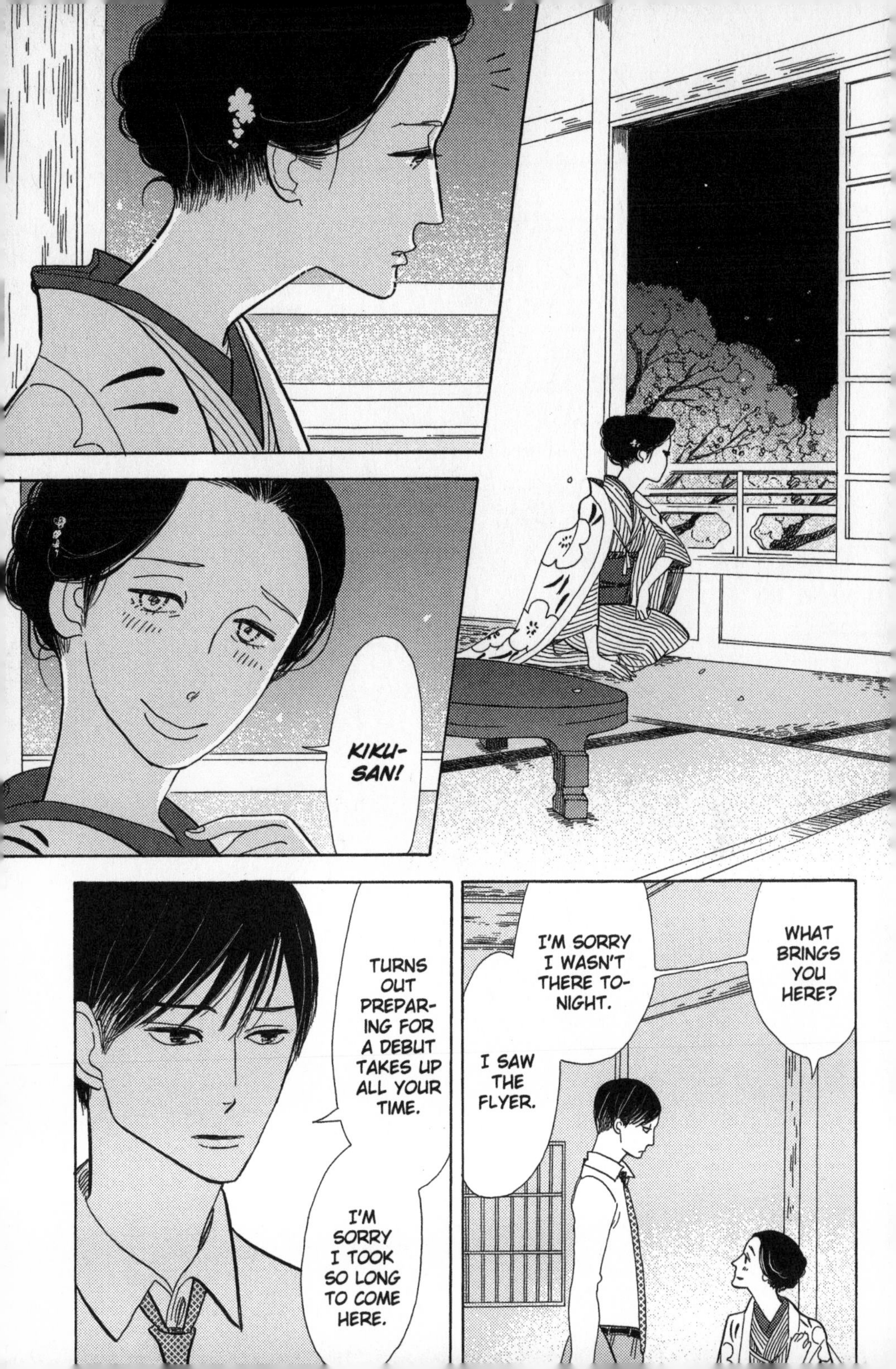
KIKU-SAN!
WHAT BRINGS YOU HERE?
I'M SORRY I WASN'T THERE TO-NIGHT.
I SAW THE FLYER.
TURNS OUT PREPARING FOR A DEBUT TAKES UP ALL YOUR TIME.
I'M SORRY I TOOK SO LONG TO COME HERE.

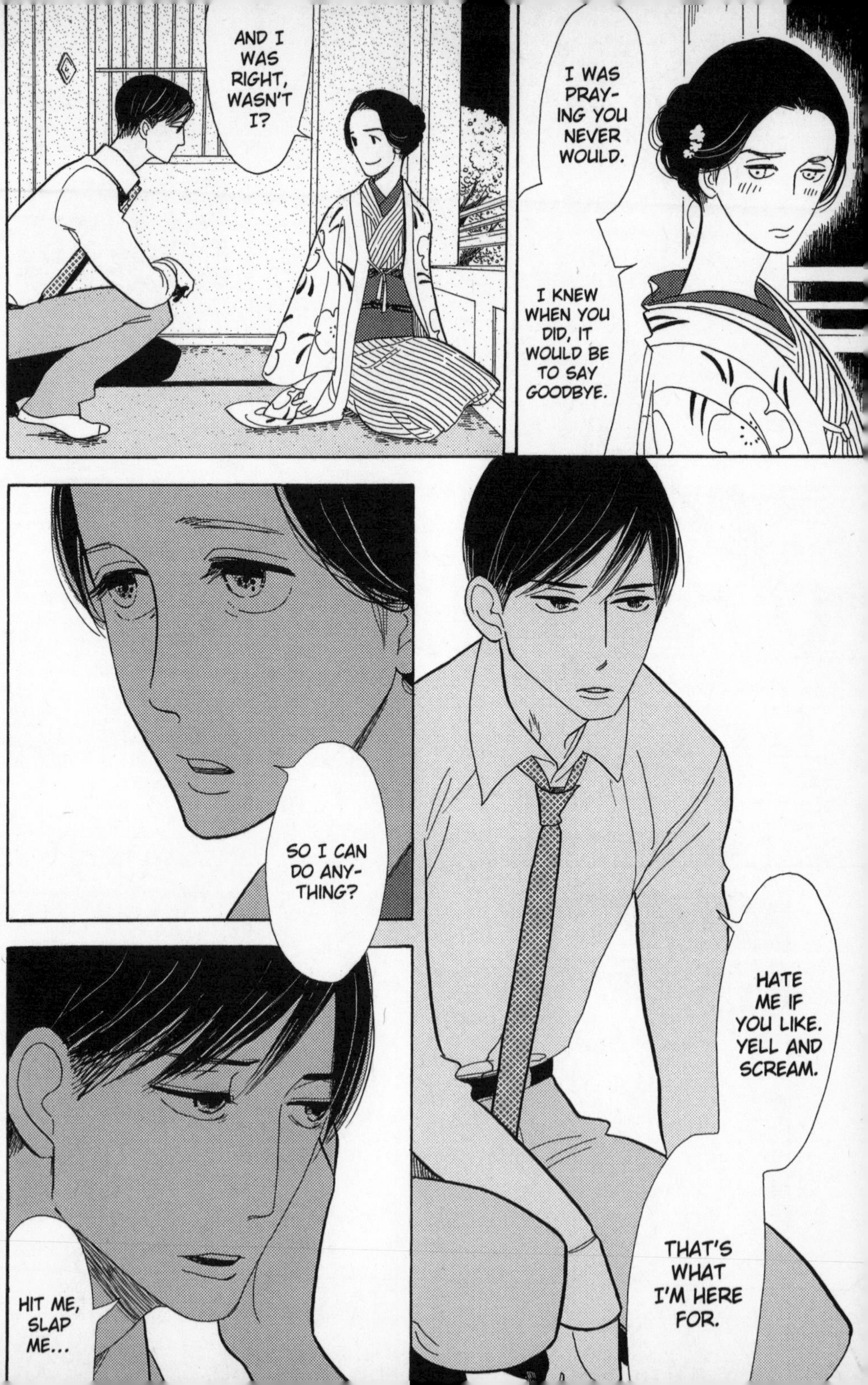
I WAS PRAY-ING YOU NEVER WOULD.
I KNEW WHEN YOU DID, IT WOULD BE TO SAY GOODBYE.
AND I WAS RIGHT, WASN'T I?
SO I CAN DO ANY-THING?
HIT ME, SLAP ME...
HATE ME IF YOU LIKE. YELL AND SCREAM.
THAT'S WHAT I'M HERE FOR.

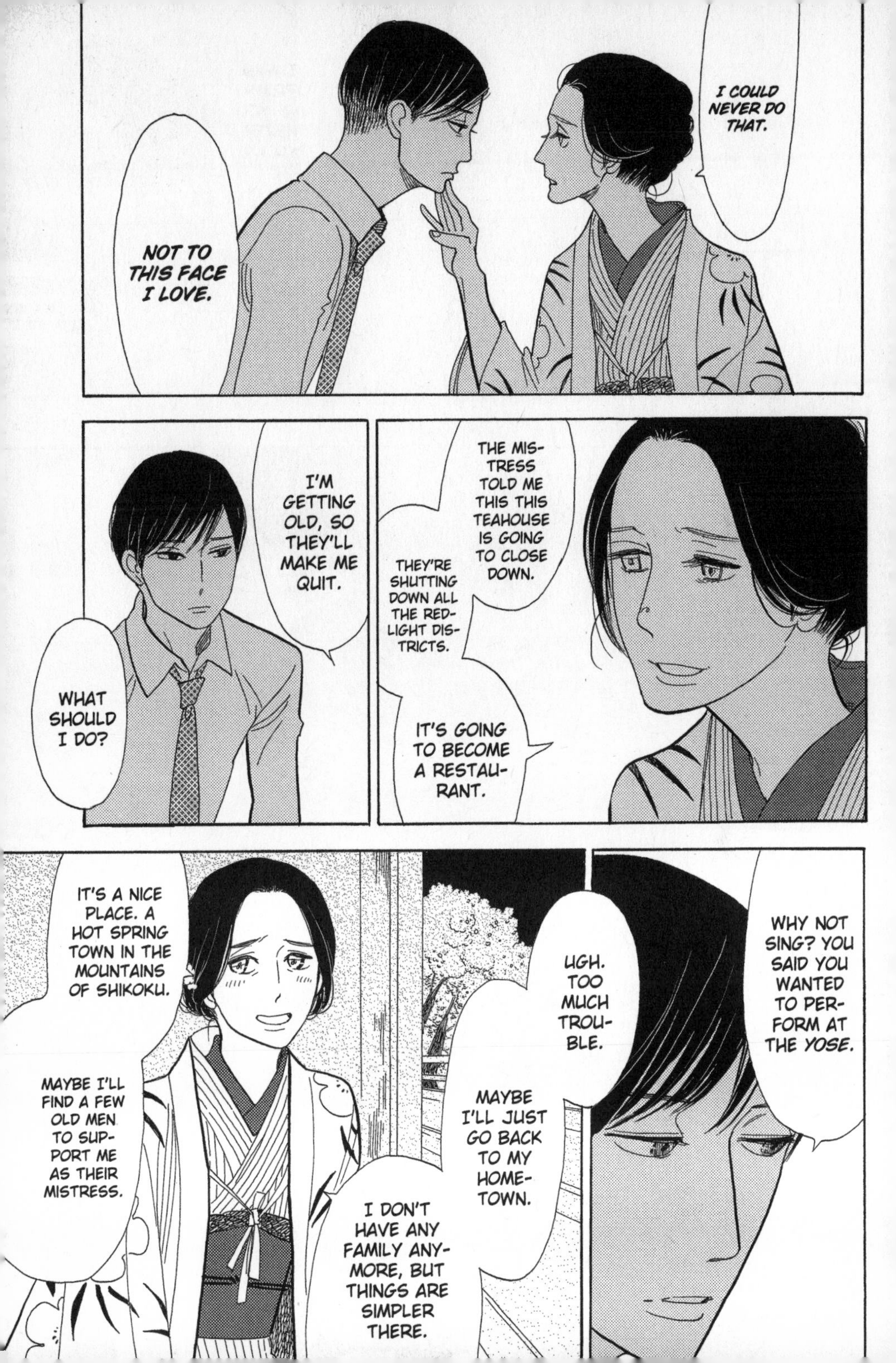
I COULD NEVER DO THAT.
NOT TO THIS FACE I LOVE.
THE MISTRESS TOLD ME THIS THIS TEAHOUSE IS GOING TO CLOSE DOWN.
THEY'RE SHUTTING DOWN ALL THE RED-LIGHT DISTRICTS.
IT'S GOING TO BECOME A RESTAURANT.
I'M GETTING OLD, SO THEY'LL MAKE ME QUIT.
WHAT SHOULD I DO?
WHY NOT SING? YOU SAID YOU WANTED TO PERFORM AT THE *YOSE*.
UGH. TOO MUCH TROUBLE.
MAYBE I'LL JUST GO BACK TO MY HOMETOWN.
I DON'T HAVE ANY FAMILY ANYMORE, BUT THINGS ARE SIMPLER THERE.
IT'S A NICE PLACE. A HOT SPRING TOWN IN THE MOUNTAINS OF SHIKOKU.
MAYBE I'LL FIND A FEW OLD MEN TO SUPPORT ME AS THEIR MISTRESS.

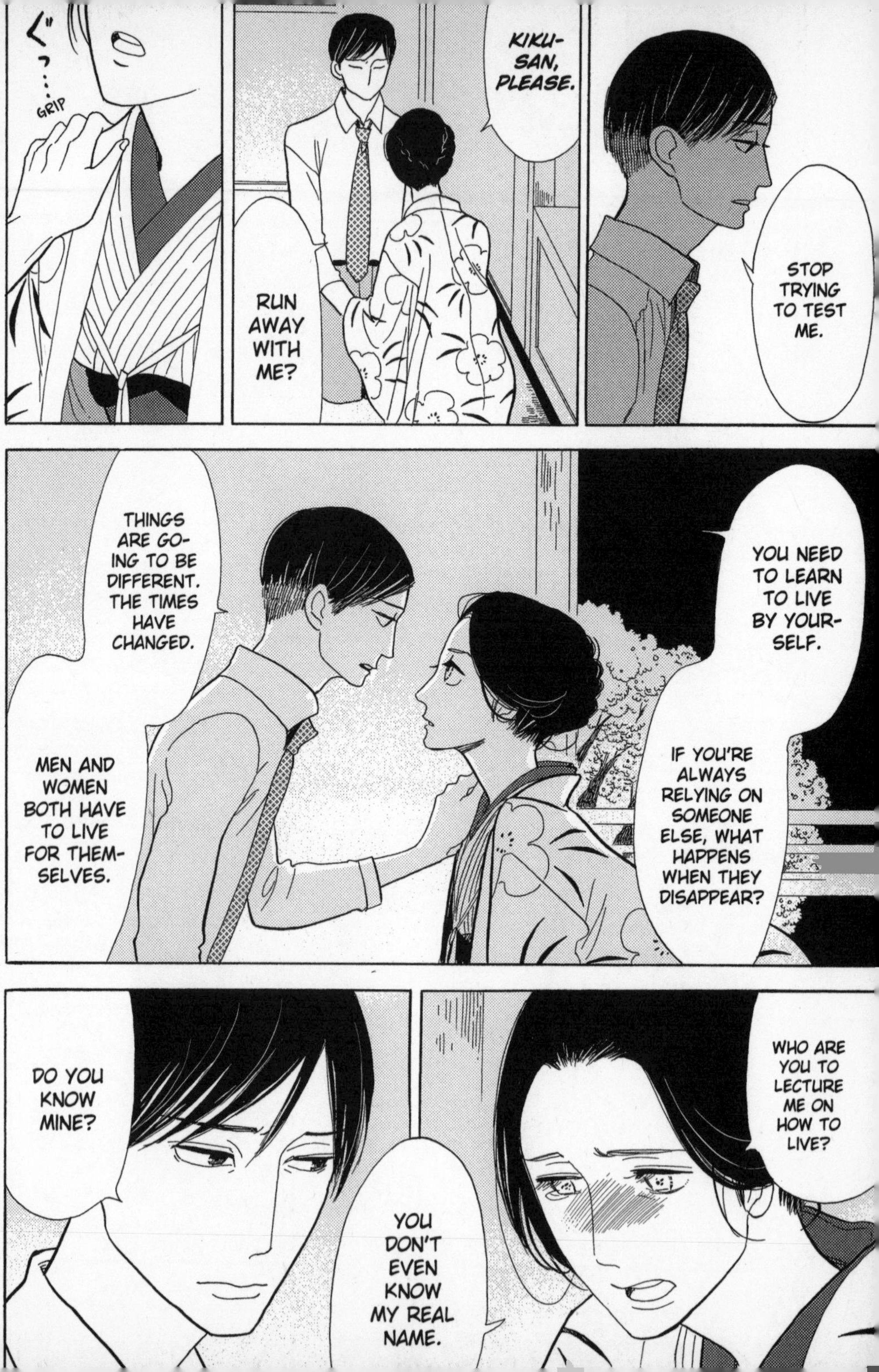
STOP TRYING TO TEST ME.
KIKU-SAN, PLEASE.
RUN AWAY WITH ME?
ぐっ…
GRIP
YOU NEED TO LEARN TO LIVE BY YOURSELF.
IF YOU'RE ALWAYS RELYING ON SOMEONE ELSE, WHAT HAPPENS WHEN THEY DISAPPEAR?
THINGS ARE GOING TO BE DIFFERENT. THE TIMES HAVE CHANGED.
MEN AND WOMEN BOTH HAVE TO LIVE FOR THEMSELVES.
WHO ARE YOU TO LECTURE ME ON HOW TO LIVE?
YOU DON'T EVEN KNOW MY REAL NAME.
DO YOU KNOW MINE?

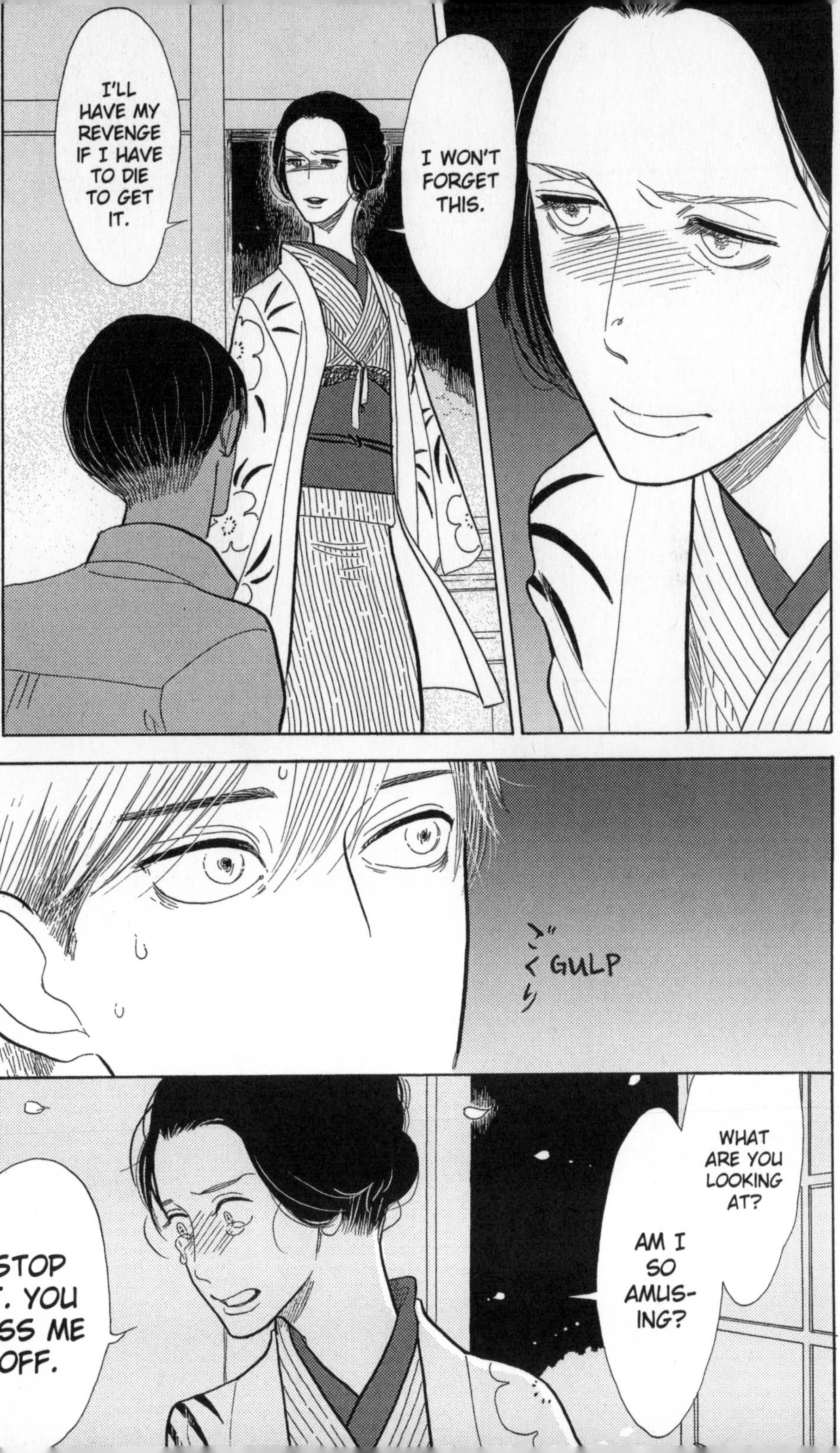
I WON'T FORGET THIS.
I'LL HAVE MY REVENGE IF I HAVE TO DIE TO GET IT.
GULP
WHAT ARE YOU LOOKING AT?
AM I SO AMUSING?
STOP IT. YOU PISS ME OFF.

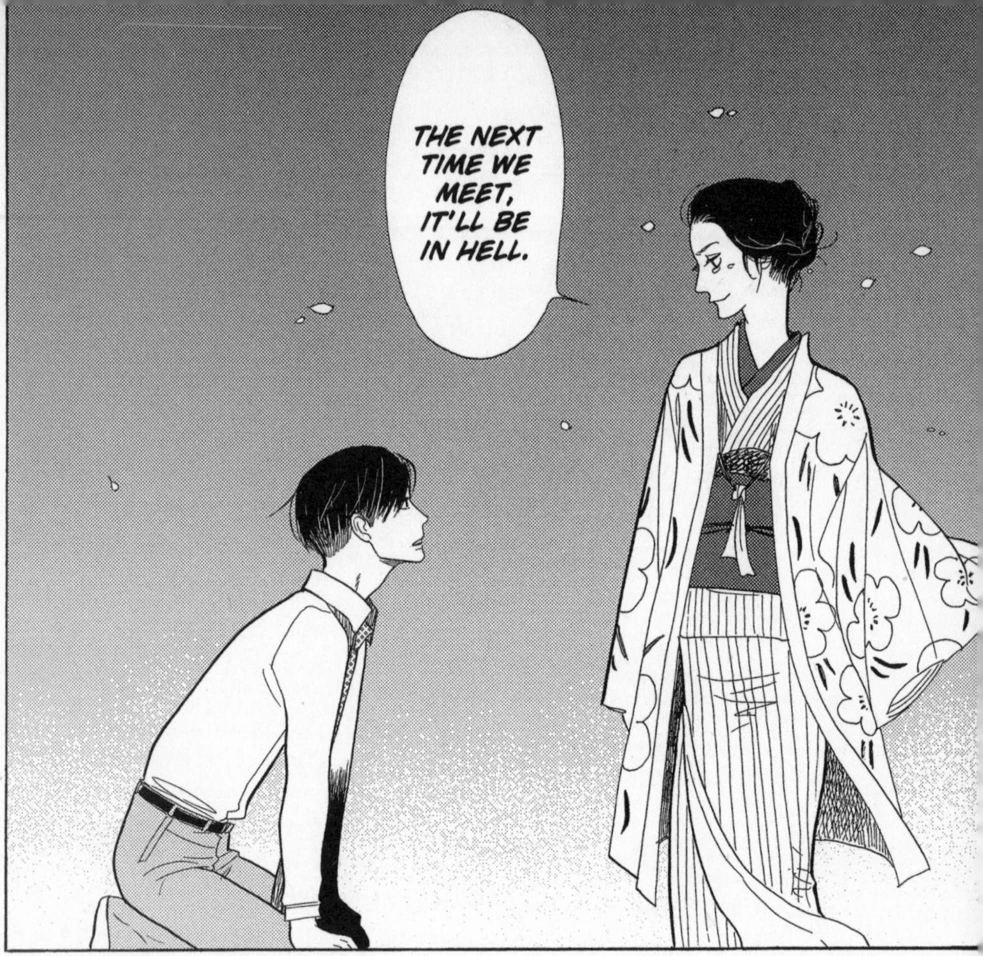
THE NEXT TIME WE MEET, IT'LL BE IN HELL.
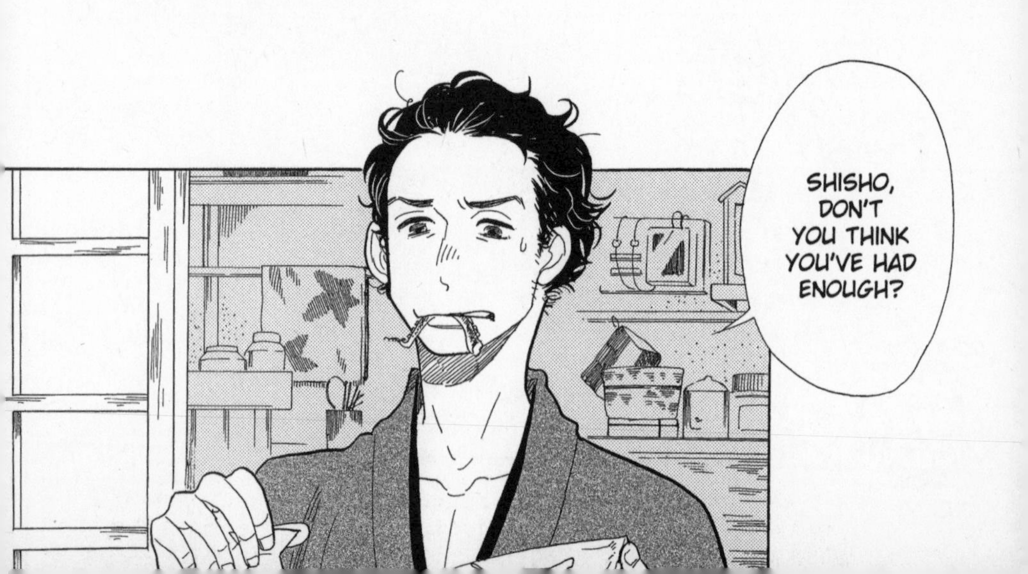
SHISHO, DON'T YOU THINK YOU'VE HAD ENOUGH?

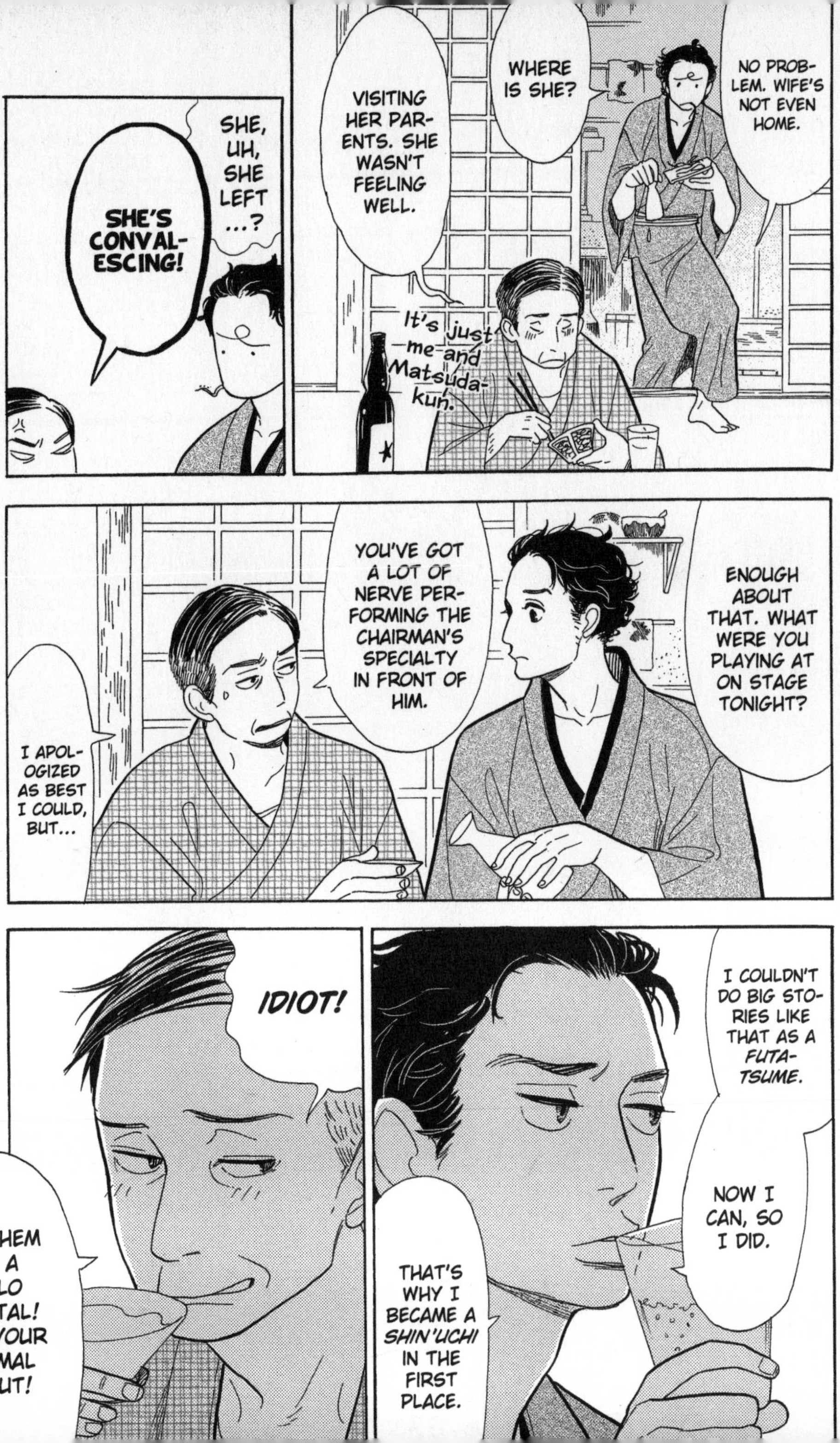
NO PROBLEM. WIFE'S NOT EVEN HOME.
WHERE IS SHE?
VISITING HER PARENTS. SHE WASN'T FEELING WELL.
It's just me and Matsuda-kun.
SHE, UH, SHE LEFT ...?
SHE'S CONVALESCING!
ENOUGH ABOUT THAT. WHAT WERE YOU PLAYING AT ON STAGE TONIGHT?
YOU'VE GOT A LOT OF NERVE PERFORMING THE CHAIRMAN'S SPECIALTY IN FRONT OF HIM.
I APOLOGIZED AS BEST I COULD, BUT...
I COULDN'T DO BIG STORIES LIKE THAT AS A *FUTATSUME*.
NOW I CAN, SO I DID.
THAT'S WHY I BECAME A *SHIN'UCHI* IN THE FIRST PLACE.
IDIOT!
DO THEM AT A SOLO RECITAL! NOT YOUR FORMAL DEBUT!

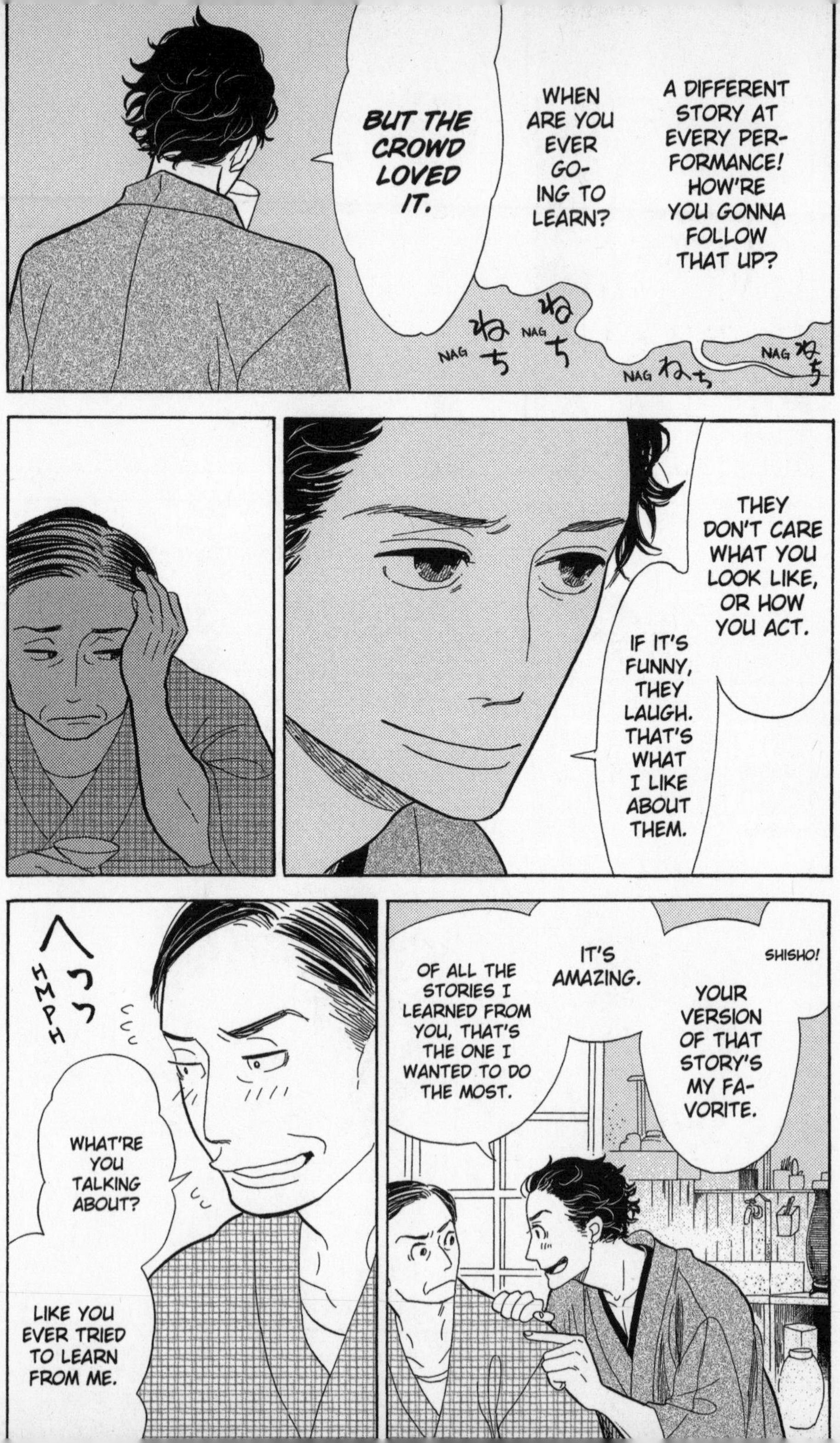
A DIFFERENT STORY AT EVERY PERFORMANCE! HOW'RE YOU GONNA FOLLOW THAT UP?
WHEN ARE YOU EVER GOING TO LEARN?
BUT THE CROWD LOVED IT.
NAG ねち NAG ねち NAG ねち NAG ねち
THEY DON'T CARE WHAT YOU LOOK LIKE, OR HOW YOU ACT.
IF IT'S FUNNY, THEY LAUGH. THAT'S WHAT I LIKE ABOUT THEM.
SHISHO!
YOUR VERSION OF THAT STORY'S MY FAVORITE.
IT'S AMAZING.
OF ALL THE STORIES I LEARNED FROM YOU, THAT'S THE ONE I WANTED TO DO THE MOST.
HMPH へっ
WHAT'RE YOU TALKING ABOUT?
LIKE YOU EVER TRIED TO LEARN FROM ME.

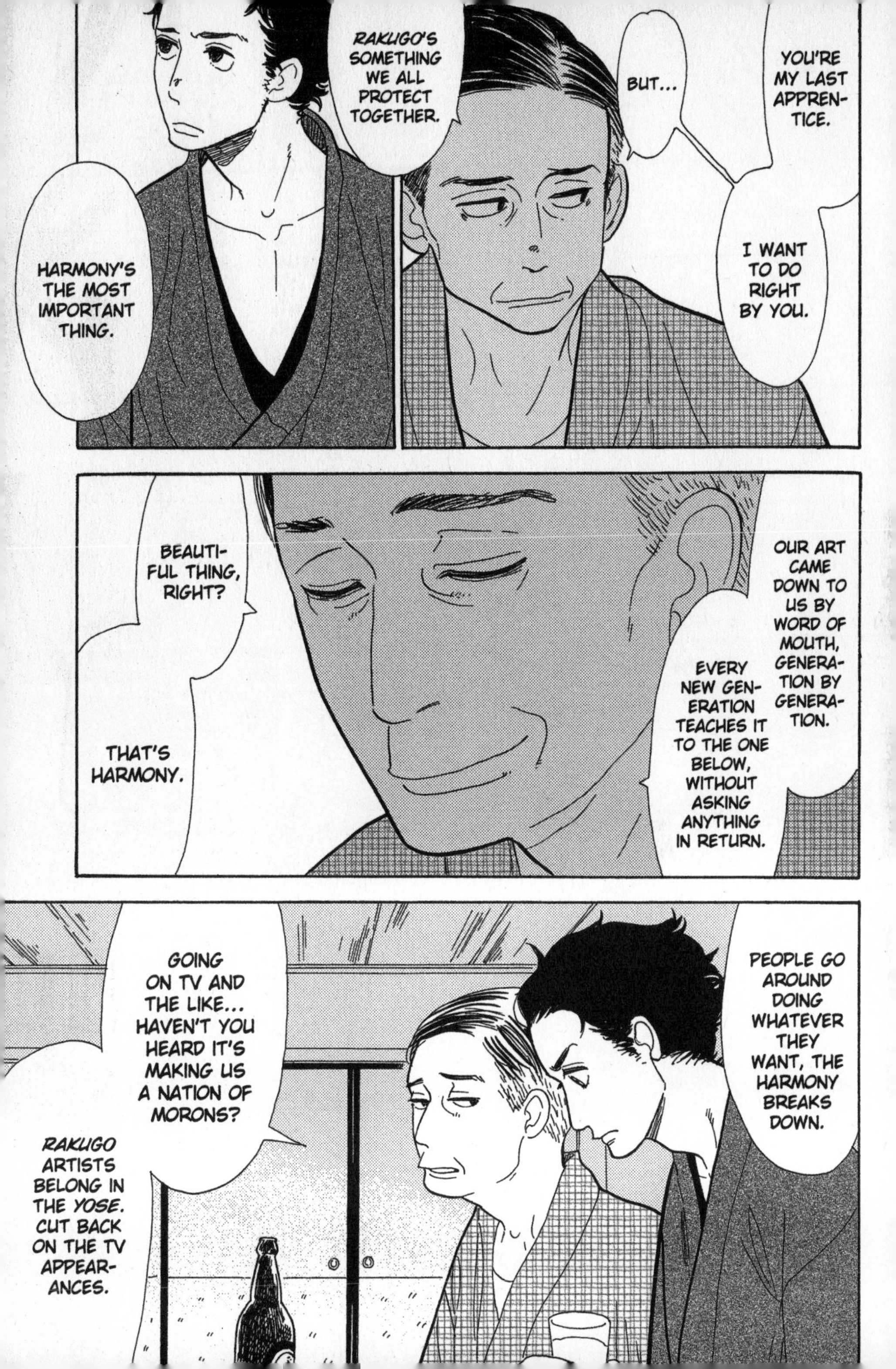
YOU'RE MY LAST APPRENTICE.
I WANT TO DO RIGHT BY YOU.
BUT...
RAKUGO'S SOMETHING WE ALL PROTECT TOGETHER.
HARMONY'S THE MOST IMPORTANT THING.
OUR ART CAME DOWN TO US BY WORD OF MOUTH, GENERATION BY GENERATION.
EVERY NEW GENERATION TEACHES IT TO THE ONE BELOW, WITHOUT ASKING ANYTHING IN RETURN.
BEAUTIFUL THING, RIGHT?
THAT'S HARMONY.
PEOPLE GO AROUND DOING WHATEVER THEY WANT, THE HARMONY BREAKS DOWN.
GOING ON TV AND THE LIKE... HAVEN'T YOU HEARD IT'S MAKING US A NATION OF MORONS?
RAKUGO ARTISTS BELONG IN THE *YOSE*. CUT BACK ON THE TV APPEARANCES.

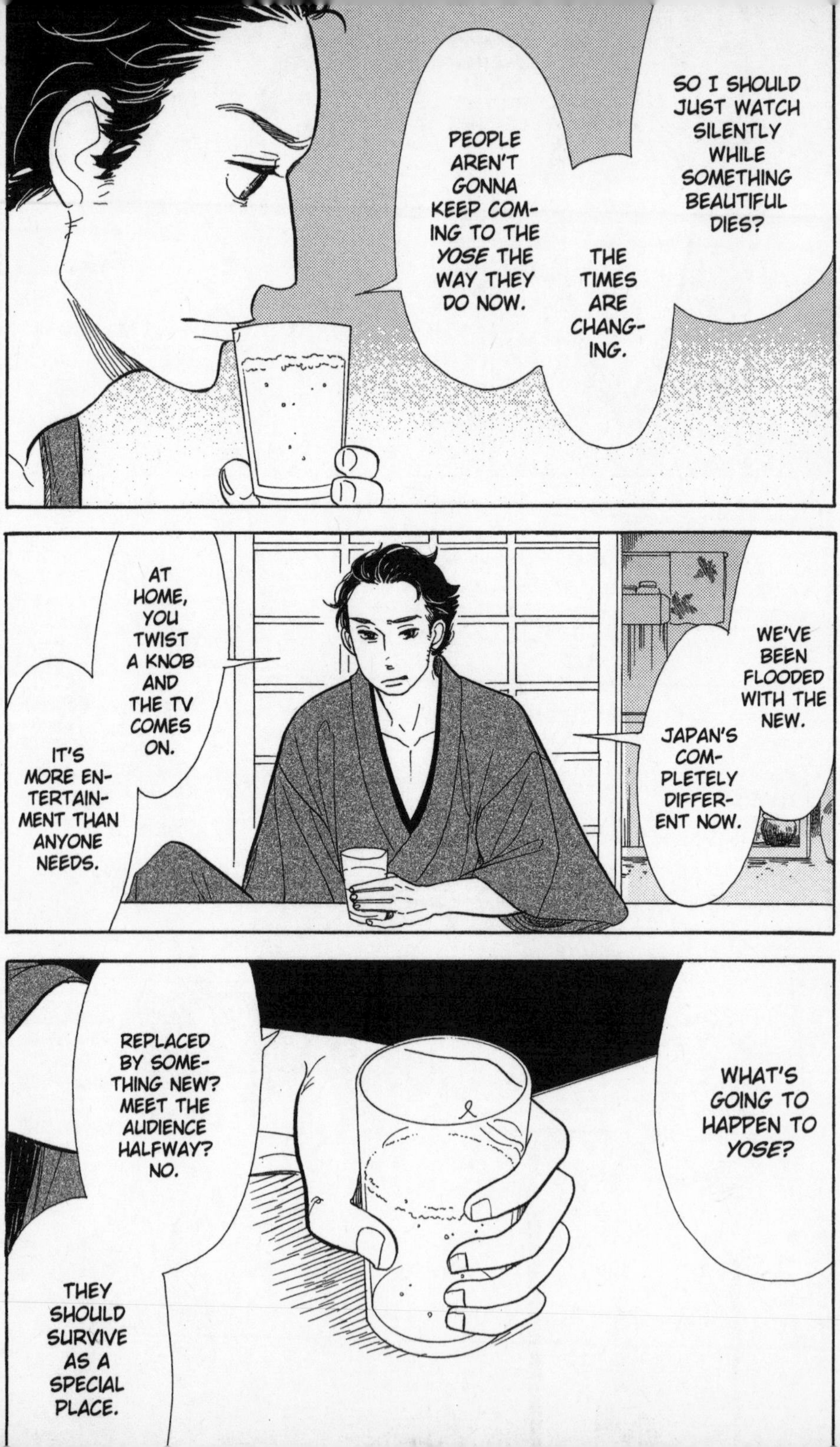
SO I SHOULD JUST WATCH SILENTLY WHILE SOMETHING BEAUTIFUL DIES?
THE TIMES ARE CHANGING.
PEOPLE AREN'T GONNA KEEP COMING TO THE *YOSE* THE WAY THEY DO NOW.
WE'VE BEEN FLOODED WITH THE NEW.
JAPAN'S COMPLETELY DIFFERENT NOW.
AT HOME, YOU TWIST A KNOB AND THE TV COMES ON.
IT'S MORE ENTERTAINMENT THAN ANYONE NEEDS.
WHAT'S GOING TO HAPPEN TO *YOSE?*
REPLACED BY SOMETHING NEW? MEET THE AUDIENCE HALFWAY? NO.
THEY SHOULD SURVIVE AS A SPECIAL PLACE.

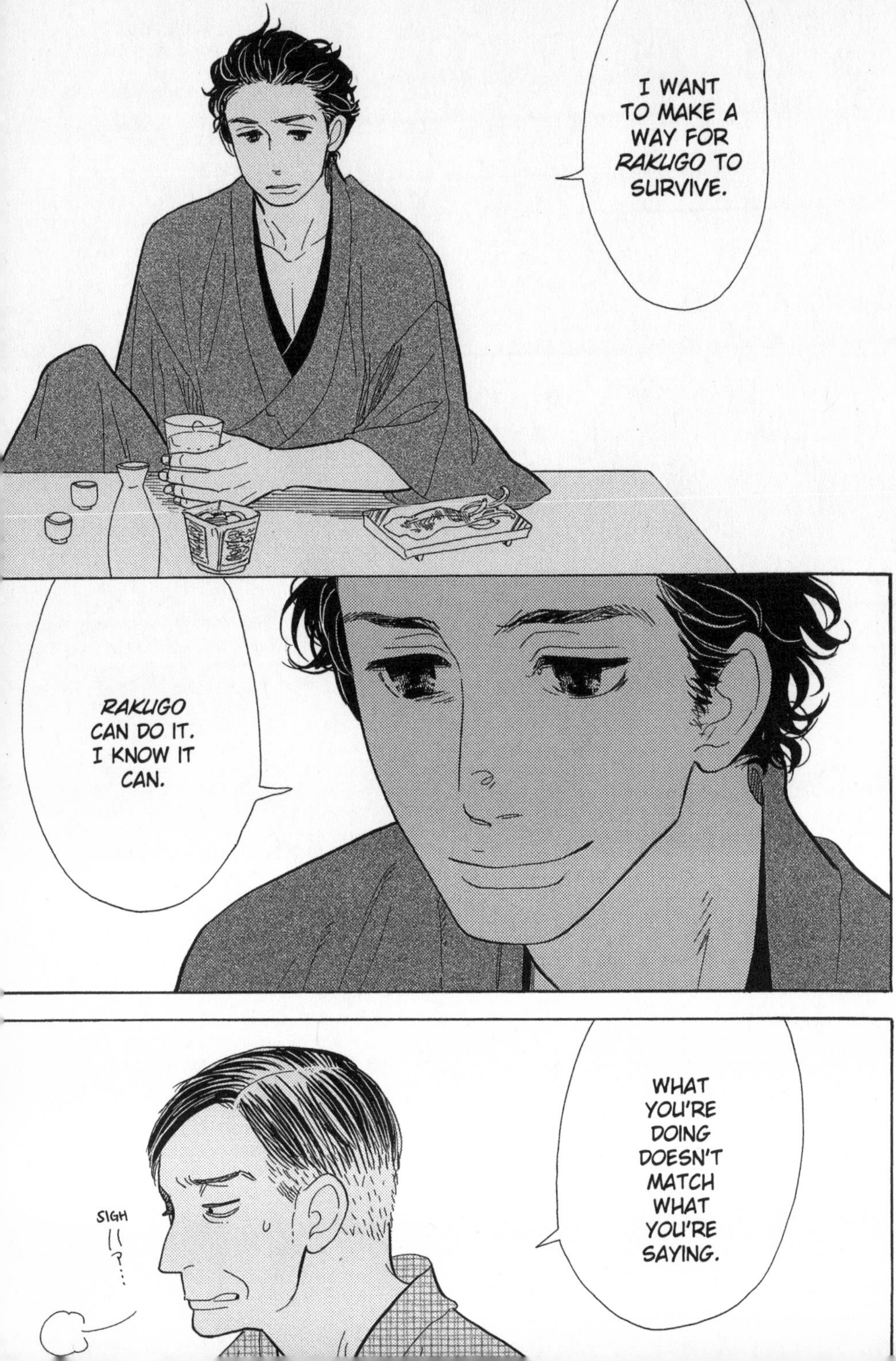
I WANT TO MAKE A WAY FOR *RAKUGO* TO SURVIVE.
RAKUGO CAN DO IT. I KNOW IT CAN.
WHAT YOU'RE DOING DOESN'T MATCH WHAT YOU'RE SAYING.
SIGH

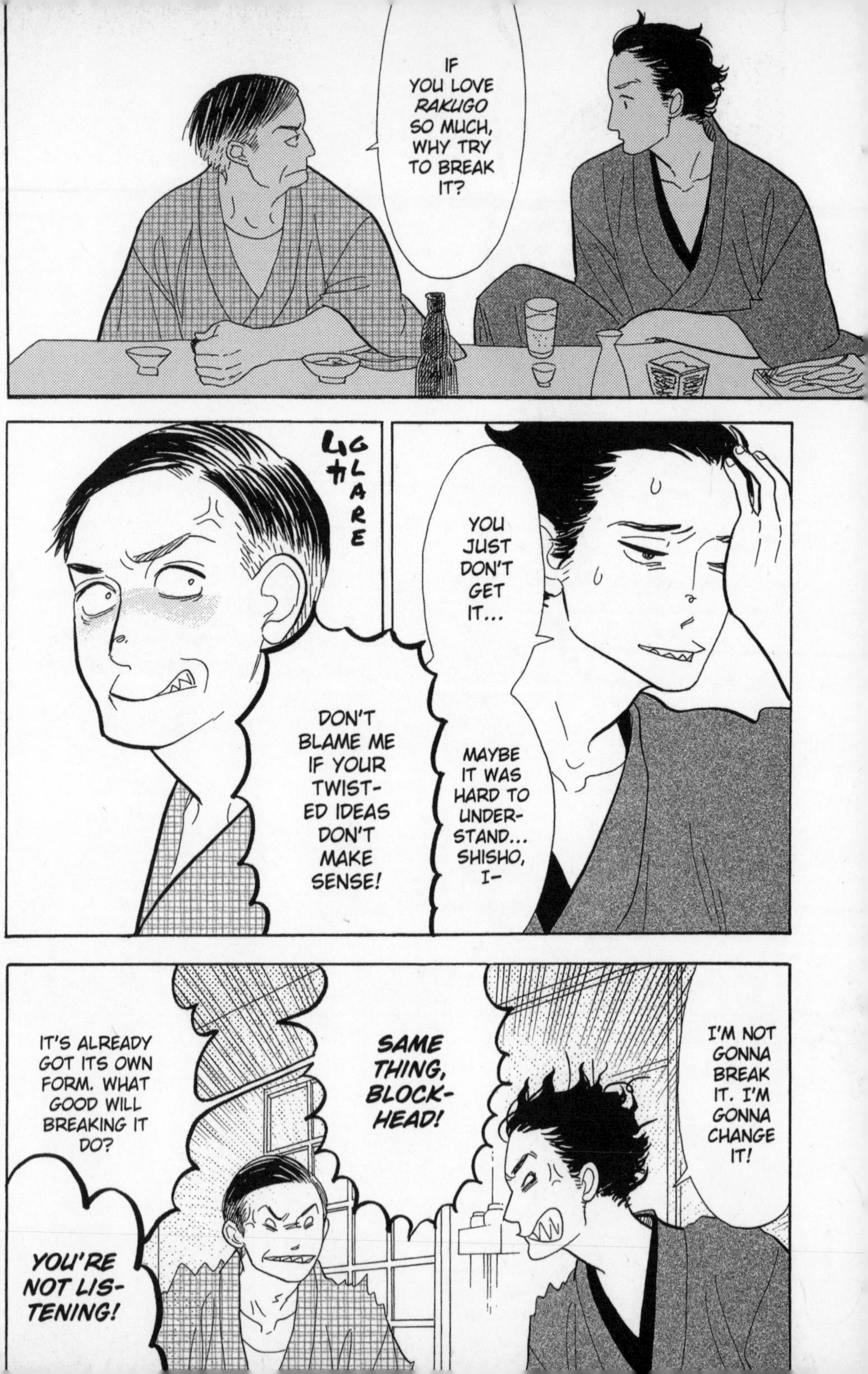
IF YOU LOVE *RAKUGO* SO MUCH, WHY TRY TO BREAK IT?
YOU JUST DON'T GET IT...
MAYBE IT WAS HARD TO UNDERSTAND... SHISHO, I-
GLARE
DON'T BLAME ME IF YOUR TWISTED IDEAS DON'T MAKE SENSE!
I'M NOT GONNA BREAK IT. I'M GONNA CHANGE IT!
SAME THING, BLOCKHEAD!
IT'S ALREADY GOT ITS OWN FORM. WHAT GOOD WILL BREAKING IT DO?
YOU'RE NOT LISTENING!

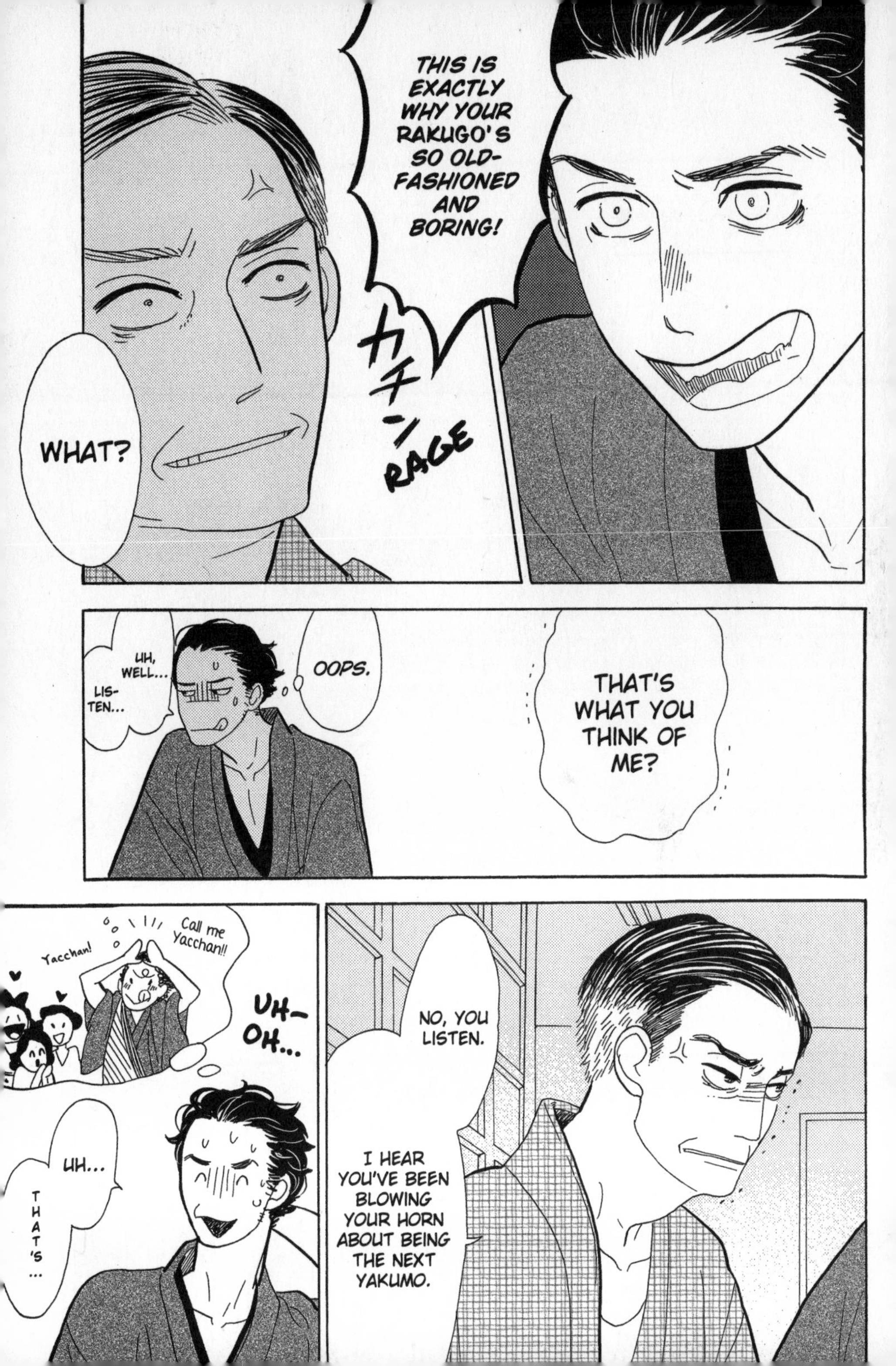
THIS IS EXACTLY WHY YOUR RAKUGO'S SO OLD-FASHIONED AND BORING!
カチン
RAGE
WHAT?
THAT'S WHAT YOU THINK OF ME?
OOPS.
UH, WELL...
LISTEN...
NO, YOU LISTEN.
I HEAR YOU'VE BEEN BLOWING YOUR HORN ABOUT BEING THE NEXT YAKUMO.
Call me Yacchan!!
Yacchan!
UH-OH...
UH...
THAT'S...

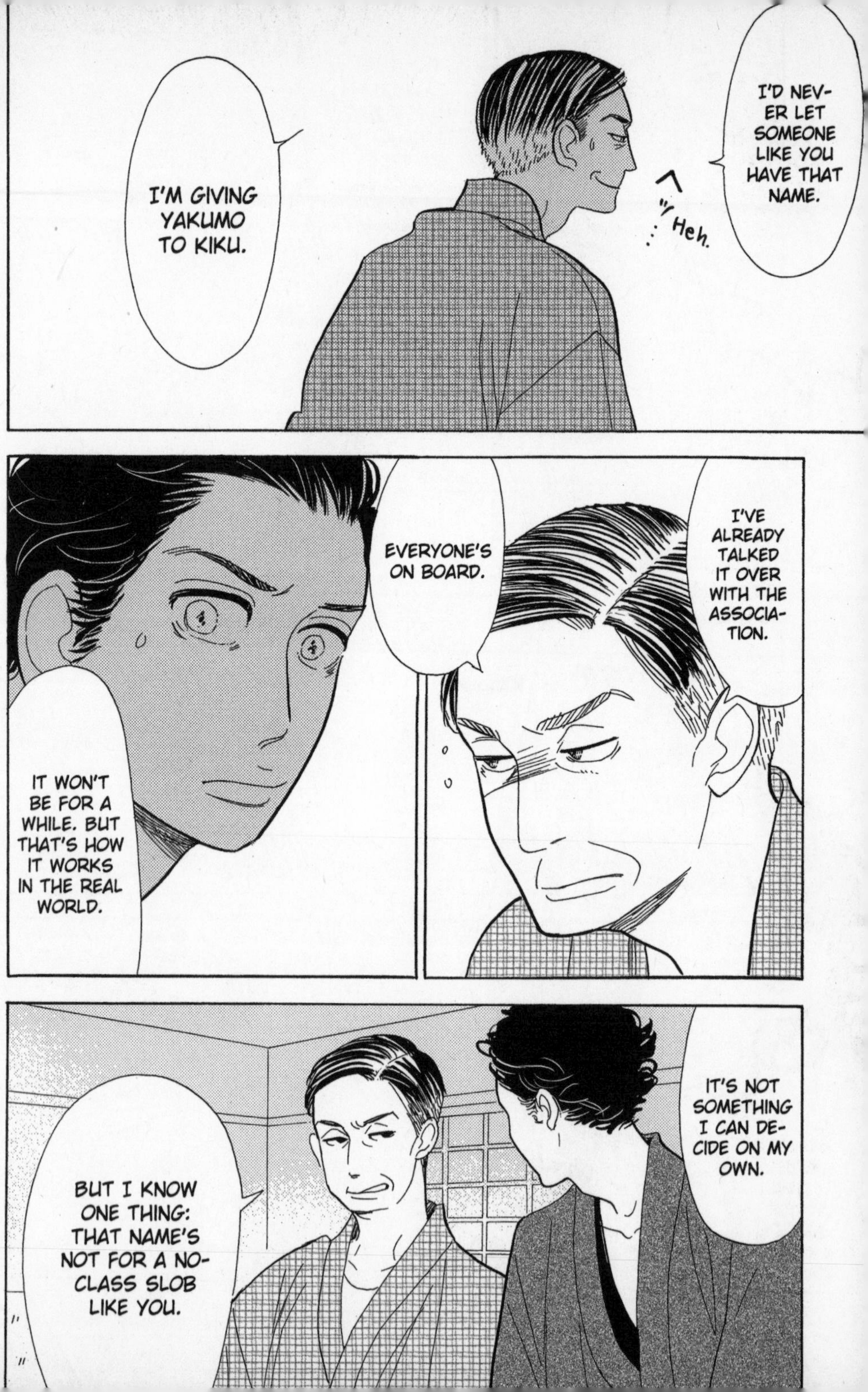
I'D NEVER LET SOMEONE LIKE YOU HAVE THAT NAME.
...Heh.
I'M GIVING YAKUMO TO KIKU.
I'VE ALREADY TALKED IT OVER WITH THE ASSOCIATION.
EVERYONE'S ON BOARD.
IT WON'T BE FOR A WHILE. BUT THAT'S HOW IT WORKS IN THE REAL WORLD.
IT'S NOT SOMETHING I CAN DECIDE ON MY OWN.
BUT I KNOW ONE THING: THAT NAME'S NOT FOR A NO-CLASS SLOB LIKE YOU.

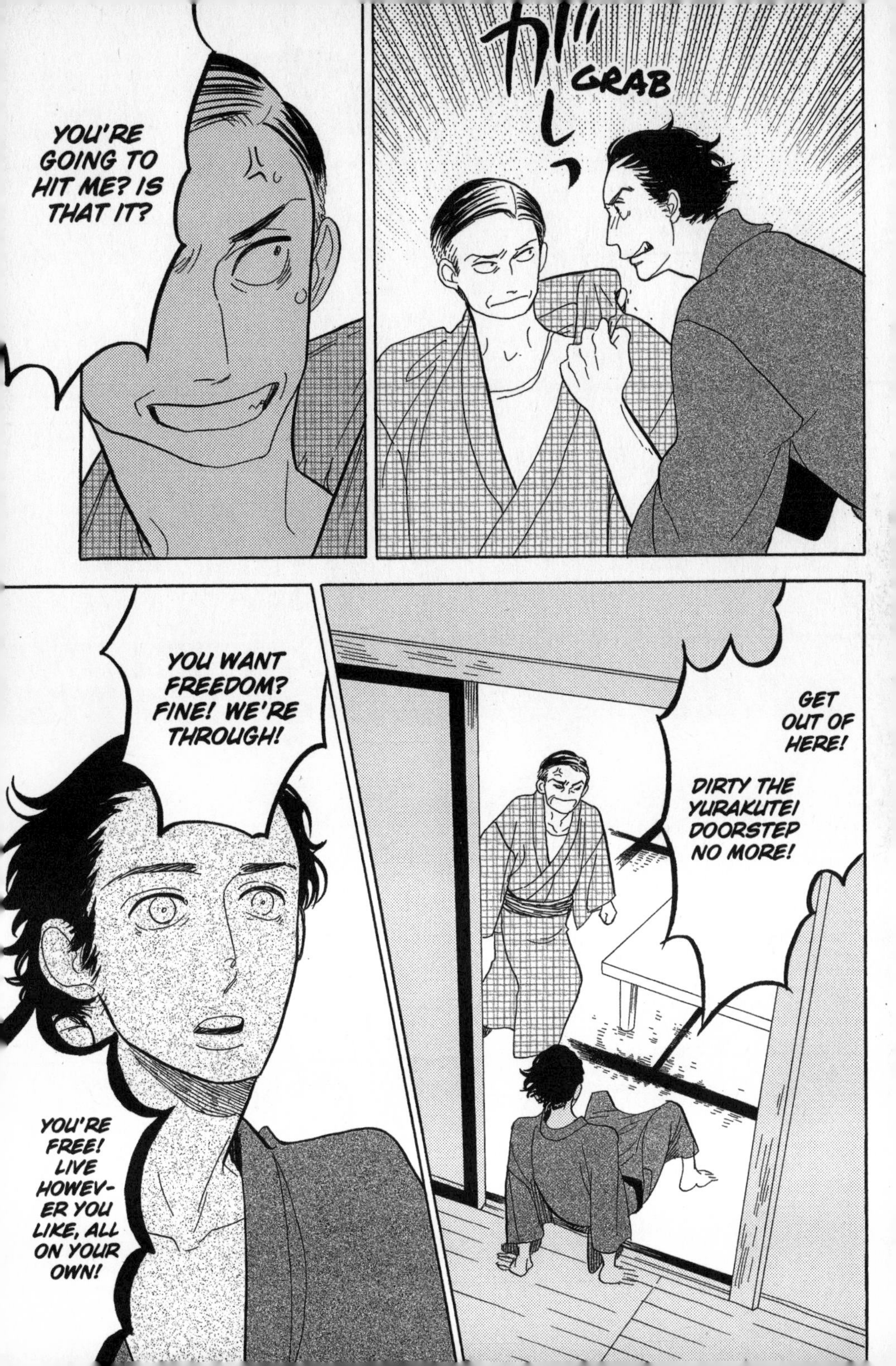

ガしっ
GRAB
YOU'RE GOING TO HIT ME? IS THAT IT?
GET OUT OF HERE!
DIRTY THE YURAKUTEI DOORSTEP NO MORE!
YOU WANT FREEDOM? FINE! WE'RE THROUGH!
YOU'RE FREE! LIVE HOWEVER YOU LIKE, ALL ON YOUR OWN!

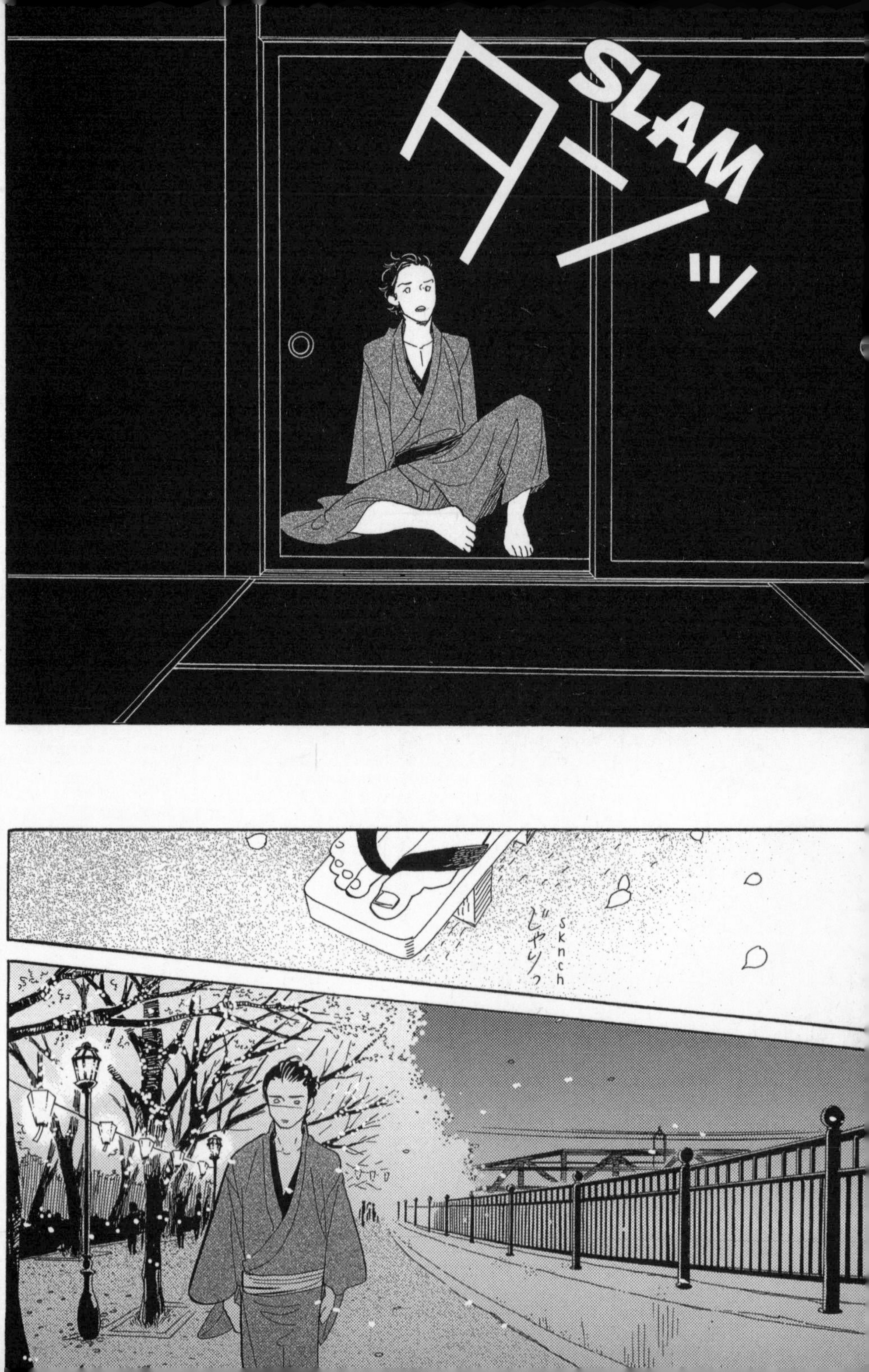
SLAM
じゃりっ
sknch

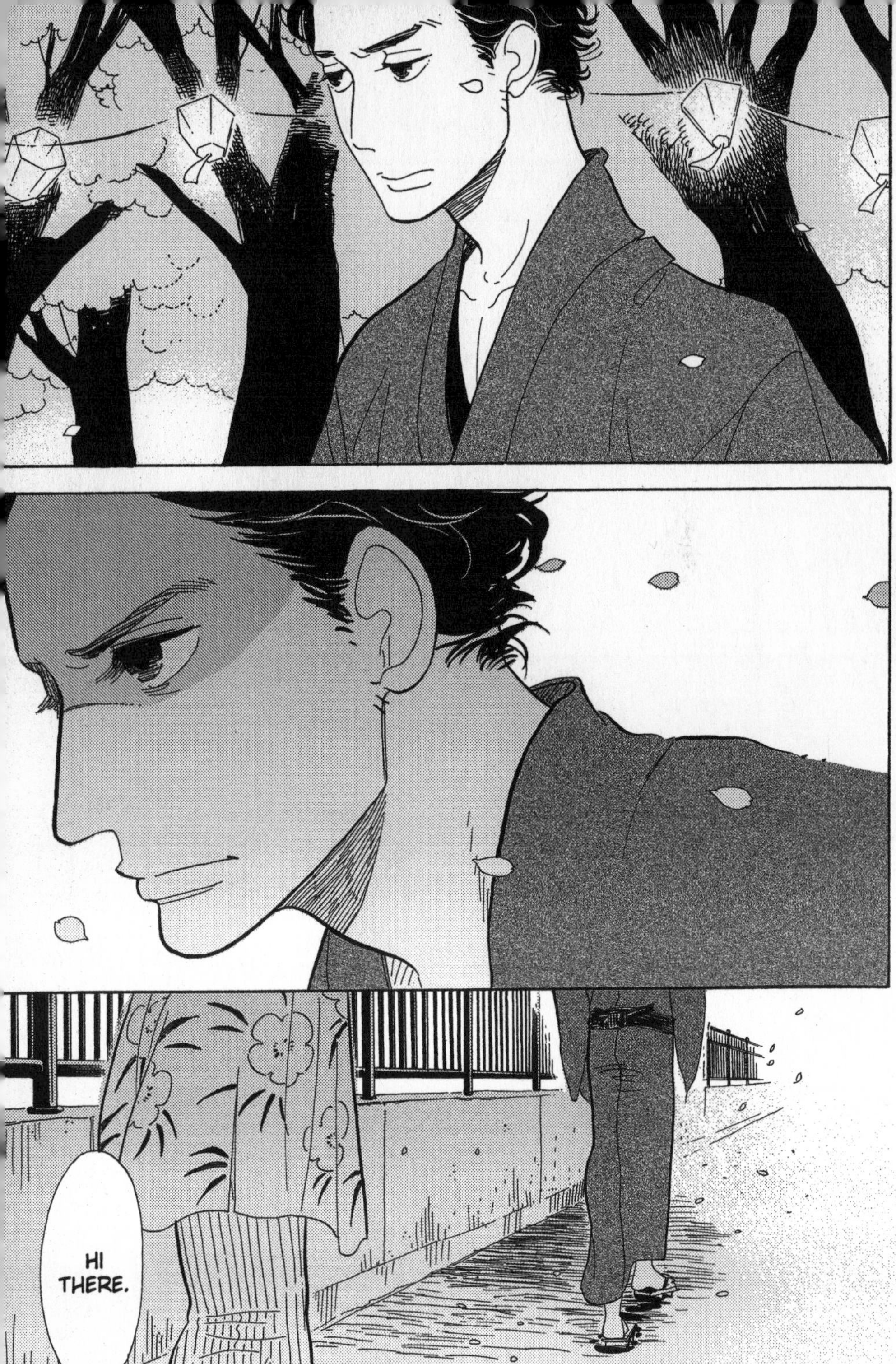
HI THERE.

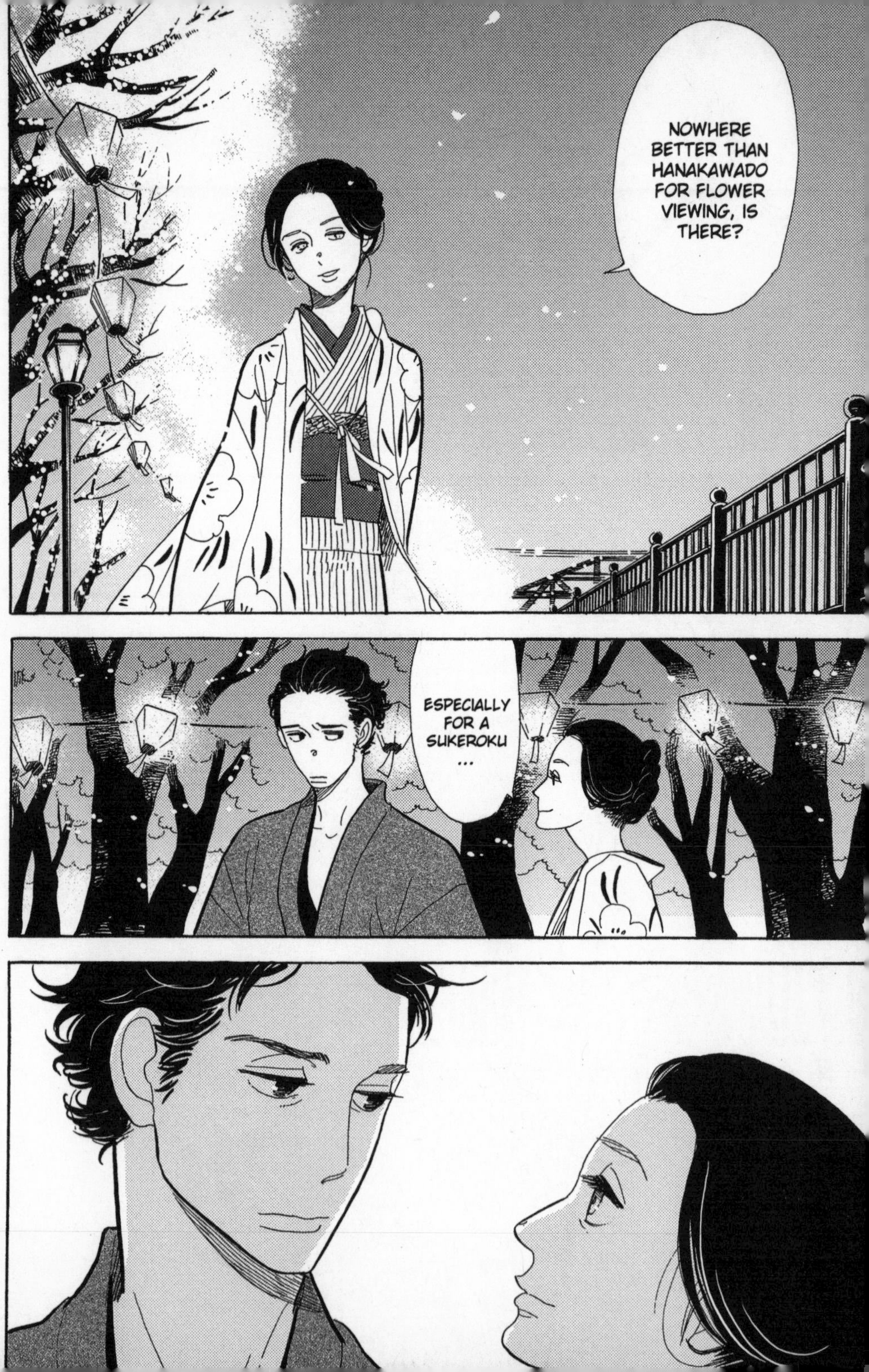
NOWHERE BETTER THAN HANAKAWADO FOR FLOWER VIEWING, IS THERE?
ESPECIALLY FOR A SUKEROKU ...

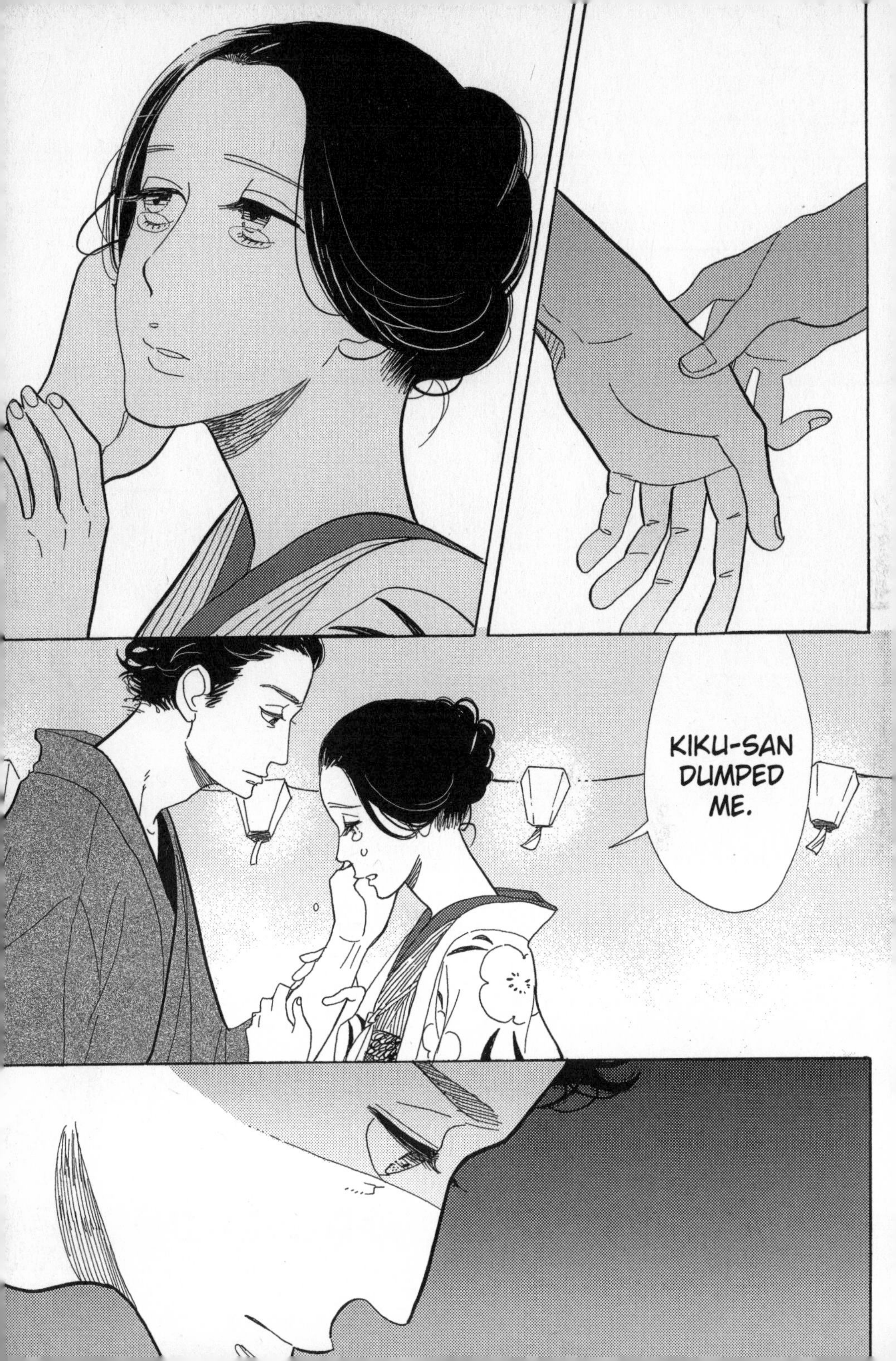
KIKU-SAN DUMPED ME.

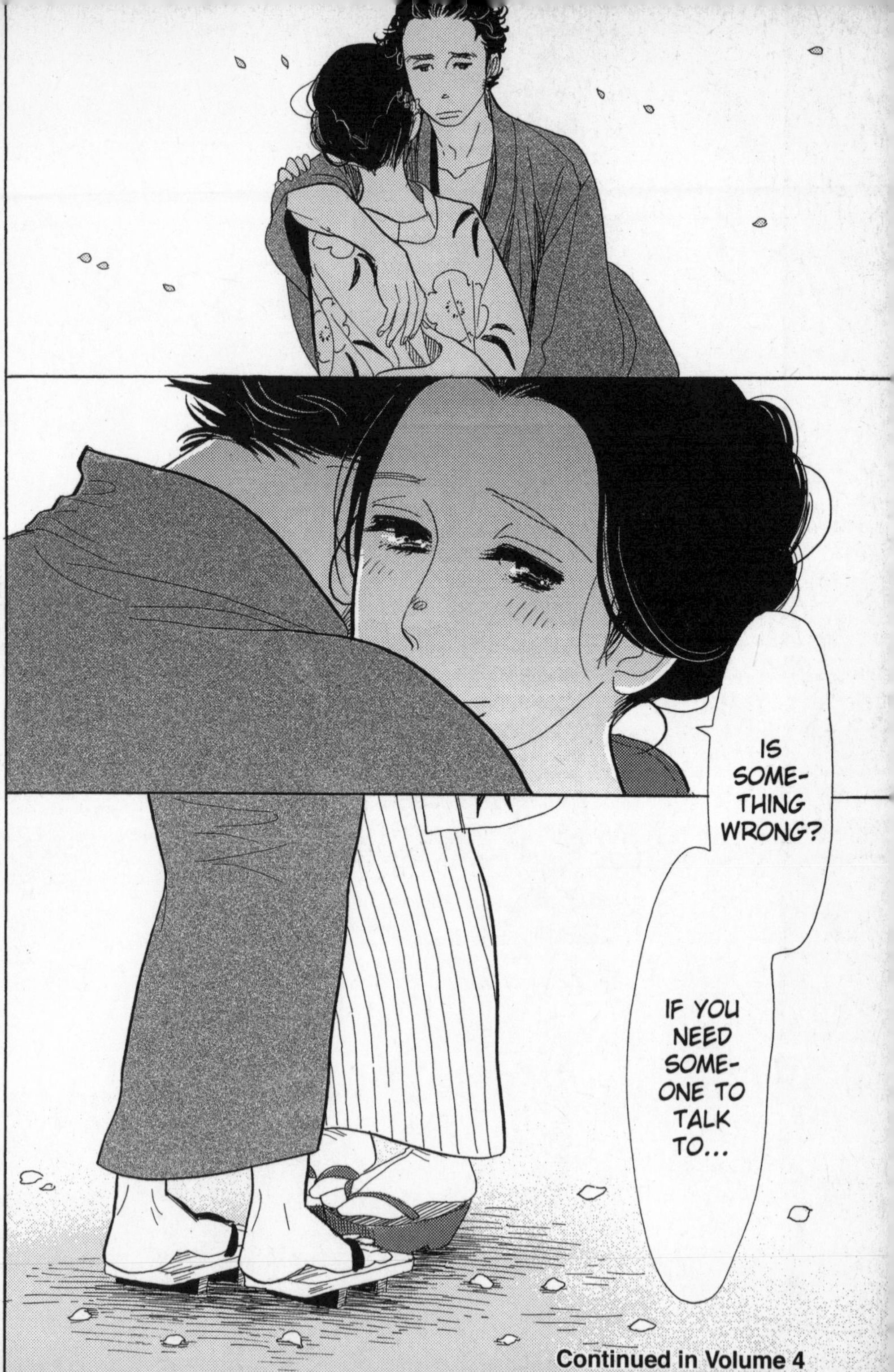
IS SOMETHING WRONG?
IF YOU NEED SOMEONE TO TALK TO...

Continued in Volume 4

Sources

Rakugo Tokusen (Special *Rakugo* Selection), vol. 1 and 2: Chikuma Shobo
Meisaku Rakugo Zenshu (Complete Masterworks of *Rakugo*), vol. 3: Sojinsha Shokyoku
Rakugo: Showa no Meijin Kanketsuban (*Rakugo*: Showa Masters, Complete Edition), vol. 2: Shogakukan

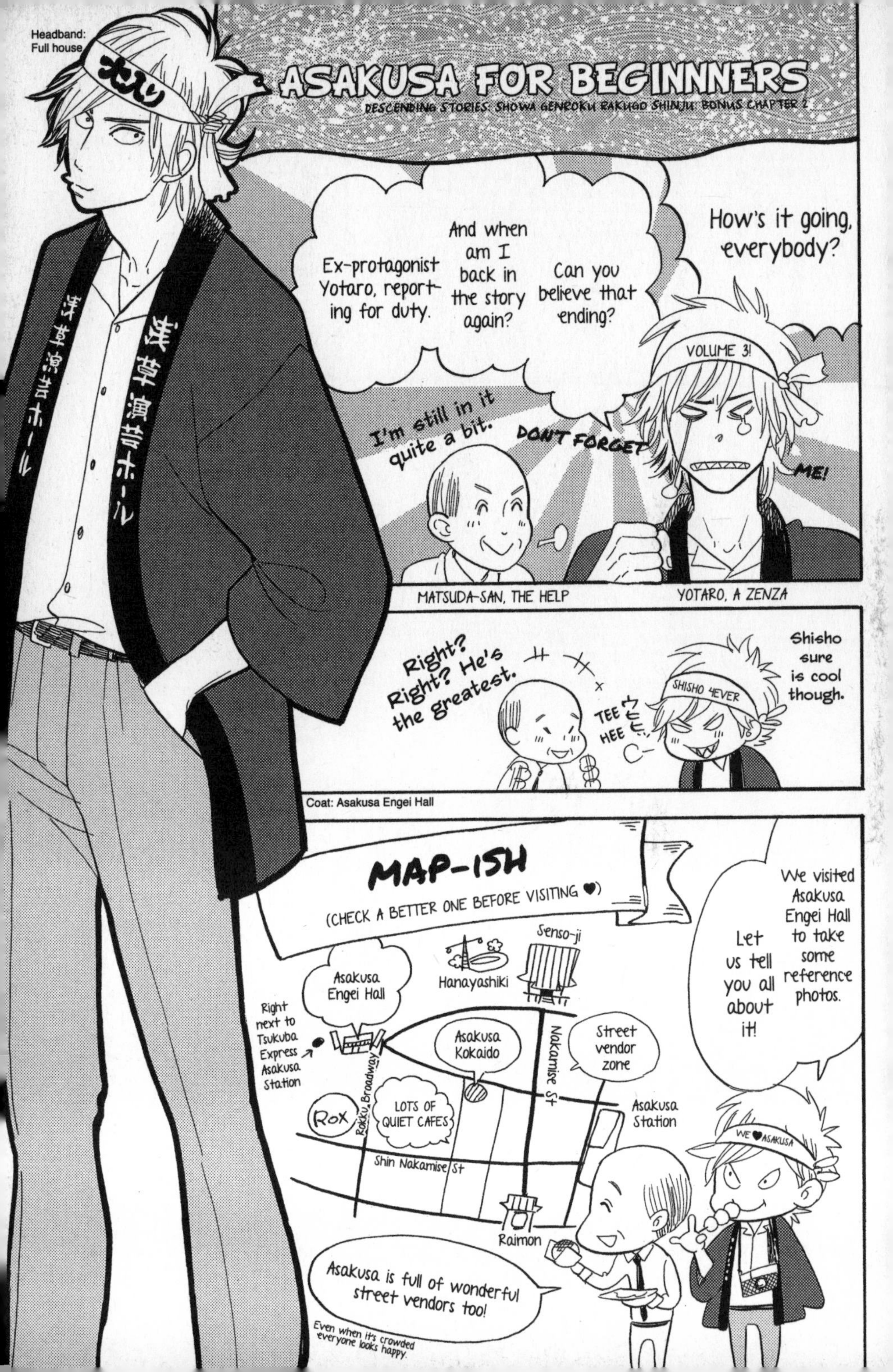
ASAKUSA FOR BEGINNNERS
DESCENDING STORIES: SHOWA GENROKU RAKUGO SHINJU: BONUS CHAPTER 2
How's it going, everybody?
Can you believe that ending?
And when am I back in the story again?
Ex-protagonist Yotaro, reporting for duty.
VOLUME 3!
DON'T FORGET ME!
I'm still in it quite a bit.
YOTARO, A ZENZA
MATSUDA-SAN, THE HELP
Shisho sure is cool though.
SHISHO 4EVER
TEE HEE
Right? Right? He's the greatest.
We visited Asakusa Engei Hall to take some reference photos.
Let us tell you all about it!
MAP-ISH
(CHECK A BETTER ONE BEFORE VISITING ♥)
Senso-ji
Hanayashiki
Asakusa Engei Hall
Right next to Tsukuba Express Asakusa Station
Asakusa Kokaido
Nakamise St
Street vendor zone
Rokku Broadway
Rox
LOTS OF QUIET CAFES
Asakusa Station
Shin Nakamise St
Raimon
WE ♥ ASAKUSA
Asakusa is full of wonderful street vendors too!
Even when it's crowded everyone looks happy.
Headband: Full house
Coat: Asakusa Engei Hall

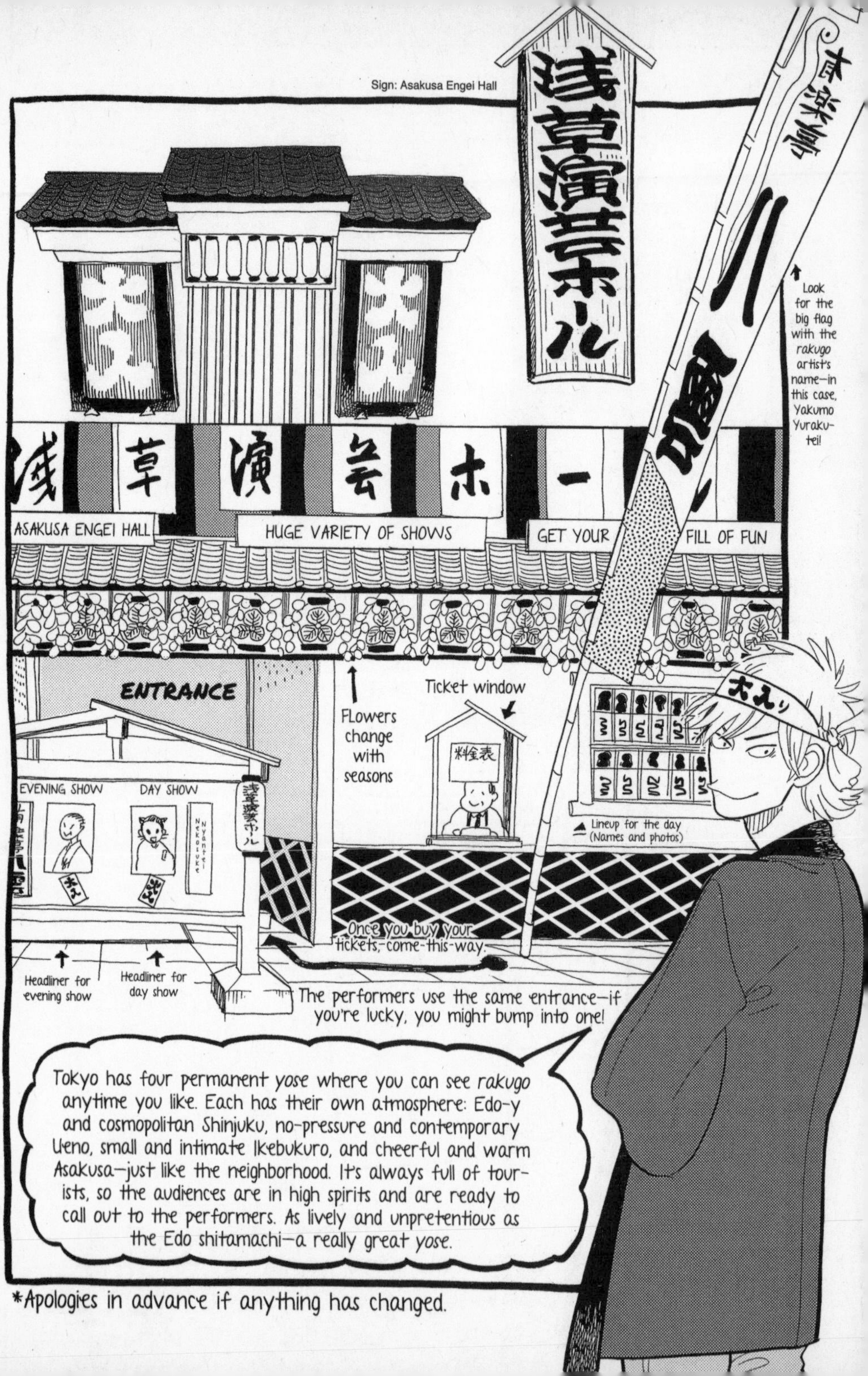
Sign: Asakusa Engei Hall
浅草演芸ホール
Look for the big flag with the rakugo artist's name—in this case, Yakumo Yurakutei!
ASAKUSA ENGEI HALL
HUGE VARIETY OF SHOWS
GET YOUR
FILL OF FUN
ENTRANCE
Flowers change with seasons
Ticket window
料金表
EVENING SHOW
DAY SHOW
Nyantei Nekosuke
Lineup for the day (Names and photos)
Once you buy your tickets, come this way.
Headliner for evening show
Headliner for day show
The performers use the same entrance—if you're lucky, you might bump into one!
Tokyo has four permanent yose where you can see rakugo anytime you like. Each has their own atmosphere: Edo-y and cosmopolitan Shinjuku, no-pressure and contemporary Ueno, small and intimate Ikebukuro, and cheerful and warm Asakusa—just like the neighborhood. It's always full of tourists, so the audiences are in high spirits and are ready to call out to the performers. As lively and unpretentious as the Edo shitamachi—a really great yose.

*Apologies in advance if anything has changed.

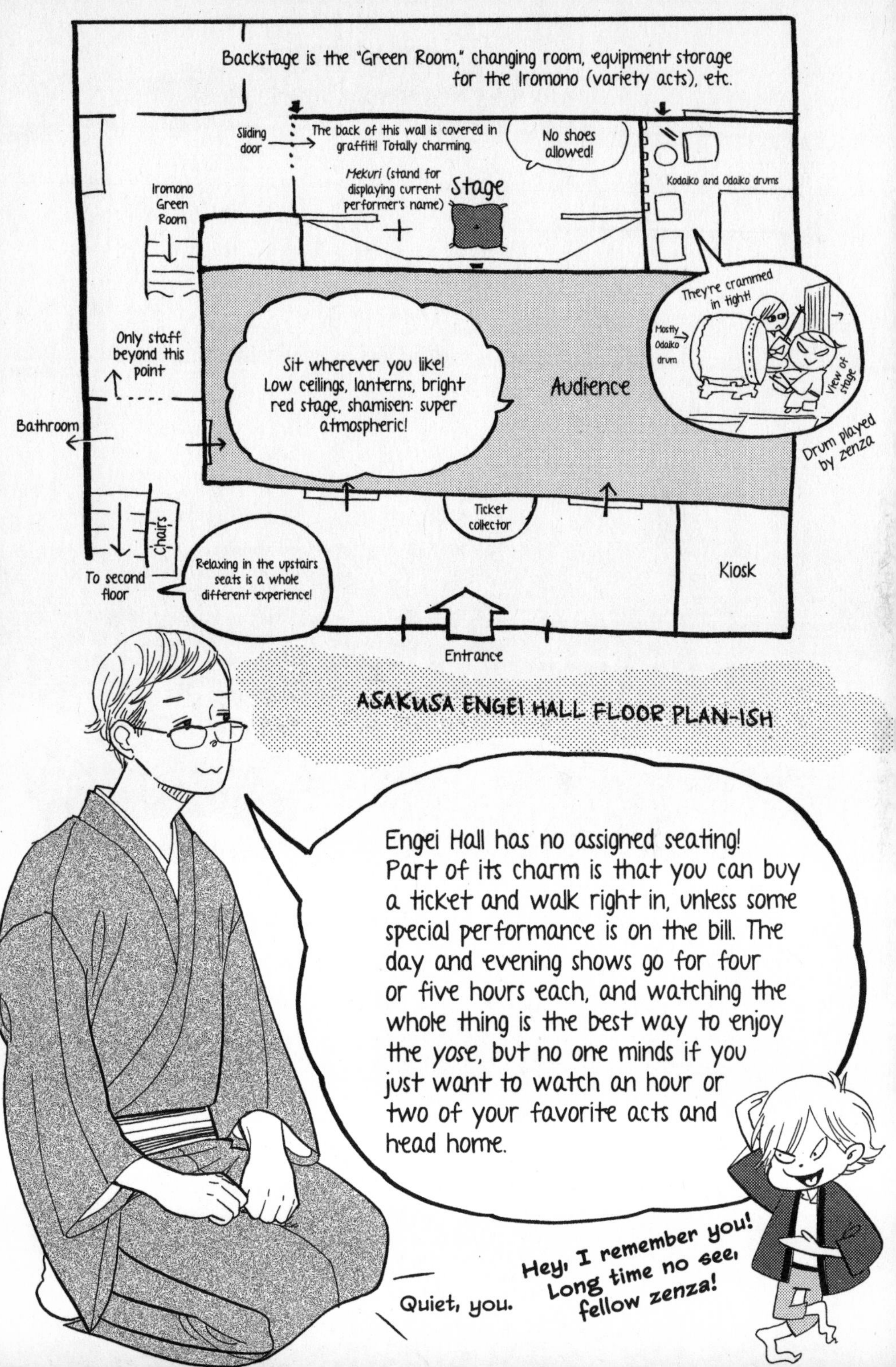
Backstage is the "Green Room," changing room, equipment storage for the Iromono (variety acts), etc.
Sliding door
The back of this wall is covered in graffiti! Totally charming.
No shoes allowed!
Mekuri (stand for displaying current performer's name)
Stage
Kodaiko and Odaiko drums
Iromono Green Room
They're crammed in tight!
Mostly Odaiko drum
View of stage
Only staff beyond this point
Sit wherever you like! Low ceilings, lanterns, bright red stage, shamisen: super atmospheric!
Audience
Bathroom
Drum played by zenza
Ticket collector
Chairs
To second floor
Relaxing in the upstairs seats is a whole different experience!
Kiosk
Entrance
ASAKUSA ENGEI HALL FLOOR PLAN-ISH
Engei Hall has no assigned seating! Part of its charm is that you can buy a ticket and walk right in, unless some special performance is on the bill. The day and evening shows go for four or five hours each, and watching the whole thing is the best way to enjoy the *yose*, but no one minds if you just want to watch an hour or two of your favorite acts and head home.
Hey, I remember you! Long time no see, fellow zenza!
Quiet, you.

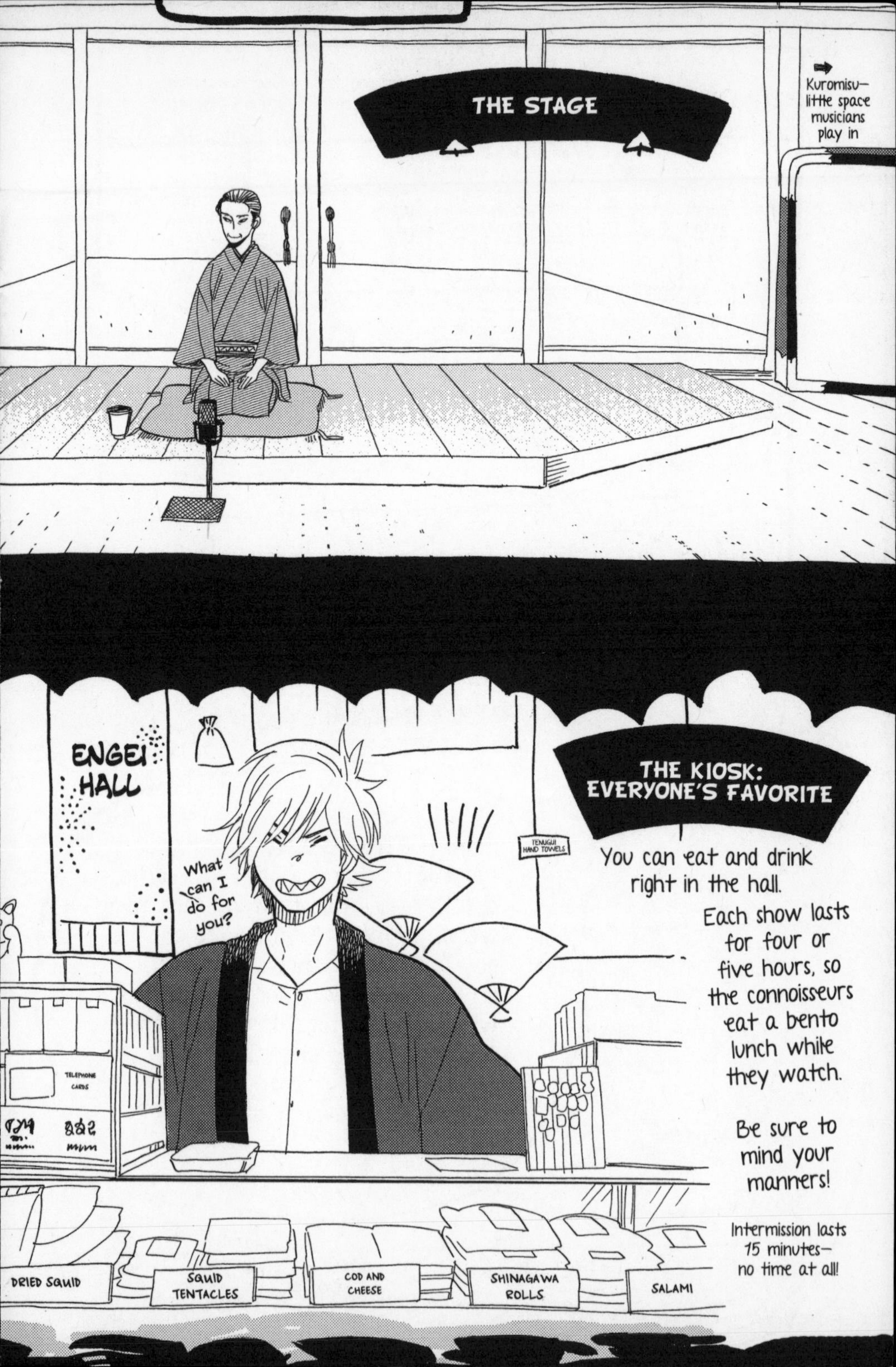
Kuromisu—little space musicians play in
THE STAGE
THE KIOSK: EVERYONE'S FAVORITE
You can eat and drink right in the hall.
Each show lasts for four or five hours, so the connoisseurs eat a bento lunch while they watch.
Be sure to mind your manners!
Intermission lasts 15 minutes—no time at all!
TENUGUI HAND TOWELS
What can I do for you?
ENGEI HALL
TELEPHONE CARDS
SALAMI
SHINAGAWA ROLLS
COD AND CHEESE
SQUID TENTACLES
DRIED SQUID

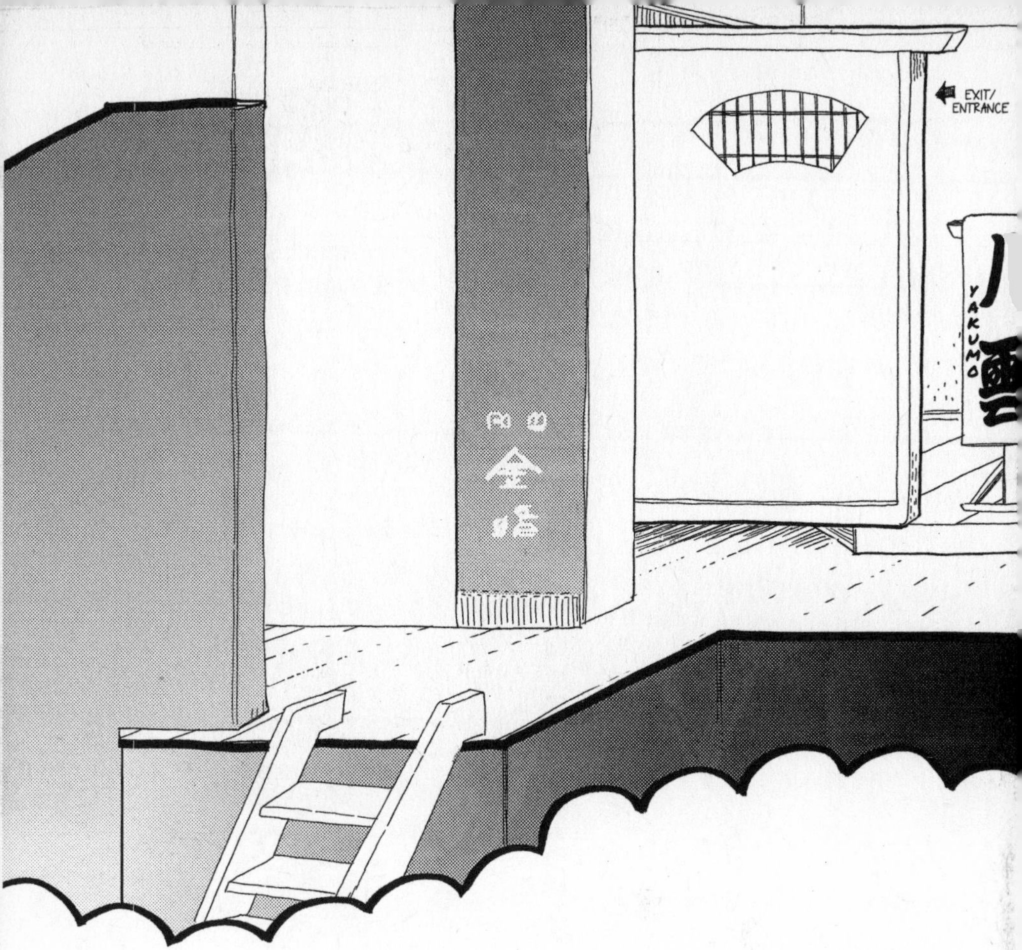
EXIT/
ENTRANCE
YAKUMO

Once they check your ticket, you get a program. This has all the performers for the day on it. The whole time you're in the hall, you're looking at your program thinking, "Oh, that guy's next," or "They were funnier than I expected," or "Huh, he's not on the program today?" and by the time you come out the program's all creased. But keep that program and you'll never forget the day. The swish of kimonos, the cheerful sound of the shamisen, the women's lovely voices, the subtle but pleasant perfume of the lady sitting next to you, the delicious Matsuya bento—all of it gets packed into your program.

HOPE TO SEE YOU ALL IN ASAKUSA SOON! —Kumota

雲田拝

Descending Stories: Showa Genroku Rakugo Shinju
Haruko Kumota
Thank you for reading!

We're finally at the half-way mark of Yakumo and Sukeroku's story. Please bear with me for the rest!

Yotaro is diligently rehearsing his *rakugo* while he waits.

2012
A fine autumn day, listening to the crickets chirp.

HARUKO KUMOTA

雲田はるこ拝

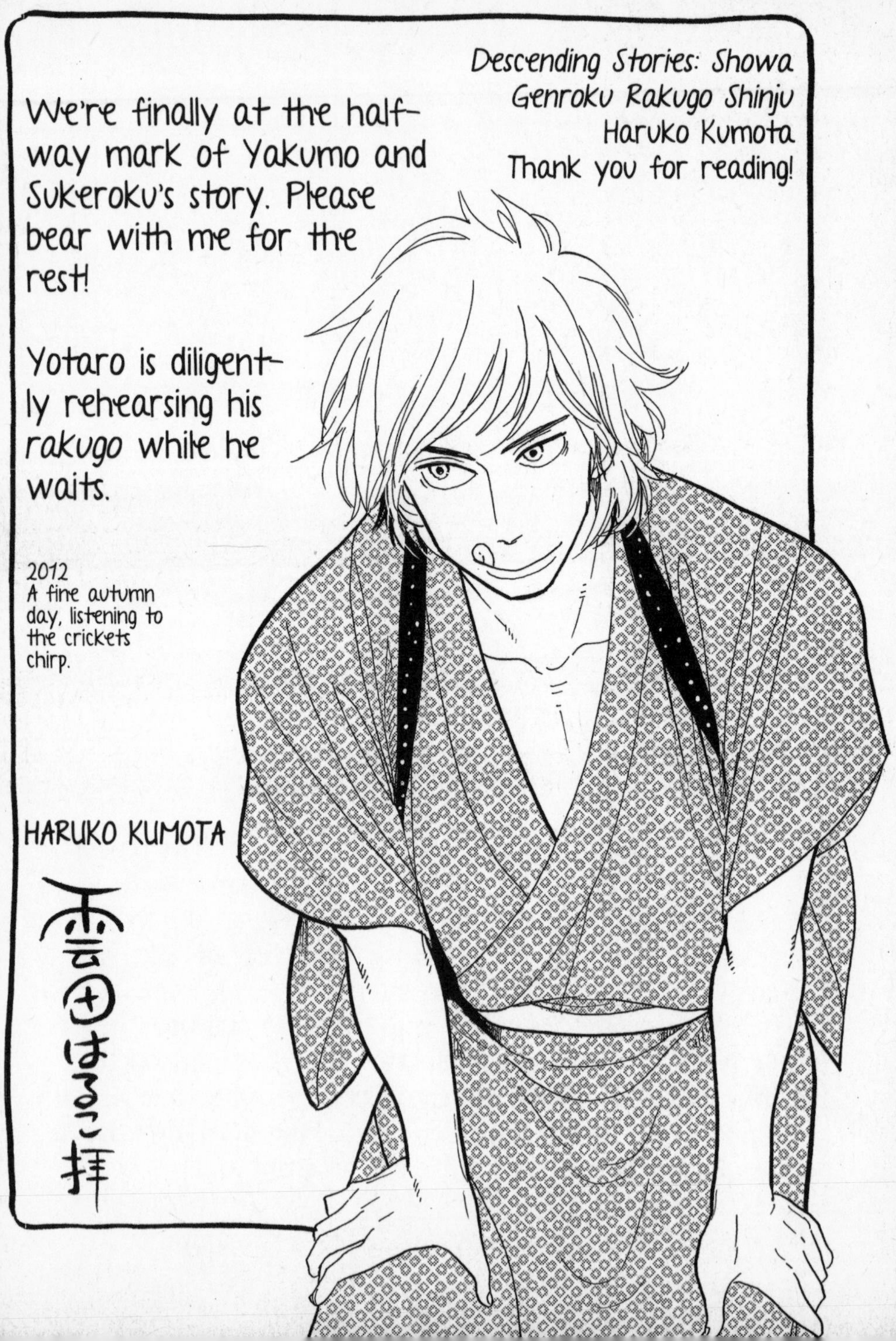

DESCENDING STORIES

SHOWA
GENROKU
RAKUGO
SHINJU

Haruko Kumota

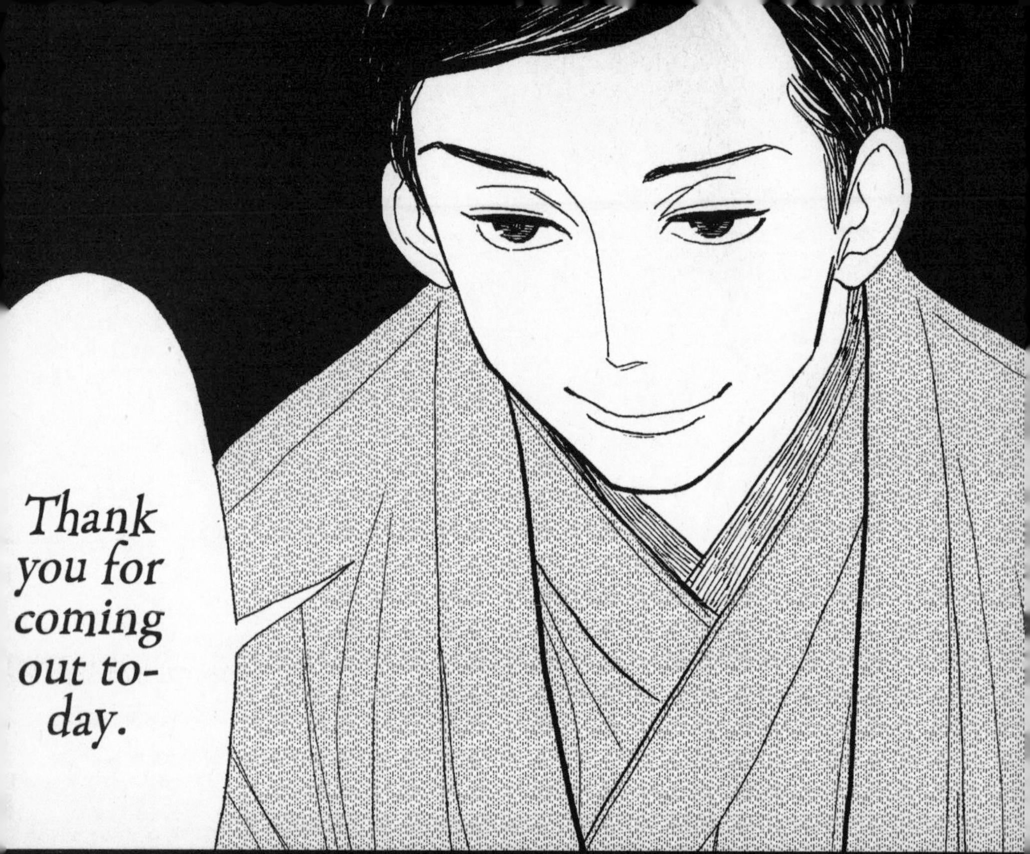
Thank you for coming out to-day.

HOW WILL IT CHANGE THEIR RAKUGO?

AND MIYOKICHI:

LOVE TRIANGLE END?

SUKEROKU REACHES A CLIMAX!

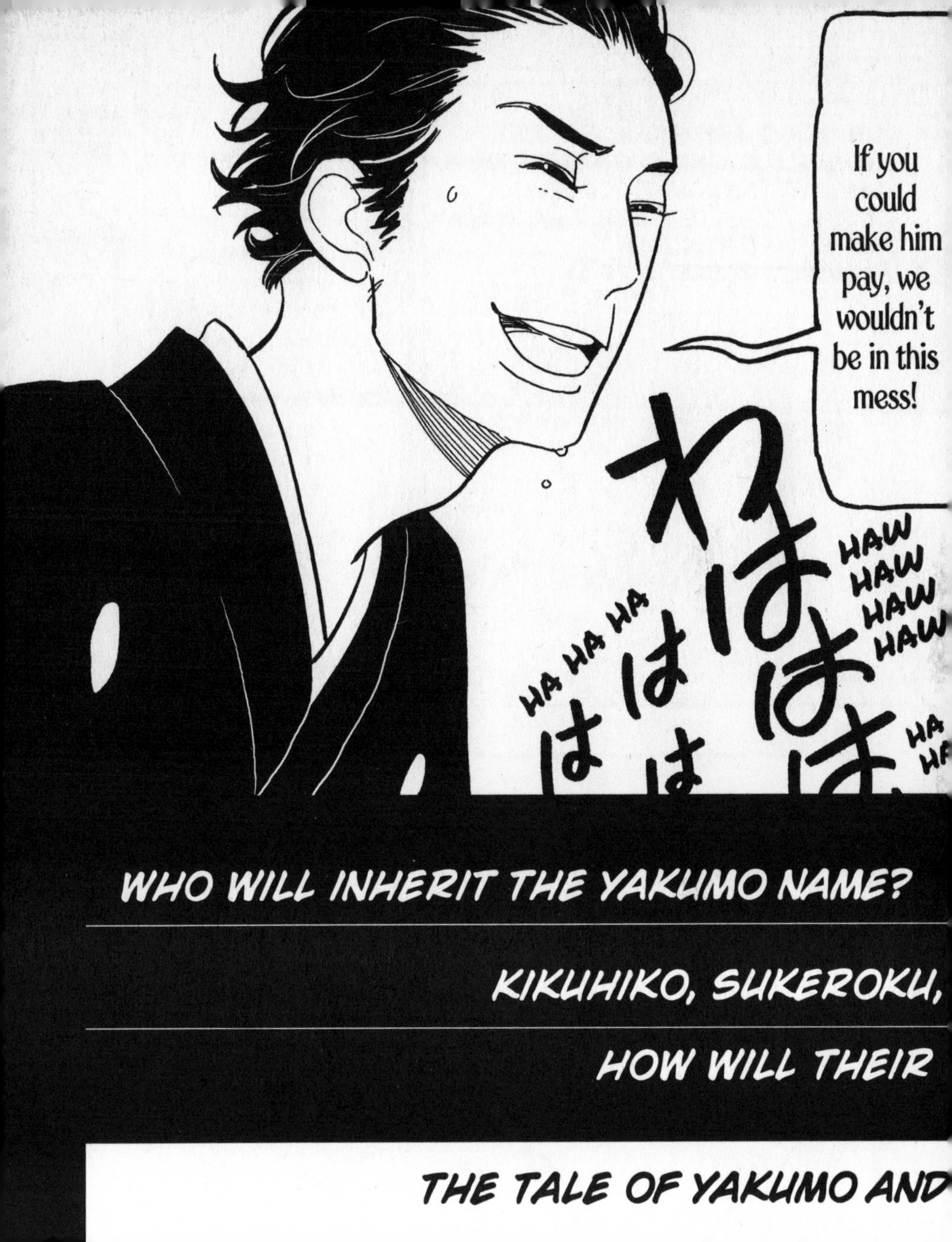
If you could make him pay, we wouldn't be in this mess!
HAW HAW HAW HAW
HA HA HA

WHO WILL INHERIT THE YAKUMO NAME?

KIKUHIKO, SUKEROKU,

HOW WILL THEIR

THE TALE OF YAKUMO AND

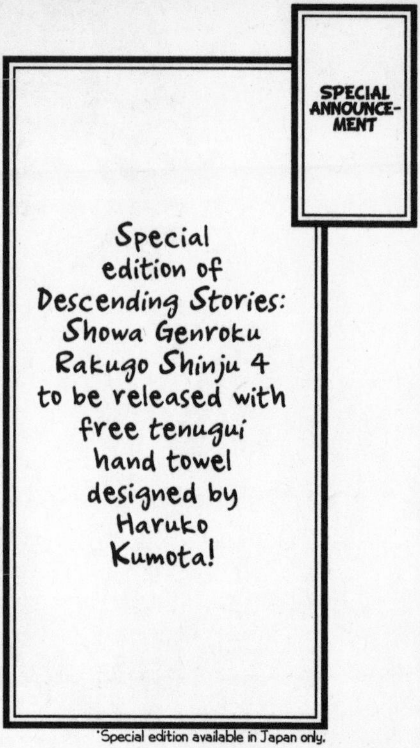
SPECIAL ANNOUNCE-MENT
Special edition of Descending Stories: Showa Genroku Rakugo Shinju 4 to be released with free tenugui hand towel designed by Haruko Kumota!

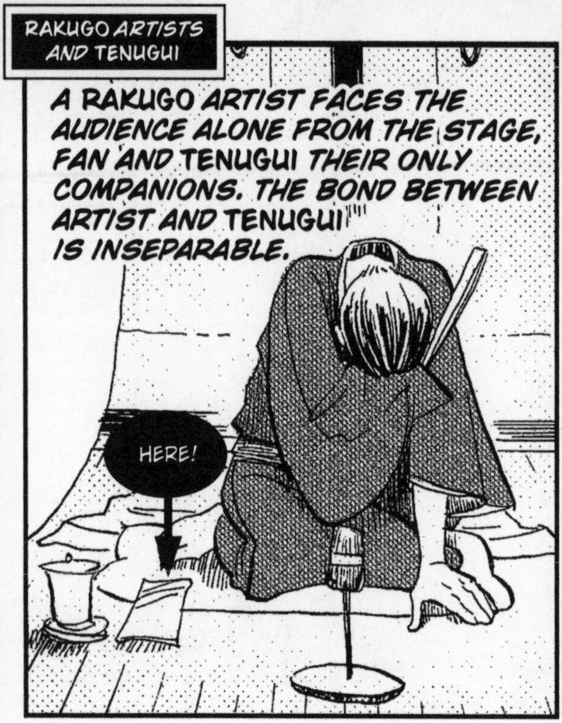
RAKUGO ARTISTS AND TENUGUI
A RAKUGO ARTIST FACES THE AUDIENCE ALONE FROM THE STAGE, FAN AND TENUGUI THEIR ONLY COMPANIONS. THE BOND BETWEEN ARTIST AND TENUGUI IS INSEPARABLE.
HERE!

*Special edition available in Japan only.

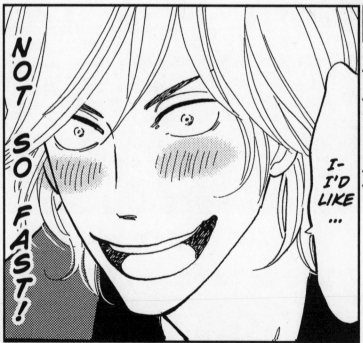

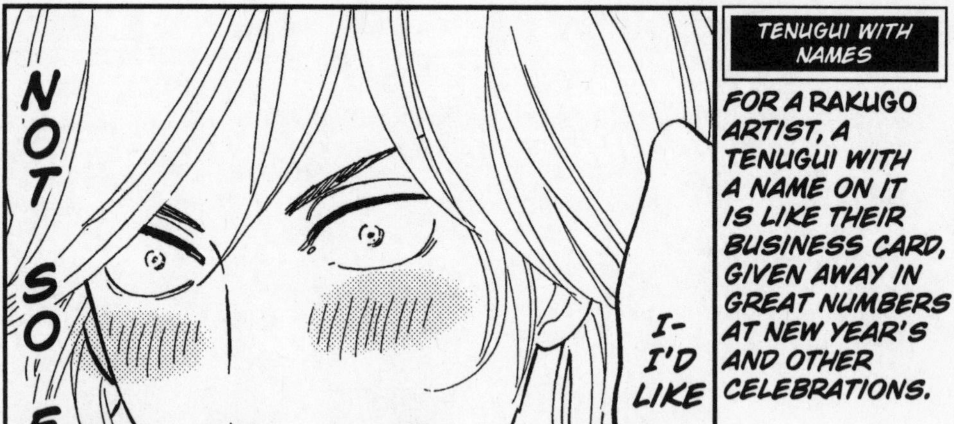
TENUGUI WITH NAMES
FOR A RAKUGO ARTIST, A TENUGUI WITH A NAME ON IT IS LIKE THEIR BUSINESS CARD, GIVEN AWAY IN GREAT NUMBERS AT NEW YEAR'S AND OTHER CELEBRATIONS.
I- I'D LIKE...
NOT SO FAST!

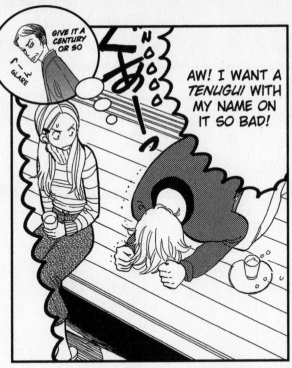

YOU CAN'T PUT YOUR NAME ON YOUR TENUGUI UNTIL YOU REACH AT LEAST FUTATSUME LEVEL. THINK OF IT AS A LICENSE YOU EARN ONLY AFTER FINISHING YOUR TOUGH ZENZA TRAINING.

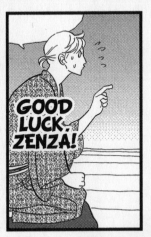

GOOD LUCK, ZENZA!

AW! I WANT A TENUGUI WITH MY NAME ON IT SO BAD!
NOOOOOO
GIVE IT A CENTURY OR SO
GLARE

USING YOUR TENUGUI

NATURALLY, TENUGUI ARE USEFUL IN DAILY LIFE TOO.

AS A HEADBAND

IN THE BATH

AGAINST THE COLD

WHAT KIND OF TENUGUI WILL IT BE?

LOOK FORWARD TO FINDING OUT!

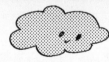

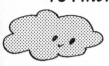

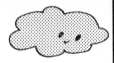

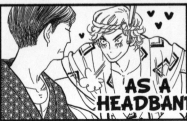

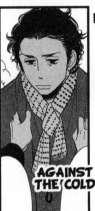

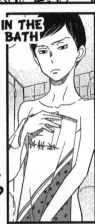

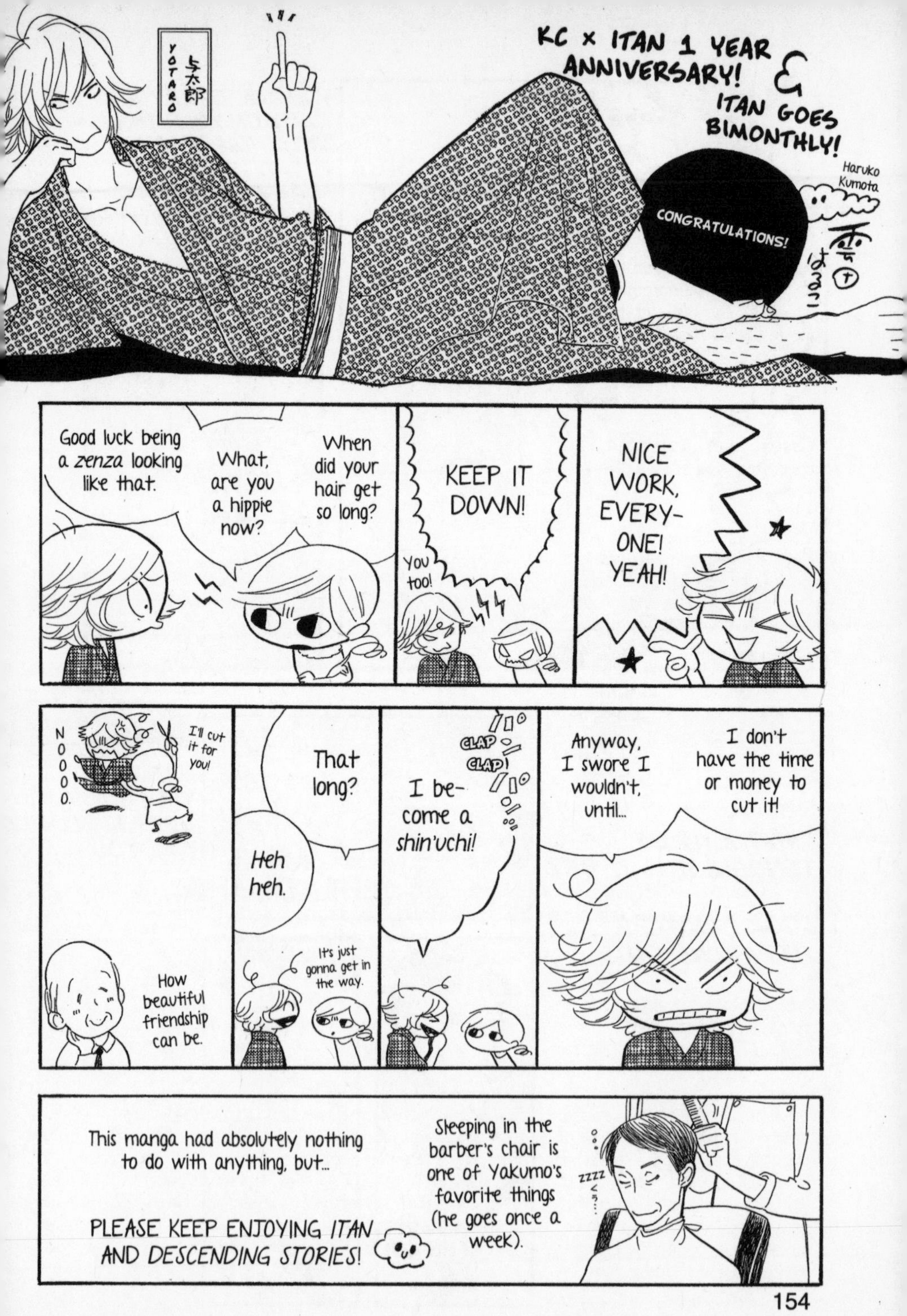
KC × ITAN 1 YEAR ANNIVERSARY! & ITAN GOES BIMONTHLY!
Haruko Kumota
CONGRATULATIONS!
与太郎 YOTARO
NICE WORK, EVERY-ONE! YEAH!
KEEP IT DOWN!
You too!
When did your hair get so long?
What, are you a hippie now?
Good luck being a *zenza* looking like that.
I don't have the time or money to cut it!
Anyway, I swore I wouldn't, until...
CLAP CLAP
I be-come a *shin'uchi*!
That long?
Heh heh.
It's just gonna get in the way.
I'll cut it for you!
NOOOOO.
How beautiful friendship can be.
Sleeping in the barber's chair is one of Yakumo's favorite things (he goes once a week).
ZZZZ
This manga had absolutely nothing to do with anything, but...
PLEASE KEEP ENJOYING *ITAN* AND *DESCENDING STORIES*!

Translation Notes

Sukeroku's Makeout Den, page 6
By today's valuation, 500 yen per night doesn't seem so bad, but at the time 500 yen would have been around $10-$15. Triple the price for women would have been steep for young *rakugo* artists!

If we don't hurry, it won't be there at all, page 8
By the end of the Edo period, Yoshiwara was no longer the cultural force it had once been. Still, it continued to operate throughout the Meiji period and beyond, surviving fire, earthquake, and even bombing, as well as criticism from reformers, and waning interest in traditional performing arts. Even after the US occupying forces abolished Japan's system of formally licensed prostitution in 1946, Yoshiwara remained an *akasen,* or "red-line" district, until the passage of the Anti-Prostitution Law in 1956 dealt the final blow.

I'm a ma-a-an..., page 9
A *dodoitsu* (short song in 7-7-7-5 form) celebrating the ideal of being desirable to all but remaining free nevertheless.

That part, page 10
In the *rakugo* "Shinagawa *Shinju*" ("Shinagawa Double Suicide"), the ageing courtesan O-Some, facing money troubles and mocked by younger courtesans, resolves to die. Afraid to commit suicide alone, she persuades the mild-mannered bookseller Kinzo to form a double-suicide pact with her. She pushes him off the bridge first, but decides not to jump in after him when a messenger arrives from the teahouse saying that her money troubles are over. Kinzo survives the fall and gets his revenge on O-Some by convincing her that he has returned as a ghost to haunt her. The terrified O-Some is convinced to shave her head and take Buddhist vows, upon which Kinzo reveals all and says that for her sin of "fishing" him she has been "made into a fish basket" (*biku ni sareta*, implying a pun on *bikuni* ("nun")).

Tenbeni scroll, page 10
Literally a "crimson top" scroll, *tenbeni* were used by courtesans to write letters to patrons and customers.

Saruwaka, page 14
A famous theater district in Tokyo. As part of the Tenpo Reforms of the early 1840s, the shogunate forced all of the kabuki and puppet theaters to relocate to an area just northeast of Asakusa Temple. The area was named after Saruwaka Kanzaburo (later Nakamura Kanzaburo I), founder of the Nakamura-za theater and a key figure in the development of Edo-style kabuki.

Fukagawa! Impressed?, page 14
Particularly towards the end of the Edo period, as Yoshiwara fell into decline, the geisha of Fukagawa were viewed as especially refined, accomplished, and fashionable.

Benten Kozo, page 18
The main protagonist of a famous kabuki play by Mokuami Kawatake (1816–1893) known variously as *Aoto Zoshi Hana no Nishiki-e* ("Glorious picture-book of Aoto's exploits"), *Shiranami Gonin Otoko* ("Five men of the white waves") or simply *Benten Kozo* ("The Benten kid"); in English it is sometimes known as *Benten the Thief,* or *Benten the Male-Female Bandit.* "Benten *kozo*" refers to the character's origins on the island of Enoshima, sacred to the goddess Benten. The most famous scene in the play involves Benten *kozo* entering the Hamamatsuya apparel shop disguised as an upper-class woman, only to eventually reveal his true identity in one of the most famous monologues in the kabuki repertoire.

Street signs, page 21
The signs crowding the street here are all for cheap and not necessarily high-minded public entertainments, including theaters, cinemas, night clubs, and strip clubs, reflecting the role this area played in Tokyo city life at the time.

Misuzu-za Public Theater, page 21
The Misuzu-za theater advertises *taishu engeki*, or "popular plays," as opposed to more formal (and expensive) forms of theater.

***Kyogen* performers, page 22**
Kyogen is a comedic form that developed alongside noh theater, and also had an influence on kabuki. The short *kyogen* skits are often used as an intermission in noh, though its unclear if this *shika-shibai* will have intermissions, or if the actors are joining in on the play itself.

Fox . . . tanuki, page 25
In the Japanese, the full insults exchanged are *bake-gitsune,* "transformed fox," and *chiri-chiri-danuki,* "curly-haired tanuki." Both *kitsune* (foxes) and *tanuki* (sometimes known as "raccoon dogs") were known as shape-shifting tricksters in folklore, but where foxes were depicted as subtle and cunning, *tanuki* were generally earthy and crude.

Winter cherries for your altar, page 71
Winter cherries (*hozuki*) are a traditional decoration for family altars during the summer Bon festival, most likely because they resemble the lanterns that are lit so that ancestral spirits can find their way home.

I keep it in the altar, page 91
Traditionally, most Japanese households kept a *butsudan*, or "Buddhist altar," containing a Buddhist icon or statue and other religious paraphernalia. Also kept in or near the *butsudan* are items of family significance, including memorial tablets for departed relatives.

Yurakutei family tree, page 92

THE FIRST YURAKUTEI WAS IN THE KANSEI PERIOD.*
EVERYONE SINCE THEN, ALL THE NAMES ARE IN HERE. GRAND MASTERS, THE LOT OF THEM.
Yakumo I
Rokusuke
Mamesuke
Yakumo II
Nanasuke
Yakumo III
Yakumo IV
Yakumo V

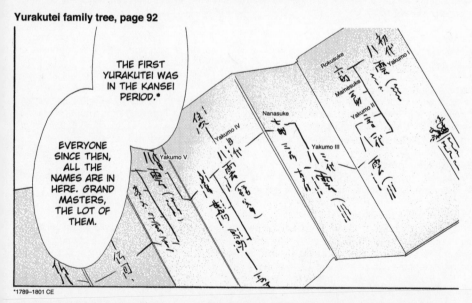

*1789–1801 CE

The names have been added to the above version of the family tree for the reader's convenience. Not all of these may be blood relatives of Yurakutei I—some may have been adopted through marriage, or were bestowed the name after ascending through the ranks.

A *hokan*, page 112
A *hokan*, also known as a *taikomochi* ("drum bearer"), are essentially the male equivalent of a geisha—although they predated female geisha by hundreds of years. In earlier centuries they served as advisors and conversation partners to feudal lords, but by the Edo period, the job chiefly involved keeping party guests entertained with jokes, skits, and games.

I was light-fingered even as a lad…, page 115
A famous monologue by Rihei Tadanobu from *Benten the Thief* (see p. 18).

Especially for a Sukeroku, page 138
The name "Sukeroku" is a reference to Sukeroku Hanakawado, beloved hero of the kabuki play *Sukeroku Yukari Edo-Zakura* ("Sukeroku, the Flower of Edo"), first staged in 1713. The name "Hanakawado" is itself a reference to the Hanakawado district of Tokyo, known for its sakura blossoms (particularly in Hanakawado Park).

RAKUGO STORIES IN THIS VOLUME:

Shinagawa Shinju (品川心中) - Double Suicide at Shinagawa (pages 10, 44)
Inokori Saheiji (居残り佐平次) - Saheiji is Kept Behind (page 107)

It is said that the roots of the current *Rakugo Kyokai* Association can be traced to the Tokyo *Rakugo Kyokai* formed thanks to the efforts of Ryutei Saraku V following the 1923 Great Kanto Earthquake. Yanagiya Kosan IV was later appointed its chairman and established it anew as the *Rakugo Kyokai* Association. It received permission to become an incorporated association with the Agency for Cultural Affairs acting as its competent authority in 1977, and its stated goal was to "advance the spread of popular performing arts with a focus on classical *rakugo*, contributing to the cultural development of our country in the process." It later became the general incorporated association it is today in 2012. It conducts performances in four theatres (*yose*) in Tokyo, as well as in halls, assembly spaces, schools, and more around the country.

For an overview of the *Rakugo Kyokai* Association, please visit:
http://rakugo-kyokai.jp/summary/

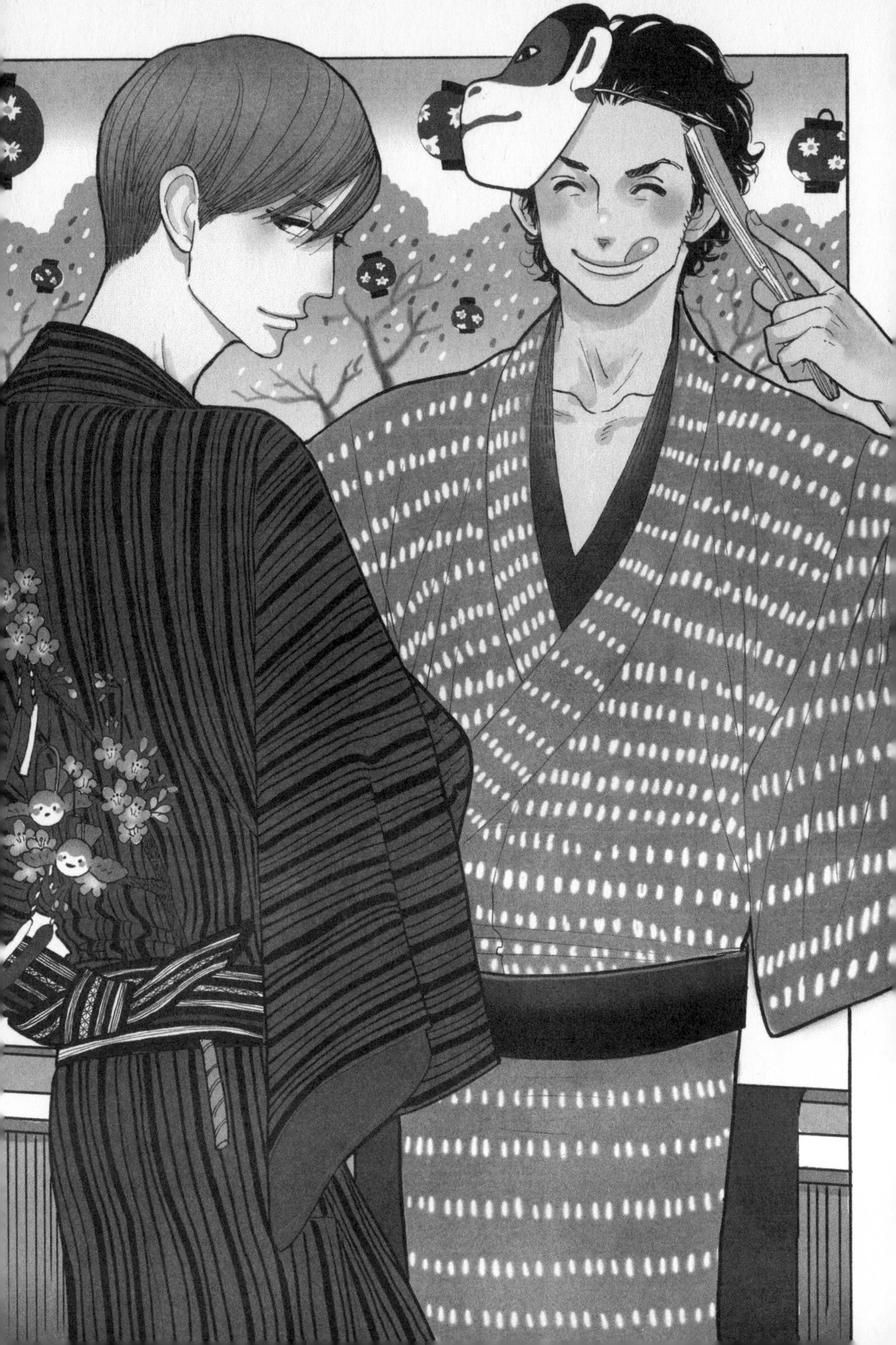

Descending Stories: Showa Genroku Rakugo Shinju volume 3 is a work of fiction. Names, characters, places, and incidents are the products of the author's imagination or are used fictitiously. Any resemblance to actual events, locales, or persons, living or dead, is entirely coincidental.

A Kodansha Comics Trade Paperback Original.

Published in the United States by Kodansha Comics, an imprint of Kodansha USA Publishing, LLC, New York.

Publication rights for this English edition arranged through Kodansha Ltd., Tokyo.

First published in Japan in 2012 by Kodansha Ltd., Tokyo.

ISBN 978-1-63236-471-5
Printed in the United States of America

www.kodanshacomics.com

9 8 7 6 5 4 3 2 1

Translation: AltJapan Co., Ltd.
Lettering: Andrew Copeland
Editing: Lauren Scanlan
Rakugo term supervision: Japan Rakugo Association
Kodansha Comics edition cover design: Phil Balsman